TIME ON OUR SIDE

Dorothy Rowe was born in Australia in 1930, and worked as a teacher and child psychologist before coming to England, where she obtained her PhD at Sheffield University. From 1972 until 1986 she was head of the North Lincolnshire Department of Clinical Psychology. She is now engaged in writing, lecturing and research. Her work is concerned with the questions of how we communicate and why we suffer.

DOROTHY ROWE

Time on Our Side

Growing in Wisdom, Not Growing Old

HarperCollinsPublishers

To my dear and ageless friends
Craig, Jacqui and Harriet
Kevin, Hilary and Kieran

HarperCollins*Publishers*
77–85 Fulham Palace Road,
Hammersmith, London W6 8JB

This paperback edition 1994
1 3 5 7 9 8 6 4 2

First published in Great Britain by
HarperCollins*Publishers* 1993

Copyright © Dorothy Rowe 1993

The Author asserts the moral right to
be identified as the author of this work

ISBN 0 00 638084 0

Set in Galliard

Printed in Great Britain by
HarperCollinsManufacturing Glasgow

CONTENTS

'Write a book about getting older,' Imogen, my agent, said to me. Imogen was then past twenty-eight and, in her eyes, rushing on to the dreaded age of thirty. When I did take her advice she had passed thirty and now sees that age and much else in her life very differently.

Mike, my editor, liked the idea of a book about time but said, 'Not a long book.'

After all time is short.
Time is passing.

Time passes relentlessly.
Time is our enemy.

Or is it?

'I'm middle aged. The body is packing up. I can't see one redeeming feature in getting older. You just think, "Nature's had you. You're on the scrap heap."'

Jean Shrimpton, aged forty-eight

'Years following years steal something every day;
At last they steal us from ourselves away.'

Alexander Pope, 'Imitations of Horace'

'When I turned sixty what I felt was like grief.'

A seventy-year-old woman

'All my possessions for a moment of time.'

The last words of Elizabeth I, aged seventy

'Before I sign off I want to wish Mrs Jean Willmington happy birthday. Welcome to the downhill side of your allotted three score and ten.'

Quantas pilot giving flight information to passengers aboard a 747 bound for Australia

'Youth is a blunder; manhood a struggle; old age a regret.'

Benjamin Disraeli, *Coningsby*

'Why can't we start old and get younger?'

A forty-year-old woman remembering the sixties

'Time is the only true purgatory.'

Samuel Butler, *Notebooks*

But at my back I always hear
Time's winged chariot hurrying near
And yonder all before us lie
Deserts of vast eternity.

Andrew Marvell, 'To His Coy Mistress'

'The clear message of our society is that youth is best, middle age is worse and old age is the pits. And for older women, ageism carried to its logical extension tells her that the best thing she can do for society is to die.'

Louise Anike

'Get time, the old arch enemy, well and truly on your side.'

Sharp Personal Computer advertisement

'As a person gets older he is less and less at home in the world.'

Enoch Powell

'I think when the full horror of being fifty hits you, you should stay at home and have a good cry.'

Alan Bleasdale

We had a lot of old people going to Back to the Future. *When I say old, I mean over eighteen.'*

Bob Zemeckis, director

We fear time passing.
We fear growing old.
Why are we afraid?
Because we think that time, our lived time, is real
and that the world must be the way we see it.
Do we need to be afraid?
No.
Because we fear old age we fear life, and, fearing life,
we fear death.
Time is not our enemy.
Our enemy is the ideas we have about time, and our
fear of growing old.

ACKNOWLEDGEMENTS

The author and publishers should like to thank the following for their permission to reproduce copyright material:

FOR THE CARTOONS:

Charles Addams, The New Yorker Magazine Inc, David Austin, *Weekend Guardian*, Fiona Buckland, Calvin & Hobbes, Universal Press Syndicate, Michael Leunig, Pat McNeill.

FOR THE PUBLISHED EXCERPTS:

Louise Anike and Lynette Ariel, Melissa Benn, Piers Dudgeon, U. A. Fanthorpe, Marjorie Hill, Michael Ignatieff, *Observer*, Candida Lacey, Nigella Lawson, Alysdair Maclean, Daniel Massey, Andrew Motion, Pamela Nowicka, Claire Rayner, Jay Rayner, Professor John J. Sparkes, Jill Tweedie, A. N. Wilson, *Evening Standard*, *Yours*.

Bellew Publishing Co. Ltd for Lloyd de Mause, *The History of Childhood*.
Faber & Faber for Ros Coward, *Our Treacherous Hearts*.
Alfred A. Knopf Inc. for Wilfred Sheed, *The World of Charles Addams*.
Oxford University Press for John D. Barrow, *Theories of Everything*.
Oxford University Press for Roger Penrose, *The Emperor's New Mind*.

Oxford University Press for G. J. Whitrow, *The Natural Philosophy of Time*.

Penguin Books Ltd for John Boswell, *The Kindness of Strangers*.

Faber & Faber for Emma Tennant, *Faustine*.

Viking Penguin for Roger McGough, *Defying Gravity*.

Random House Inc. for Daniel J. Boorstin, *The Americans: The Democratic Experience*.

Random House UK Ltd for Sigmund Freud, *Infantile Mental Life: Two Lies Told by Children*, Collected Works trans. and ed. by James Strachey.

Random House UK Ltd for Margaret Forster, *Have the Men Had Enough*.

Routledge for Lionel Rose, *The Erosion of Childhood: Child Oppression in Britain 1860–1918*.

Transworld Publishers Ltd for Stephen Hawking, *A Brief History of Time*.

FOR THE PUBLISHED ARTICLES:

Independent:
Ruth Hughes – The One Thing They Never Tell You About HRT; Liz Hunt – His Brain Forgot About His Body; Paul Thomas – A Letter; Charles Glass – The Revolution in Iran Is Over; Matthew Gwyther – Britain Bracing for the Age Bomb; Melanie McFadyean – A Vision in the Mirror of Sex; Karl Maier – Free-market Africa's Age of Disrespect; Lynn Barber – The Price of Genius; Sheila Kitzinger – A Child's View of a Terrible War; Zoë Heller – The Road to Recovery.

Observer:
Peter Hillmore – A Child Quietly Starves to Death; Mat Coward – Cross Purposes; Caroline Carrl – Rock of Ages; Colin Macilwain – High-flyer at 40, Has-been at 45; Preamble.

Guardian:

Geraldine Bedell – Out of the Ordinary; Richard West – Convert a Third Kill a Third; Suzanne Moore – Everything You Never Wanted to Know About Sex; Richard Ehrlich – Is There Soup on Your Itinerary; Judith Williamson – Never Mind the Quantity – Think for Yourselves; Anne Karpf – New Face of Ageism; Fintan O'Toole – From Absolute Time to Created Time; Ian Katz – Despair of Children Who See No Point in Living; Martin Walker – American Diary; Margaret Forster – Menopause: Mid-life Crisis or Cause for Celebration; John Palmer – Pensioner Power Moves in on Euro Parliament; David Brindle – Dramatic Rise in Male Suicides; Chris Mihill – Third World Rise in Birth Control; Jan Rocha – Boy 'Sacrificed for Poll Success'; Derek Brown – Bombay Diary; Maggie O'Kane – Serb Jihan in a Bosnian Town; Ryszard Kapuscinski – Canyons of the Mind; Alan Moore – Sex and the Abandoned Child; Edward Pilkington – Why the Dead Don't Like Tuesdays; Joanna Smith – At a Loss; Efua Dorkenoo and Scilla Elworthy – A Cry in the Dark; Deng Yingchao – From the Awakening Society to Tiananmen Square; Marat Akchurin – Wake in the Cool of Dawn; Derel Brown – Hindu Regime Lets Shia Bleed in Peace; Susie Mackenzie – Answering a Divine Call; Tatyana Tolstaya – Tsar of All the Answers; Wendy Moore — Rhyme and Reason; John Willcock – Maxwell Declared £406m Bankrupt; Maggie O'Kane – Cake, Milk and Captivity; Falih 'Abd al-Jabbar – Saddam's Spoils of War; Owen Bowcott – Tensions Run High at Coalisland Funeral of IRA Men; Joanna Lyall – Out of the Shadows; Andrew Anthony – Wild at Heart.

Over the many years when I was talking to depressed and anxious clients they would tell me how they feared getting old. For
many of these people reaching a certain age – thirty, forty, fifty,
sixty – destroyed their last hope and plunged them into the
chaos against which depression was their only defence.

Over these same years I was finding that my friends, colleagues and myself harboured the same fear. What age we feared
depended on how old we were.

In our twenties we feared turning thirty. In our thirties we
feared turning forty. In our fifties we feared, not merely turning
sixty and becoming an old age pensioner, but becoming one
of those forgetful, incapacitated, ludicrous figures which our
parents, aunts and uncles, once so young and vigorous, had
become. Often, I observed, we let our fear of ageing spoil our
present life.

When, six years ago, my agent Imogen Parker, then twenty-
eight, asked me to write a book on how we feel about getting
old, I did not feel old in any way at all. Now I am at a stage
of discontinuity. I feel at one with my friends who are in their
twenties, thirties and forties, yet, when I survey my thoughts
and fantasies about the future, I feel that something is changing.
The future does not have the same importuning demand as it
once did. The future was once so important to me. Now when
I want to get something done, like this book, it is not because
future promises or commitments are so pressing, but because
once the general housekeeping which goes with the production
of a book is completed, I can concentrate on the present. When

I am engaged in the actual writing of a book I live entirely in the present, and that is wonderful. That's the main reason why I write. (Earning money is also a good incentive.) But, of course, at every moment of our lives everything is changing. I intend, in twenty years' time, to write a definitive text about what it means to grow very old. In the meanwhile I am reporting that our fears about growing old are greatly exaggerated. Like most of the fears we have, they are entirely in our head.

The beliefs and attitudes we hold are never separate entities in themselves but are always bound up in what we think, feel and do. Our fears about ageing are bound up with how we see ourselves and our world, and are part of the conclusions we have drawn from all our experiences including our earliest. It was in this context that I examined our fears about ageing.

I began by asking everyone I could, from five-year-old Stephie Fraser to my ninety-five-year-old aunt, Mrs Margaret Clyde, how they saw ageing, time and death. I talked to people who lived in societies which were reputed to honour old age. I looked, as I have always done, at how people live their lives. I am over sixty, so there are many people whose lives I have observed for up to six decades. I know how things have been turning out for them and why the chickens they hatched early in their lives came home to roost as vultures. I could see and question the principles by which they lived their lives. What principles, I asked them, do you still hold to and which have you changed? Is there a list of principles by which we all might live our lives successfully and happily?

I asked too how they saw time. Was time a path they walked along, a river that flowed by, or something else? Our image of time, I discovered, has much to do with why we fear the passing of time.

In discussing our fears about ageing a constant theme, especially for older people, was why in our society old people are treated so badly. They are excluded, treated with disregard, even contempt. The answer, I decided, lay in how we bring up our children. If we understand our children, then perhaps when we get old our children will understand us.

If we fear getting old, whatever 'old' is for us, we fear life, and if we fear life we cannot live it but merely survive in misery. We can be happy living in time only so long as we can live in the present, neither regretting the past nor fearing the future.

My thanks to all those people who took the time to talk to me about time.

Dorothy Rowe
Sheffield
12 August 1992

CHAPTER 1

The fearful passage of time

TIME IS an old familiar that we never get to know. Friends and family may leave you, but time never goes away. Seek solitude on a desert island and time keeps us company. We can find time and lose time, but never lose it completely. We can measure time, mark time and beat time. We can spend time, save time and waste time. Time can be good and time can be bad. Time can fly, and time can crawl. Time can tell, and time can see. We can tell *the* time, but we cannot speak *to* time. Time always eludes us and is deaf to our entreaties. We can cry 'Stop!', but time pays no attention. Time always rushes on, and we are dragged along too, helpless passengers in a speeding train, fragile leaves in a torrent of wind and water.

Even when time is ordinary it's strange. We say, 'What time's dinner?', 'Don't be late,' 'The train was on time.' To make sense of such common questions, demands and statements we need to agree on some quite complex methods of measuring time. In such ordinary exchanges we often use time as a metaphor that conveys very briefly a great deal of meaning.

What do we mean when we say, 'The train was on time'? Is the train on time in the same way as it is on rails? Of course not. 'On time' is a quick way of referring to a correspondence between the arrival of the train and a list of numbers called a timetable. But doesn't 'on time' also give a picture of the train racing along beside time and then leaping on time's back so that time and the train arrive at the station together?

There's finding time and making time. When Barry Norman was talking to Gloria Hunniford on BBC Radio 2 about his latest novel he said, 'To write a novel you don't find time, you make it.'[1] A literal meaning of this statement would be something like, 'I am always very busy with my other work, so I have to reorganize my activities in order to write a novel.' But doesn't 'making time' give the impression of being in control of time? Instead of being helplessly swept along by time we might, fortuitously, find a piece of time, or, even better, we might make a few pieces of time. If only we could. If only between midnight and six in the morning I could get ten hours sleep!

We like to think that we have time under our control. We talk about 'passing time', as if we can do what we like with time. But it isn't so. When Vladimir says in *Waiting for Godot*, 'That passed the time,' Estragon points out that the time would have passed in any case.[2]

How is it that something we can neither see, nor hear, nor touch, nor smell dominates our lives and permeates our very being? Does time actually exist, or is it just a figment of our imagination, a fairy story we tell ourselves in order to organize and explain our lives? If all of us, time measurers and time keepers, disappeared, would the universe behave in a time-bound way, from the Big Bang to the Big Crunch or whatever, or would it exist in timeless majesty? Even the physicists, who are supposed to know about these things, cannot agree. In fact, all that physicists can tell us about time only makes it all the stranger.

We exist in time and space. We can go forward and backward in space, but we can't go back in time. I can go from Sheffield to London and back again, but I cannot return to Sheffield at the time I left.

The great theories of science – Newton's mechanics, Einstein's relativity, and the quantum mechanics of Heisenberg and Schrödinger – all seem to work just as well with time running backwards as well as forwards. But this isn't what we see. All our experience agrees with the Second Law of Thermodynamics which states that, when a process is irreversible, entropy, or the capacity for the system to change, always increases, so that the system in the future will have higher entropy than in the present or the past. Cold milk cools hot tea, ice melts, and mountains crumble. I can't go back in time, so I'm increasing my capacity for entropy, something I confirm every time I look in the mirror.

How do physicists reconcile the timelessness of the great theories with the time-suffused Second Law of Thermodynamics and our experience of time?

Their answers often seem to have more to do with the personal meaning they have given to life and death than with their knowledge of physics.

There are those physicists who dismiss our perception of time with their most damning word, 'subjective'. For such physicists subjective observations are at best unreliable and at worst totally untrue. Science, so they believe, is concerned only with 'objective' truth and the real world. Such thinking is not confined to physicists. Psychiatrists traditionally take little account of their patients' subjective experience. The renowned psychiatrists Eliot Slater and Martin Roth in their *Clinical Psychiatry*, the psychiatrists' bible, advised, 'It is the objective world in which we live and to which the subjective world must pay deference. It is even more important to know what the facts are than what the patient makes of them.'[3] But who decides what is a fact? And isn't that decision based on the subjective experiences of seeing, hearing and thinking?

These denigrators of our experience (usually men) often have difficulty in coping with their own personal experience, but they find comfort in believing in the objective world of classical physics which, in theory, wrote Roger Penrose,

> evolves in a clear and deterministic way, being governed by precisely formulated mathematical equations. This is true for the theories of Maxwell and Einstein as it is for the original Newtonian scheme. Physical reality is taken to exist independently of ourselves; and exactly how the classical world 'is' is not affected by how we might choose to look at it. Moreover, our bodies and our brains are themselves part of that world. They, also, are viewed as evolving according to the same precise and deterministic classical equations. All our actions are to be fixed by these equations – no matter how we might feel that our conscious wills may be influencing how we behave.[4]

That is, you can't think anything other than what you think because everything you do is determined by the laws of physics.

In contrast, there are physicists who, in trying to grapple with the paradoxes of quantum theory, have decided, as Roger Penrose said, 'to take the strongly subjective view that there is, in actuality, *no* real world "out there" at all!'[5] Strangely, just as those who reject the subjective experience of time still use clocks, calendars and teaching timetables, which are simply ways of co-ordinating our subjective experiences, so those who reject the objective world take good care when crossing the road.

Then there are the believers in the *strong anthropic principle* which reconciles timelessness with timefulness in the belief that everything happens for the best in this best of all possible universes. The *weak anthropic principle* is simply that human life evolved only in that part of the universe which provides the conditions necessary for life. Obvious, really. Whereas 'the strong anthropic principle,' wrote Stephen Hawking in his famous book *A Brief History of Time*, 'would claim that this whole vast construction exists simply for our sake',[6] exponents of the strong anthropic principle always involve God or Nature in their explanations.[7]

It has always bothered me, ever since I was a child in Sunday school, that God took so long to prepare for our arrival in comparison to the time our species has actually existed. It is hard to comprehend the immensity of the time the universe was in existence before the human species appeared. Even the Earth took an extremely long time to come into being and for forms of life other than human to inhabit it. One way of imaging this comparison was suggested by John McPhee.

'Imagine the Earth's history as the old measure of the English yard, the distance from the king's nose to the tip of his outstretched hand. One stroke of a nail file on the king's middle finger would then erase human history.'[8]

But at least the strong anthropic principle brings comfort to those physicists whose courage fails them and whose vanity is insulted when they glimpse their tiny existence in the context of the universe's space and time.

Bill Gates, the thirty-six-year-old billionaire founder and owner of the software company Microsoft, was interviewed by Henry Porter who asked him 'about Einstein who once said that after exploring the order of the universe he had become aware of the supreme architect. Did Gates believe in God? He replied: "Well, Einstein may have believed in God but it didn't help him any. I mean, look at his work." It was as if Gates had asked himself what God could do for him and answered that it was very little.'[9]

Of course theologians and physicists who believe in the strong anthropic principle would argue that Einstein and Gates couldn't have done what they did if God hadn't been there as the First Cause. Physicists would do well to avoid the strong anthropic principle totally, otherwise they will find themselves in the same confusion as theologians. Belief in God as the First Cause forces theologians to believe in a strictly deterministic world, yet they are also expected to believe that God gave human beings Free Will. Not that God's idea of Free Will coincides with my idea of free will. I think that we are free to create, from the whole array of our past experience, whatever interpretation we want of what happens to us. By contrast, saying to a person, 'You have the freedom to choose how you live your life but if I do not approve of your choices I will punish you' is hardly allowing that person a free choice. God apparently behaves just like those parents who say to their children, 'You can do whatever you like with your life, darling, just *so long as you're happy*,' and the child knows that he'd better not be unhappy or his parents will be disappointed.

The strong anthropic principle is just one attempt by physicists to put together all the theories which explain parts of the universe into one unified theory, a Theory of Everything. Such theorists sometimes feel the need to keep their spirits up by claiming to be on the verge of a breakthrough. Stephen Hawking wrote, 'I still believe that there are grounds for cautious optimism that we may now be near the end of the search for the ultimate laws of nature.'[10]

But he threw caution to the winds in his conclusion to *A Brief History of Time*.

If we do discover a complete theory, it should in time be understandable in broad principle by everyone, not just a few scientists. Then we shall all, philosophers, scientists, and just ordinary people, be able to take part in the discussion of the question of why it is that we and the universe exist. If we find an answer to that, it would be the ultimate triumph of human reason – for then we would know the mind of God.[11]

I think he wrote this last paragraph simply to make a strong ending to his book. The unified theory he proposes makes God unnecessary and he doesn't even include God in the book's index. However, the phrase 'the mind of God' has been seized upon by those people who try to compensate for the way the world has disappointed them by believing that there must be something more which is beyond our world and far better than our world. However, those who talk of how the theories created by physicists will reveal the mind of God are not the first to entertain such hopes. For Florence Nightingale statistics were more than a study. To her they were a religion because, so she thought, they revealed 'the thought of God'.[12]

Florence Nightingale and many of the people who talk of 'the mind of God' imagine God to be a person, and persons have minds and thoughts. The image we have of something determines the kind of theory we create about that thing. John Barrow, Professor of Astronomy at Sussex University, has made a study of what would be needed for a Theory of Everything. He pointed out that:

The current breed of candidates for the title of a 'Theory of Everything' hope to provide an encapsulation of all the laws of nature into a simple and single representation. The fact that such a unification is even sought tells us something about our expectations regarding the Universe. These we must have derived from an amalgam of our previous experience of the world and our inherited religious beliefs about its ultimate Nature and significance. Our monotheistic traditions reinforce the assumption that the Universe is at root a unity, that it is not governed by different legislation in different places, neither the residue of the clash of Titans wrestling to impose their arbitrary wills upon the Nature of things nor the compromise of some cosmic committee. Our Western religious tradition also endows us with the assumption that things are governed by a logic that exists independently of those things, that laws are externally imposed as though they were the decrees of a transcendent divine legislator. In other respects, our prejudices reflect a mixture of different traditions. Some feel the force of the Greek imperative that the structure of the Universe is a necessary and inflexible truth that could not be otherwise, while others inherit the feeling that the Universe is contingent.[13]

His examination of the complex matters which relate to Theories of Everything led John Barrow to conclude that

The scope of Theories of Everything is infinite but bounded; they are necessary parts of a full understanding of things but they are far from sufficient to unravel the subtleties of a Universe like ours. In the pages of this book, we have seen something of what a Theory of Everything might hope to teach us about the unity of the Universe and the way in which it may contain certain elements that transcend our present compartmentalized view of Nature's ingredients. But we have also learnt that there is more to Everything than meets the eye. Unlike many others we can imagine, our world contains prospective elements (those which we cannot recognize or generate by a series of logical steps). Theories of Everything can make no impression upon predicting these prospective attributes of reality; yet, strangely, many of these qualities will themselves be employed in the human selection and approval of an aesthetically acceptable Theory of Everything.

There is no formula that can deliver all truth, all harmony, all simplicity. No Theory of Everything can ever provide total insight. For, to see through everything, would leave us seeing nothing at all.[14]

So if a Theory of Everything cannot explain why we experience time differently from the way physicists describe it, perhaps we need to look at explanations in terms of the way we human beings make sense of our experience of the real world. In the real world a vast multitude of events occur, and when we encounter an event we can make sense of it in terms of a vast multitude of meanings. Our meanings can never describe exhaustively all aspects of every single event, but the multitude of possible meanings we can create allows us to glimpse the rich diversity of the world. Or, as the Nobel Laureate Ilya Prigogine said, 'The world is much richer than is possible to express in any single language. Music is not exhausted by its successive stylisations from Bach to Schoenberg. Similarly we cannot condense into a single description the various aspects of our experience.'[15]

There is no way we can condense into a single description our own subjective experience of time. Even though we know, intellectually, how our day is divided evenly into hours and minutes, we never actually experience time proceeding in such an orderly fashion. Minutes can drag and hours pass in a twinkle, so that time does not seem to proceed at an even pace. However, time never seems to stop completely. We see no gaps in time. Time, it seems to us, always flows.

Roger Penrose made what he called 'an alarming suggestion' about this.

I suggest that we may actually be going badly wrong when we apply the usual physical rules for time when we consider consciousness! There is, indeed, something very odd about the way that time enters into our conscious perception in any case, and I think that it is possible that a very different conception may be required when we try to place conscious perceptions into a conventionally time-ordered framework. Consciousness is, after all, the one phenomenon that we know of, according to which time needs to 'flow' at all! The way in which time is treated in modern physics is not essentially different from the way in which space is treated and 'time' of physical descriptions does not really 'flow' at all; we just have a static-looking fixed 'space-time' in which the events of our universe are laid out. Yet, according to our perceptions, time does flow. My guess is that there is something illusory here too, and the time of our perceptions does not really 'flow' in quite the linear, forward-moving way that we perceive it to flow (whatever that might mean!). The temporal ordering that we 'appear' to perceive is, I am claiming, something we impose on our perceptions in order to make sense of them in relation to the uniform forward time-progression of an external reality.[16]

Consciousness flows like time. The 'stream of consciousness' is a constant flow of thoughts, feelings and images. For most of us the stream is always continuous, but some people experience a stopping of their thoughts on some occasions. Psychiatrists talk of 'thought stopping' as being a symptom of schizophrenia, but some people who have never experienced the confusion and fear which is called psychotic have described to me how, when they are tired, or simply need to withdraw briefly from the turmoil of daily life, they actually stop thinking. Other people have to practise meditation for a long time before they can achieve the aim of meditation, the stilling of the chatter of consciousness.

As this chatter goes on we are always seeing things that aren't there and hearing things that haven't been said in order to make sense of our experience in a way which is somehow consonant with the real world. We look at a picture and see what isn't there. Perhaps we might see a triangle

Can you see a white triangle, lying above another triangle to which it is held by a ring? The borders of the white triangle are not drawn in everywhere, yet there are cells in the brain which respond to these invisible but perceived lines.

or beauty?

People rarely say what they mean, but the listeners fill in the gaps. Someone says, 'Tea?', and we say, 'Yes' or 'No', responding to what hasn't been said. So perhaps we also fill in any gaps in time's flow so that we can keep ourselves in some relationship with the real world.

We always try to keep ourselves in relationship to time. Even when we are asleep we are aware of time passing. If we wake during the night most of us can tell what time it is, approximately, without looking at a clock. Some people don't need an alarm clock. They just tell themselves what time to wake and they do. However, we lose this connection with time passing when we are under general anaesthesia. On a number of occasions I have watched the anaesthetist align a needle in my arm and the very next moment I've heard a nurse telling me to wake up. On other occasions I've been at the bedside of someone waking from anaesthesia. Each time we struggle into consciousness, and once assured that we are still alive, we ask, 'What time is it?'

We need to know what time it is now, in the present, so we can align ourselves with what has happened in the past and what might happen in the future. It is curious how our thoughts are always taken up with memories of the past and with plans, hopes, fears for the future, yet all we ever actually experience is the present. Just as we cannot go back to the past so we can't go forward to the future. All we ever know is a series of present moments.

Many people, perhaps most of us, are always turned towards the future. I am always making plans, promises, appointments, and these move like a wave across the blank pages of my diary, filling every space. I organize my future as time moves relentlessly on, and this gives me the feeling that I have my life under my control. This is a delusion, because most of the events which could affect my life are beyond my control.

The society I live in looks towards the future. Some societies look to the past. In a rare television programme on the Hasidic Jews in north London a police officer who knew them well said, 'All of us live on the edge of for ever. I think you can say that traditional western thought is forward. My humble interpretation is that this particular community are on the edge of for ever but their for ever is back. It's almost as if their future is irrelevant. Apart from the Messiah of course.'[17]

For the Hasidic Jews alive now, history as told in the Bible and (possibly) the coming of the Messiah lie outside that stretch of time which they can ever experience, just as the story of my convict great-grandfather and the events of the year 2050 lie outside the stretch of time I can experience.

This, I find, is the strangest part of time.

You wake up in this theatre, and out of the darkness you see this story going on, all these people doing incomprehensible things. You watch it, you take part in it, and gradually, after a very long time, you start to make sense of it. If you're lucky, you stick around long enough to think you've made some sense of it, and then, just as you think you might be getting to understand it, you're thrown out – out into the complete, utter, absolute blackness. What, I ask you, was that all about?

Don't tell me we wake up then in some wonderful, comprehensible, beautiful place which goes on for ever and ever. Millions of us? Millions and millions of us? Or only those who were born after 1AD and had the chance to hear and accept Jesus's message? What happens to those millions who went before, or lived elsewhere? Or is it only those who happened to hear what Muhammad had to say? I don't think so. They said important things, but Jesus, Muhammad and the rest of the religious leaders were simply part of our species' story whose significance we nearly get to understand, provided we live long enough and have the chance to get some kind of liberal education, that story about which we tell ourselves many stories in order to make some kind of sense of what happens to us between one darkness and another. The stories we create can come out of fear – fear of vanishing into the unknown, an unknown into the unknown, fear that can make us behave like obedient children before some supposedly grand, wise, powerful figure, the epitome of what we wanted our parents to be but weren't, or the epitome of what our parents threatened us with in order to make us obedient – or our story can come out of courage, the courage to say that against the blackness, 'I am here, a uniqueness which can observe and respond to, if not comprehend, that moment in time in which I, a comprehending being, exists. I do not have to apologize for or earn my right to exist. *I* exist and *I* observe. That is enough.'

But most of us don't have so much courage. For many people the events of their childhood and the demands and limitations of their society rob them of the unselfconscious self-confidence with which they were born.

And because of this they fear the passing of time and growing old.

CHAPTER 2

Fearing to grow old

IT WAS winter in Sheffield and I was wearing what I always wear when I don't have to dress up – jeans, a shirt and sweater. I'd gone to ask Judith, my accountant, about the financial implications of a project I was planning. I talked about what I was doing – as usual, travelling, teaching, writing – and she, as ever, was enthusiastic. She said, 'Look at you there in your blue sweater and jeans. You're an inspiration to me.'

I knew Judith meant this as a compliment, but it didn't feel like one. Not that I'm averse to compliments. I'm always pleased when someone tells me they find my books useful, because I sometimes wonder whether I'm just writing about matters which concern only me. I'm always pleased when someone tells me I write well, because I always feel that my writing could be better. But to be complimented for dressing comfortably and doing what I want to do felt like being complimented for breathing.

But I'm not telling you the full story. Here's the rest of it – what was implied in what she said.

Judith found me an inspiration not because of what I did, but because I did it *at my age*.

Sixty-one-year-old women are not supposed to dash around the world and insist on informing everyone of their strongly held views. They are supposed to live circumspectly and keep their views to themselves. Sixty-one-year-old women are not supposed to wear what teenagers wear. They should choose clothes which shroud their bodies and not attract attention.

The rules about what sixty-year-old women should and

shouldn't do have always been strict. When my mother turned sixty she decided to defy convention. She would not, she told me, go into all black as her mother-in-law had done on her sixtieth birthday. Mother would continue to wear the pretty pastel-coloured dresses she had always worn. She also continued to wear the whalebone corsets she had worn all her adult life, through each hot and sticky Australian summer. She never accepted trousers as a female garment. Whenever she saw me wearing a dress she would say, 'I always like you in a skirt.' My mother was the supreme artist of the implied criticism.

Mother is no longer here to criticize me directly or indirectly, but other relatives in Australia do. (Why do relatives feel that they have the right to say anything without regard to your feelings while friends are much more tactful?) I am asked directly or indirectly, 'When are you going to retire?' when what is meant is, 'Isn't it time you stopped gallivanting around and came home to die?' Of course I could be useful there before I died – looking after the youngest and oldest members of the family – but I should realize that turning sixty means that you leave life's race, pack up your things, and prepare to die. Many of my contemporaries are doing this. They are leaving the work that absorbed them for so many years, the homes they've filled with possessions, meaning and memories, and moving into retirement villages where they can occupy their time by laying bets on who is going to die next. This is not for me. I'm still part of life's race and I've just got into my stride. I come from a long-lived family and, barring accidents, I've got another twenty or thirty years to go.

Of course I have some anxieties about the future. I would hate to become incapable of looking after myself and fall into the hands of that multitude of carers for the elderly who so successfully combine sentimentality and savagery. They present to the world the sentimentality of caring for these poor old dears, and to the people in their care that lack of understanding and those daily humiliations which soon convince the strongest of us that life is not worth living. Such a conviction hastens death. Society connives at such 'caring' institutions – and there are many of them – because they dispose of those human beings who are seen as being of neither use nor ornament.[1]

I don't fancy dying of cancer. Where physical pain is concerned I am a coward. Whenever I read a death notice which says, 'Died after a long illness bravely borne' I know that could never be said of me. I comfort myself with the knowledge that if I die of an illness it won't be a long one. I've had a lifelong battle with bronchiectasis and chronic sinusitis, and in so doing acquired a remarkable tolerance for antibiotics. At the end pneumonia will be my friend just as it was my father's.

My general practitioner tells me that antibiotics always work. I believe that slightly more than what psychiatrists say, that antidepressants always work. I know that not to be true at all. I hope that my GP knows that there are situations where she should not attempt to see whether an antibiotic works. After all, these drugs cannot give any of us eternal life. I hope that, having assured me that antibiotics always work, she does not feel the need to prove it, and so prolong a process which must sooner or later come to an end. I hope that whoever is there has the good sense of the nurse and the daughter-in-law in Margaret Forster's autobiographical novel *Have the Men Had Enough?*

> As I left I stopped at the door of the Sister's office, feeling I should make some enquiries about Grandma's condition. The relief Sister was there, busy with paperwork, but she invited me in, indicated a chair. She said that she wanted to catch me anyway, just 'to make things clear'. Grandma was not eating, and more importantly, hardly drinking. The infection of her lungs was worse. The Sister was watching me closely as she said, 'The doctor isn't sure if it would respond to antibiotics.' Messages seemed to flash with every movement she made – the lowered head, the careful outspread hand, the gesture she made with her pen. Nothing explicit was said at all. I said it might be better to wait, to see if nature would clear the infection on its own and what about something for the pain. Sister raised her eyebrows. She said that perhaps that might be a good idea but she didn't think Grandma was in any pain at the

moment. Then she asked if all the family were in agreement.[2]

Nothing that happens in life is ever totally good or totally bad. Take, for example, the way in which invisibility increases with age. This for me is also an example of George Bernard Shaw's dictum that in life there are only two tragedies – not getting what you want and getting it. As a child and especially as a teenager I longed to become invisible. That or dying were the only ways I could see of escaping the endless stream of criticism I received from my family and teachers. I could never please them so I thought that I might as well disappear. Instead, growing into womanhood, I became more and more visible. Men looked, and wanted a response from me. Much as I wanted to be loved and admired I found the endless pressure from men wearying and irritating. In my late forties I discovered that the pressure was decreasing. Travelling on my own became safer and easier. However it wasn't just that I was no longer attracting attention. It took me a while to realize that I was becoming invisible. Now I am completely invisible, except to a few wise folk who can actually see me.

Let me give you an example.

In Johannesburg two years ago I was standing at the reception desk of a splendid hotel waiting for the receptionist to finish her phone call. I wanted to ask her for a safe deposit box. Across the huge foyer I saw an airline captain striding towards the desk. He reached it just as the young woman finished her call. With a smile that said, 'I'm wonderful and so are you' he demanded, ever so charmingly and confidently, instant attention from her. I said, 'I have been waiting some time. I need a deposit box.'

He looked around, startled. Had one of the pot plants spoken? Had this voice come from a radio? He was puzzled. He could see no one else at the desk. The young woman who had undoubtedly encountered many airline captains, smiled at me, rose, and asked me to accompany her to the safe room. He, still looking puzzled, trailed behind us.

This young woman was one of the wise folk. There was

something conspiratorial in our smiles. I think that we had summed up this airline captain in the same way. I suspected that she was as weary of the pressure from men like him as I was at her age.

Being invisible can be physically hazardous. People whose eyes I can see have not registered my presence walk into me or let doors close in my face. But for someone whose daily delight is observing people being invisible is just marvellous. What a lot I learn about people when they don't realize I'm watching and listening!

For example.

I boarded the Highland Express at King's Cross and sat in one of the groups of four seats in a first-class carriage. I was going to Perth, and I came equipped with newspapers, books, my writing folder, a packed lunch and a mug of tea, all of which I spread over the table. This expanse of property and myself were quite invisible to the two young men who entered the carriage and took the two seats across the aisle from me. I knew I was completely invisible because, for the whole of their journey from King's Cross to York, they never lowered their voices no matter how delicate the subject they discussed. If I had paid continuous and careful attention to their conversation I could have identified which firms they worked for, and I could have written a very interesting and revealing report for their bosses and colleagues whom they discussed in detail. As it was, my attention drifted in and out of their conversation while I read or worked on this chapter.

These were two men in their late twenties who were already well up the ladder of entrepreneurial success. At first I thought they must be computer wizards, but as they went on to talk about using electron microscopes and scanners I realized that, as well as being computer wizards, their basic training was in science. However, they were planning careers which would take them into top management. They were obviously very competent chaps. The kind of chaps who, if a woman can't get her car to start or a computer programme to run, would sort the problem out for her.

From a discussion about their technical prowess they examined the question of how long they should spend in the sales department to acquire the essential experience. Then they went on to discuss the most exciting subject of all. No, not sex. Something far more important than that. Their expense accounts. Not complaints about how unfair or tardy the accounts departments were, but how to manipulate the system to make a profit.

Such a sharing of secrets brought them closer together. The discussion about travel expenses brought them to telephones and answerphones, and, suddenly, I was aware that they were sharing a deeply personal secret. Each of them was laughing the way we do when we tell someone something we wouldn't reveal to anyone else. Each of them had at home one of those answerphones which, if you have a remote control and the code, you can phone from anywhere and get your messages. Now I heard them share a confession which they would never want to reach a woman's ears. They confessed to each other that they did not know how to operate their remote control to get their messages.

Ever helpful, I was tempted to offer to show them just how to do this. But that would have blown my cover and embarrassed them dreadfully. There are times when a woman must not reveal to a man that she knows his weaknesses.

I don't feel myself to be invisible. When I look in the mirror I see someone there. This is just another example of how we are always aware of two sets of perceptions – how we perceive ourselves and how we perceive other people's perceptions of us. These two sets of perceptions rarely fit comfortably together. From our earliest childhood we see ourselves in one way and other people persist in seeing us differently.

We all want to be accepted, loved and admired as the person we know ourselves to be, but this rarely happens, not even when we are tiny babies. Loving parents might give their baby unqualified acceptance, but they can't force the rest of society to do the same. Little Miles was only two hours old when his mother heard a visitor scolding him for having hurt his mother when he was being born. The next morning she heard the nurses scolding Miles for keeping his mother awake at night, when in fact both of them had been too excited by their new situation to sleep. Babies in the womb, so the research shows, hear music and prefer the sweet melodies of Mozart or, if their mothers watch television, the theme song of *Neighbours*, to the sharpness of Stravinsky. Miles mightn't have recognized the actual words that were said to him in his first twelve hours, but he would have recognized the tones and in response to the scoldings felt sad and confused.

At first the difference between how we see ourselves and how we perceive other people's perception of us is very confusing. Babies puzzle over, 'Why does my lovely mother disappear and this screaming harridan come in her place? Why do I cry for comfort and company and no one hears me?'

Then we work out a way to end this confusion. One young woman, chatting to me about her childhood in Australia, said, 'You know how when you're children and you sit in the back seat of the car and your parents sit in the front, and everything they say is right and everything you say is wrong?' She showed how we end our childhood confusion. We accept what our parents tell us. They are right and we are wrong. And when they tell us we are just not acceptable to them – we are dirty, greedy, selfish, bad-tempered, stupid, ugly, the cause of all their misery – we believe them.

Children are usually wise to accept what their parents say because, if they don't attempt to fit in with their family, life will be very difficult for them. However, accepting without question what your parents say can create the bad habit of not questioning what other people say, especially those people whom you see as more powerful or more knowledgeable than you.

Through our family we discover that in the society we live in there is a collection of rules, attitudes and beliefs which have developed over the centuries and which, if we make them our own, will enable us to behave in ways which are acceptable to our family, friends, colleagues, and society at large. If we don't accept these rules, attitudes and beliefs and instead insist on working things out for ourselves we find that we are then faced with those very difficult questions, 'How should I make sense of my life?' and 'How ought I to live my life?'

It is so much easier just to accept the rules, attitudes and beliefs that most people hold than to think for yourself, even though the rules, attitudes and beliefs of every society have the function of shaping individuals to fit the society. Fitting into your society means giving up or hiding part of yourself. Most of us, whether we question society's rules, attitudes and beliefs or accept them wholeheartedly, try to fit into society, for not to do so means being seen as mad or bad, the consequences of which are very unpleasant.

Society's rules, attitudes and beliefs serve to classify its members and define how the people in each classification should behave. One important classification is according to age. Whenever we meet, or hear about, another person we want to know how old that person is. We think of ourselves always in terms of how old we are.

Every society divides its members into the young, the middle-aged and the old. However, just where these demarcations fall depends on how long the people in that society expect to live. Up to the beginning of this century life expectancy in industrialized countries was little more than about forty years. Our society's rules, attitudes and beliefs have not yet allowed for the fact that life expectancy is now seventy or more.[3] Consequently anyone who makes it past sixty is regarded as a living fossil.

Even though each society determines some external markers with regard to who is called young, middle-aged and old – the age you are allowed to leave school, have your bar mitzvah, vote, marry, retire – what you actually see as young, middle-aged and old depends on how old you are. When I asked Josh, aged ten, and Jaime, aged eight, what they saw as young, middle-aged and old they were agreed that thirty is middle-aged. Their parents, Kate and David, both aged thirty-four, were definitely middle-aged. But to me Kate and David are in that group I call young. (When I asked Stephie, aged five, the youngest in the family, whether she was young, middle-aged or old, she said, 'I don't really know. Mum and Dad don't tell me those things about me,' thus exemplifying how, as children, we rely on our parents to tell us who we are.)

It wouldn't matter how we divided people into age groups

if we didn't then evaluate each age group and decide what was good and what was bad.

There are society's evaluations and our own evaluations. If your evaluation and society's evaluation of your age group don't agree certain awkwardnesses always arise. I like the age I'm at, but I still have to put up with being invisible or, if seen, being patronized. If your evaluation and society's evaluation of your age group do agree it can still be difficult. If society says, as it does, that middle-aged people are past their best and in middle age you believe that you are past your best, then life is indeed miserable for you. Even if society says that youth is best and you, being young, agree you can still be miserable.

You can worry about getting old.

TOO OLD AT THIRTY

The writer Kate Saunders and I were at the BBC to talk about revenge on Radio 5. I told her and the BBC researcher, Alison Potts, who was twenty-six, that I was writing a book about how we feel about getting older. Alison said, 'I was home at the weekend and do you know what my mother said? She said I was nearly thirty. I was really offended. I'm nowhere near thirty.' (Six months later Alison wrote to me to say, 'I'm all set for marriage on November 21 – a real rite of passage. I do feel older now.'[4]) Kate said, 'I tried to get used to the idea of being thirty. Six months before I was thirty I practised saying I was thirty. That was all right. The bad time was when I turned thirty-one. I'd realized that I was *in my thirties*!'

Ian McEwan, introducing the two protagonists in his novel *The Child in Time*, wrote, 'For all his worldly confidence, dark suit and handmade shirt, Darke was only six years older than Stephen. It was a crucial six years, however, dividing, on Darke's side, a reverence for maturity that made it a teenage ambition to appear twice one's age, from Stephen's conviction that maturity was treachery, timidity, fatigue, and that youth was a blessed state to be embraced for so long as it was socially and biologically feasible.'[5]

Tony Parsons, writing in the *Guardian* about meeting his Japanese in-laws to be, said, 'In Japan they say a girl is like a Kurisumas Keiki – Christmas cake. At 22 and 23 she is perfect, at 24 close to her prime, but after 25 it is all downhill.'[6]

One day a few years ago when I was still working as a therapist I realized that of the twelve clients I was seeing regularly, five were aged between twenty-six and thirty-three. They were each suffering in different ways – depression, anxiety, panic attacks, despair, self-harm – but they were all agreed on one thing. Thirty was the turning point in life. You had to have made it by the time you were thirty because after thirty you were *too old*.

The five differed on what they regarded as 'making it'.

Mary and Susan saw thirty as a biological time bomb. If a woman hadn't had her children by the time she was thirty she would never be a mother, or even if she did have children and even if the children escaped being affected by some dreadful genetic disorder which only elderly mothers (i.e. over thirty) can create, they would suffer at the hands of a decrepit, ageing mother. It was no use my pointing out that many women in their thirties and forties successfully conceive and bring up healthy, happy children. Mary and Susan had built their identity on becoming mothers by the time they were thirty.

Mary believed that the only way she could be a good woman was to become a mother. She longed to lavish on her own children the love she had been denied as a child. Her mother had been twenty when Mary was born, and died of cancer five years later. Mary spent her childhood being passed from one relative to another.

Susan really wasn't all that interested in children and demonstrated this lack of interest in many ways, but she wouldn't admit this to herself, much less to anyone else. What she wanted was her mother's approval. Her mother bestowed approval on Susan as frequently as it snows in the Sahara, but she did make it plain that it was her children's duty to provide her with grandchildren. Susan knew quite well that if she did have a baby her mother would take the child over on the grounds that Susan was as incompetent as a mother as she had been in everything else, but she clung to the hope that just by giving birth she might make her mother say for once that she was pleased with her.

Unfortunately neither Mary nor Susan had had any success in creating a stable relationship with a man and they both had the good sense to know that until they sorted out their problems – Mary her depression and Susan her habit of relieving tension by cutting herself – they could not bring up a child on their own. By believing at twenty-eight that over thirty was 'too old' they denied themselves a decade or more in which to sort themselves out and then have children. Instead each passing day brought them increasing anguish.

John was one of the most anxious people I have ever met. He said he'd always been anxious – he'd inherited it from his mother – but his anxiety had got a great deal worse over the past three years. It all had to do with work. He'd been one of the bright young trainee managers in a large firm where the competition between all the managerial staff was very keen. The trainee managers, once they finished their training, were supposed to race up the rungs of the hierarchy so that they reached a position of considerable authority by the time they were thirty. However, he had been held back for a year, the victim of a hit and run driver. It was no use my saying that he would have caught up with his fellow trainees by the time he was thirty-one or thirty-two. He was sure that if he hadn't made it by thirty he was out of the race. It was certainly no use my pointing out a parallel between the way the group of trainee managers had run away and left him and how his brothers, all older, bigger and faster than him, would tease him by handicapping him in some way and then running away and leaving him behind. Surely I wasn't suggesting that there was some connection between childhood experience and adult life! Would I please stop talking such nonsense and instead tell him how to get rid of his anxiety.

Simon had celebrated his thirtieth birthday with a party in a pub. All his friends were there, and his dad. Simon's dad loved a party, and loved being with Simon's friends who enjoyed –

or at least seemed to enjoy – his stories of his youth when he was Jack the lad *and* a very successful entrepreneur. When he was just eighteen he'd got a barrow at the local market and sold sausages and cheap cuts of meat. By the time he was thirty he owned a string of butcher's shops, a sausage-making business, a large house and a Rolls-Royce. 'I always wanted to own a Rolls-Royce,' he would say, 'and I was determined to get one by the time I was thirty and I did.'

He said this at the party, just after they'd all sung 'Happy Birthday' to Simon. He slapped Simon on the back and said, 'Well, boy, where's your Rolls-Royce? You're not keeping up with your dad, are you? Never mind. Have a cigarette. Bloody hell, the packet's finished. Get me another one, there's a good lad.'

As his friends laughed and joshed him Simon, smiling, bought his father cigarettes. When his girlfriend whispered, 'Your father's awful to you,' Simon said, 'He doesn't mean anything. It's just his way.' However, the next day, when he was taking his dog for a walk along the canal he thought about his future, working for his father, no escape until his father died. 'He treats me like a kid, works me hard, pays me a pittance. He'll die and leave me nothing,' he thought.

Simon had been in therapy for many months before he could allow himself to remember and talk about what had happened beside the canal. Initially all he would say was that he had been taking his dog for a walk, thinking about nothing in particular, when he was overcome by terrible weakness and trembling and a pain around his heart. He had collapsed in a near faint and was rescued by some passers-by. At the hospital the doctor said Simon had a panic attack.

When he finally came to look at the sequence of events he remembered how he had seen the starkness of his future, how, having failed to make it by thirty and thus earn his father's and his own respect, he was as good as dead. He had felt angry with his father, so angry he could have killed him, and then he was afraid that he might kill him and be left all alone, and afraid that his father would punish him as he had always punished him for getting angry. But even when Simon could see all this he could not move on emotionally and physically until he had revised his belief that everything worth achieving had to be achieved by the time he was thirty.

Peter had many achievements and he was only twenty-eight. He had a doctorate in mathematics and had published a number of highly regarded research papers. He was also an outstanding athlete. But for him all he had done was nowhere near enough. He had come to me with the question 'How can I further my career?', but what emerged in our discussions was not his ambition but his intense despair.

When I asked if his parents were proud of his achievements he said, 'I've done what they expected of me.' Both his parents were lawyers and they had sent him, their only child, to the best schools. They came to speech and sports days and shared the glory of the prizes he had won because they felt it was self-evident that their child would be a high achiever, but the rest of the time they gave him scant attention while they pursued their careers. Peter was no more than eight when he realized that simply achieving educationally and athletically would never gain him his parents' undivided attention. He would need to do something more.

Peter remembered how, on holiday from his prep school, he had overheard his parents talking about the death of a young musician whose concerts they had attended. They spoke of his achievements and likened him to Mozart. 'Who knows what he might have achieved if he had lived,' said Peter's father. 'I'll be wondering that for the rest of my life.' 'I'll never forget him,' said his mother.

That night Peter created a new fantasy about what his future would be. He abandoned the story about winning ten gold medals at the Olympics and, as the world's greatest scientist, finding a cure for cancer. He could never decide on the right ending of this fantasy, whether, when his parents begged his forgiveness and vowed their eternal love, he would spurn them or forgive them. Now his future was clear. By the time he was thirty his brilliant achievements would be there for all to see. Then, soon after, he would die. He wasn't sure whether he would die of a mysterious illness or in an act of extraordinary heroism, but one thing was clear. His death would impress his parents in a way that his life never did. They would discover their great love for him and they would grieve to their dying day.

As he progressed through school Peter learned that in some fields of endeavour much can be achieved in youth but in others achievements come only after many years of toil. However, mathematicians usually do their best work in their twenties, and athletes need to be young. So he decided to specialize in mathematics and running. Once he'd made some extraordinary mathematical discoveries and established some times for the 100, 500 and 800 metres which few could emulate there would be no point in living after he had turned thirty.

So convinced had he become that his fantasy was an accurate plan for his future that at twenty-eight he approached his thirtieth birthday as a condemned man approaches his execution. He was a guilty condemned man, for his achievements fell far short of what was required. His question to me was really, 'How can I achieve in the next two years everything I must achieve?'

Peter was not the first young man to believe that what he had achieved could never be enough. At twenty-three John Milton was writing,

> How soon hath Time, the suutle theef of youth,
> Stoln on his wing my three and twentieth yeer!
> My hasting dayes flie on with full career,
> But my late spring no bud or blossom shew'th.[7]

Yet he had already written 'On the Morning of Christ's Nativity', 'L'Allegro', and 'Il Penseroso'.

This sense of needing to achieve much between leaving school and reaching thirty can come in part from the way childhood is presented to children, not as a time to be enjoyed but as a preparation for growing up. Children sacrifice much in the hope of rewards in their adult life, and they want the rewards to come immediately upon reaching adulthood. Some children see the rewards as fame and riches, or undying love, and others see them as the delights of power, of imposing their ideas on other people.

Christopher was twenty-one when I talked to him. He said, 'I think you're pretty much adult by the time you're seventeen, but I'd see being an adult figure by the time you're twenty-eight. It's a stabilized age. After that your physical development starts going in another direction. You settle down. A friend of mine who is only twenty-one got married the other day and I thought that was frightful. You only do that when you're twenty-eight. By thirty I want to be in some position of influence. To be able to put things that I believe in into practice and make them happen. Whether it's academic or legislative, I don't know.'

Christopher saw 'the things I believe in' as totally beneficial. He had not yet seen how dangerous are the people who know what is best for us. When you have been brought up to believe that you have to earn by achievement the right to exist, learning to tolerate limitations and uncertainties in yourself and others can be difficult.

Christopher interpreted the doubt that experience of life engenders in many older people as being an increasing weakness that follows turning thirty. He said, 'I don't see turning thirty as going downhill. You just start climbing a different hill. It's quite hard now to visualize any positive aspects to it although there obviously are. You start to grow in different ways. You're not in such a rush to get anywhere and do everything. As you get older you could have a more measured approach to goals.'

No doubt as Christopher gets older he will come to understand how, with the passing of the years, we become less certain. Enoch Powell was far more certain of the correctness of his views when he was twenty than Christopher is at twenty-one. Interviewed shortly before his eightieth birthday, he said,

One is less sure. Having seen so many certainties overturned and judgements aborted, I am more sceptical, more mistrustful of what I think I see, or think I hear, or think I observe. One distrusts one's own perspective which is shifting, changing, and therefore one distrusts one's judgements. Indeed, I suppose one would not take life at all seriously if one were as sceptical as one had become in one's eighties.[8]

All these stories about people who had given to the age of thirty a meaning which aroused in them a feeling of dread are illustrations of how we each construct our own life story. This story, like all proper stories, has a beginning, a middle, and an end. The beginning is where we came from – our family's history, the history of our nation/race/religion as we learn it from our teachers, our personal history as told to us by our family, and, increasingly, our memories. The middle of our story is present time. From the present we see the future which stretches before us as the working out of our story. We do not see our future as simply the passing of time where anything can happen. We create expectations and predictions about our future, and these expectations and predictions evolve from the life story which we tell ourselves.

We begin creating our life story in those first moments when we discover the passing of time, a discovery which grows out of the baby's innate ability to connect one event with another and use this connection to expect the second event to occur once the first event has happened. Babies can make these connections in the womb. About eight months after birth most babies come to understand that objects and people go on existing even when they are out of sight. Some evolving sense of past and future must exist by then, though learning concepts of hours, weeks, years comes much later. The sense of self evolves with the sense of time passing, and our life story is an essential part of our sense of self.

The meanings we give to aspects of time passing, like past and future, young and old, arise out of the conclusions we have drawn from our experiences. These conclusions become predictions, part of the future in our life story. Some of these predictions we use to exclude certain possibilities. When John Williams, an ex-convict, was telling his life story on BBC radio, he said, 'It's awkward to come into gay places if you're past twenty-five.'[9] This conclusion, drawn from his experience of gay places, now forms a prediction: 'If I go to gay places I won't be accepted because I'm too old.'

Caroline Sarll set out her life story, past, present and future, when she wrote about turning thirty.

Gin and gingivitis. Couch potato-itis. That's what I thought lay ahead of me as I awoke in the early hours of my recent thirtieth birthday. Only five more years, and (biblically at least) I'd be one of the middle-aged mob. I felt depressed, decaying and, worst of all, deceived. This should not have happened to me. After all I have always taken precautions against the onset of this condition – worn miniskirts like dusters, avoided wearing slippers and going to the Garden Centre on Sundays, known what was Number One in the charts – this just had to be an accident, didn't it? Didn't it? . . .

I am definitely ageing physically. Oh bum. And yes, even that's not what it was. Once described by a boyfriend as 'two boiled eggs in a handkerchief', it's more like an undercooked omelette now.

It's not the fact that I'm starting to fall apart though that really worries me. That's been happening since I was twenty-five, when I sprouted my first grey hair. No, it's all the things that I've suddenly become aware of. Like Scott Fitzgerald's aptly described 'thinning briefcase of enthusiasm'. The fear that the fight and the fire have gone out of me a bit. And I'm seriously threatened by all those horribly uncreased twentysomethings creeping up behind me at work.

More than anything, it's the realization that thirty really is the first of the 'ominous 0s'. The first real decade of decision; twenty is so obscenely young that no one really thinks about the structure of their life, or the limitations of it at all. And when I get to forty, I'm sure I'll have gone beyond caring. Then I will definitely be ancient.

The truth is I'm shocked I'm not immune from making responsible decisions like everyone else. I thought I could float on regardless, as I did through my twenties, rehearsing for the real thing. I was always 'going to do it next year'. Move to London. Change career. Travel the world. Write my first novel. Be disgustingly famous. All by the age of thirty. Ho hum. I haven't done any of those things . . .

But why the urgency? According to the media, it shouldn't matter that I haven't 'arrived'. Everyone knows that it's the thirtysomethings who are the have-alls of our society, with career, home and family.

But something tells me I won't even 'get it all' in the next decade. OK, I do have the first two, but I don't think I want the third. Not for at least ten years. Not when all my friends with children (that's ninety per cent of them) can only hold conversations based on Calpol and kacky nappies. I'm in no hurry for that. I'm too young. The trouble is, though, by the time I get around to that and marriage, my boyfriend will probably have run off with a nubile and 'normal' girl, ready to settle down, and my reproductive store cupboard will undoubtedly be bare.[10]

However, we make a grave mistake if we think that our life story is our life. 'Life,' said John Lennon, 'is what happens while we're making other plans.'[11]

Which is what my friend Jane, my exact contemporary, discovered. She told me, 'In my early twenties my friend and I thought that it would be impossible to live beyond thirty-five and that we would go together at that stage. I thought that certainly if I hadn't achieved anything by the age of forty-five there was certainly no point in living longer. And then the delight of coming out of that and realizing that the thirties were so much better than the twenties, and the forties were delightful, better than the twenties and thirties together, and the fifties even better still and so on. It was quite a revelation.'

Not everyone believes that.

FINISHED AT FORTY

Not everyone believes that thirty is impossibly old. Only people younger than thirty believe that. Those of us who make it past thirty increasingly, as time passes, see thirty as young, amazingly young. Would that I could be thirty again – but knowing what I know now.

However, enshrined in that collection of rules, attitudes and beliefs which society demands we hold is the belief that on reaching forty we are past our best. By forty we have become a lesser being than we were. We are less fit, less able, less acceptable, less valuable.

Within society individuals are seen as valuable in terms of the work they do. Children, the old, the physically and mentally infirm, and those who cannot find work are not seen as valuable. However, different kinds of work are not equally valuable. In our society television presenters are undoubtedly more valuable than mothers.

Individuals wanting to work have to be perceived as being capable of working. Job advertisements frequently specify 'person under 45'. In the USA legislation has forbidden such ageist criteria, but in the UK the government believes that no such legislation is needed because as large numbers of 'Baby Boomers' (the generations born between 1946 and 1966) get older employers will be forced to employ them because there are significantly fewer workers in younger generations.

In Britain the Conservative government values market forces, not personal feelings and wisdom. It is as insulting to be excluded in terms of age as it is in terms of race or gender. Age, race and gender are aspects of ourselves over which we have no control, and to be discriminated against because of these aspects is to be told that we have no right to exist. It is also insulting to be told that our accumulated knowledge is not valuable. Such an attitude is also stupid because there is a vast amount of knowledge, in terms of both skills and personal wisdom, which cannot be acquired from books or through instruction but only from doing. Yet people over forty who lose their jobs find it hard, often impossible, even to be interviewed for a new job, much less employed.

In an article entitled 'High flyer at 40, has been at 45' Colin Macilwain wrote:

The Industrial Society, in an effort to counter ageism, last year commissioned and published an extensive attitude survey among members of the British Institute of Management aged 49 to 65. Broadly, the survey suggested that the talents of many such people are being squandered by industry.

One of those anonymously surveyed, a 60-year-old engineering consultant, said, 'I am self-employed due to redundancy in 1986 and the absolute refusal of companies to employ on a permanent basis people of my age. I feel that a whole life's experience has been literally thrown on the scrap heap. Yet on TV two days ago I saw an employer trying to recruit East German engineers to work in the UK.'

Sue Webb, head of policy at the Industrial Society and author of the survey, says: 'Some of those affected are horrifyingly young. You are considered an old manager at 40, but to have great potential in your late thirties. So your life as a high-flying executive can be pretty short.'

One of the root problems, Webb thinks, is that mature people start to believe some of the myths about their own potential. She cites the example of one 48-year-old who told a prospective employer he expected this to be his last move. He didn't get the job.[12]

People in their forties and fifties who seek training in some work new to them will find their potential valued in terms of how many further years they can work. An innocent might think that older, wiser, more experienced people would make excellent social workers and clinical psychologists, yet anyone over forty-five who applies for a training post might well be refused on the grounds that the employing authority would not be able to recoup the cost of the training by the time the applicant retired.

Administrators work this out just by doing sums. They don't need to be told that anyone over forty-five might not be allowed to train as a psychoanalyst. Being over forty-five might in itself prevent a person from becoming a psychoanalytic patient. Otto Fenichel in his *Psychoanalytic Theory of the Neuroses* laid down that, 'The ideal age for undertaking analysis lies between fifteen and forty-five.' He gave as the reason for this rule, 'Older people may have lost the flexibility necessary for analysis.'[13]

According to society's collection of rules, attitudes and beliefs a person's acceptability and value are measured not just by what work they do but also by their sexuality. Are they sexually active? Do they look sexually attractive?

For men being, or apparently being, sexually active is far more important than looking sexually attractive. This is because most men are more concerned with competing successfully with other men and thus gaining their admiration than they are with gaining a woman's love. So they don't bother about their appearance, or when, as readers of men's glossy magazines, they do, it is in terms of competition with other men rather than in terms of attractiveness to women.

How can a man prove he is still sexually active when, in his late thirties or early forties, he cannot hide from himself that, while his spirit is still willing, his flesh is becoming increasingly weak? The much used solutions to this problem are not particularly edifying.

1. If married, he abandons his wife and goes off with a much younger woman. He looks to men for signs of admiration and tries to avoid seeing the disdain he engenders in women.

2. If a bachelor famous for his many liaisons, he fathers a child and proclaims that he is the first man to discover the joys of fatherhood.

3. Since (1) and (2) are expensive, most men have to resort to displaying the behaviour which says, 'Given half a chance I'd put it about all the time, but the wife, the job and lack of money limit my chances.' Hence the popularity of the Page Three Girl.

Not all men feel the need to resort to any of these solutions. They have recognized that for men there is no conflict in being perceived as sexually active and attractive *and* as being good husbands and fathers. So these men present themselves as good husbands and fathers, and, indeed, some of them are. But for women such a solution is not possible.

For a woman the issue is not sexual activity but sexual attractiveness. Society says, if you are not sexually attractive you are nothing. The journalist Rosalind Coward reported:

> Diana is a researcher for the BBC. She is in her late thirties and she described to me how the whole ethos of her institution is hostile to the ageing woman. 'I've noticed how women producers and researchers mysteriously disappear in their forties. That's partly to do with the fact that many drop out to have children and then fall behind in their careers. But it's also to do with the fact that the BBC – I suppose like many establishment institutions – tends to be very prejudiced against older women. Just look at what happens on screen. Very few older women are kept on as presenters – there are hardly ever any older women on chat shows and intellectual discussions. The shows are for ever exchanging last year's model for this year's. Well, it's the same behind the scenes. It makes me feel very insecure. I never thought I'd be someone affected by growing older because I'm a strong person and I value myself. But in the last couple of years I've been assailed by doubts. I think these up-and-coming young men are going to want to surround themselves with attractive young women. I'm horrified to hear myself say that. I didn't think my confidence at work depended on my being young and attractive, but I can see that it does.[14]

When Anjelica Huston's long-time lover Jack Nicholson fathered a child with a much younger woman, she was, understandably, very upset. From what I have read it seems that she was even more upset by turning forty. She said, 'I cried for two whole days. I felt horrible, ugly and debilitated. It was a total nightmare. To me life was over when you reached forty. When I was growing up I always believed that reaching forty meant you were now old and decrepit. It meant that you were out of the running.'[15]

Anjelica, so it seems from her photographs, has maintained a youthful beauty, but, as any woman approaching forty knows, retaining youthful beauty requires much effort. Anjelica would have done this not merely because of vanity and the demands of her work as an actress, but because society demands that she should. As Emma Tennant said, 'There is no in between for women. We are either dumped-on grannies or rapacious sex-pots.'[16]

Peter Coni, chairman of Henley Royal Regatta, banned from the stewards' enclosure skirts which do not cover the knee. He said, 'There are idiot women of middle age whose legs should be concealed from the public view who insist on wearing the mini-skirt. We are really protecting the public from mutton dressed as lamb.'[17]

When Emma Tennant in her novel *Faustine* questioned whether women really want to spend their lives pursuing youthful, sexual beauty she found that American publishers rejected her novel on the grounds that it was not politically correct. She explained, 'Many believe that no woman in America should do anything other than pursue the aim of being as youthful as possible at all times. It is shocking to suggest that it might be a strain, that they might not want to.'[18]

Society says that it is not permissible for women to see the lives of Cher, Raquel Welch and Joan Collins, who have devoted themselves to remaining sexually attractive no matter how old they might get, as one of the many alternative ways that women might choose to live their lives. Women, says society, have only two choices, a granny or a sexpot.

This creates a tremendous problem for those women in their forties and fifties who wish to present themselves in ways consistent with the lives they lead and with their aspirations. Melissa Benn, interviewing the feminist writer and researcher Shere Hite, wrote,

> Then she tells me an interesting thing, how in the States a generation of women, aged about forty, are now running for political office and having terrible trouble with their TV commercials. They can't look too young, mutton dressed up as lamb. But then, 'the experts told them they had to stop looking like anybody's mother because young

women in particular won't vote for anyone who reminds them of their mother. The mother represents the trap of being female, part of a secondary class. Every generation who is young and hip wants to avoid becoming, quote unquote, middle-aged women. The thing is to change what people think of as middle-aged.'[19]

A plea for different and better meanings to be given to middle age came from a woman commenting on Germaine Greer's book on the menopause, *The Change*.[20] She wrote:

I started to have 10 hot flushes a day. You get a kind of one minute warning, like a nuclear bomb, then my hair and body would be wet with sweat. Afterwards I was freezing cold. My body felt overwhelmed. I would wake up at night and walk around and I was exhausted. Finally I decided to try HRT (hormone replacement therapy) and I grew enormous boobs but at least the hot flushes stopped and, as one dear friend said, 'Thank God. At least you don't look as if you're going mad any more.'

But as a sixties person I have terrible problems about age. The menopause told me I was getting older, that I couldn't beat the rap. Emotionally I felt that it was the end. As a forty year old you are acceptable but I am now approaching fifty and that is beyond the pale. Society tells you that at fifty you are not interesting, you're useless. There is no women's movement any more, so we have to take on these negative images alone and find positive ones for ourselves, and it's hard.[21]

It is indeed hard because for women there are not just the passing years to contend with but the inevitable menopause, the end of a woman's reproductive life. Society says that a post-menopausal woman (and the menopause can be as early as forty) cannot possibly be seen as sexually attractive or enjoying sexual activity. Couples who go on having enjoyable sex into old age are seen as quaint and cosy, not dramatic and significant as young lovers are seen. Middle-aged women with lovers younger

than themselves are seen as bad women and their lovers denigrated as 'toy boys'.

Germaine Greer agrees with society that a post-menopausal
woman ought to be as chaste as a nun. 'Some women,' she
said, 'the lucky ones, lose interest in sex after the menopause.'[22]
However, in saying that this is what women want she is simply
reflecting her own experience, not reporting a universal fact.
She is glad to be free of sexual entanglements and the messiness
of menstruation. Like her, women whose lifetime's experience
of sex was that it was unpleasant or boring are pleased to escape
it, but women who enjoyed sex do not share Germaine's views.
When I compare notes with such women who are in their fifties
and who are on their own it is not sex they reject but all the
responsibilities which, for a woman, go along with a sexual
relationship. When you've had to be responsible for others all
of your life, once the burden is lifted you don't want it back.
Such women hear their married sisters, when they contemplate
their husband's retirement, mutter, 'I married him for life but
not for lunch.'

Meanwhile, Cher, Raquel and Joan deal with the menopause
by pretending that for them it does not exist. They are for ever
young.

At least they look young to me. I wondered how they looked
to young people. Maria, a nursing student of twenty-one, told
me that she admired Cher immensely. 'She's taken charge of
her life just like she's taken charge of her body. I think she looks
great.' Her admiration for Cher did not seem to have changed
how Maria lived. Keeping a youthful appearance will be successful only if such care is started before any signs of age appear.
What did Maria do to preserve her beautiful skin and figure?
Nothing, she said. Her job was too demanding.

I asked Naomi, aged fifteen, what she thought of Cher and
women like her.

She said, 'I think they're trying to make themselves what
they're not. They're trying to make themselves look younger
and lead a younger life-style. I suppose that's the American way
of life, isn't it? The whole American way of life is that you're

younger than you are. Keep going when you're seventy. I suppose it's good in some ways, but in other ways it's silly. They are pretending to be what they're not. It's a fact of life that people get older. As you get older you can't run around and you get wrinkles. Having facelifts doesn't change the fact that you're older inside, even if they try to kid themselves. I suppose there's nothing wrong with it, but when you think of these facelifts, they're too tight, they don't look natural. It doesn't look as real.'

'What will you do when you get older?'

'I'll have to accept it. It's one of those things, isn't it? I'm not scared of getting old. I'm scared of getting really old, you know when you see a really old lady crossing the road and she takes four times longer than anyone else. I'm a bit scared of that. But if you keep yourself fit. You hear of these seventy-year-olds running marathons for charity. I don't think I'll do that much, but I'm going to try and keep myself fit and not get decrepit.

'What do your friends think of Cher?'

'I don't know. We don't really talk about it. We don't walk into school and go, "Oh my God did you see Cher's new tattoo? I wish I had that." We don't talk about it. I don't know whether they do it to please themselves or to get to the public, but to get it to people our age, I don't think they do. I don't think there's anything wrong using face creams and looking after your skin, but special operations to change the way you are, it's not natural. My grandma, she's seventy something, she looks lovely. Even though her age is showing through now. She doesn't try to hide it behind face lifts and that stuff.'

Eternal youth comes at a great price. Whenever I see photographs of Cher's amazing body, or Nancy Reagan's stitched-in smile, I think of the pain those women chose to put themselves through in body-altering operations. Often, when I am running late and know that I have to spend five minutes putting make-up on, and never perfectly, I think of how much time must be spent in front of the mirror by those women whose make-up and dress must always be perfect. How uncomfortable it must be to wear a flowing wig over thinning, dyed hair! How debilitating to worry over every wrinkle.

Pain and discomfort always make us self-regarding. Constant inspection of one's appearance, comparing how I look now with how I looked yesterday, or how other people look creates a self-absorption which excludes other people and ignores the world. For ever young means for ever selfish. This is the moral of Emma Tennant's novel *Faustine*. In this Muriel, at forty-eight ageing and invisible, gives her soul to the Devil in exchange for eternal youth. She discovers the exquisite power a beautiful woman has over men. The Devil, as generous to her as he was to Faust, gives her wealth and the power that comes with wealth as well, but what she loses is her capacity to care about other people. This is simply part of the Devil's plan to create Chaos which is unending, a world where everyone leads lives of utter selfishness, a world not unlike our own. The story ends with a warning from the Devil to us all.

> I must merely hint that the next time you happen to turn on the TV, or find yourself to be lucky enough to be in a red-light district or at the receiving end of a delivery of explosives or guns, next time you enter a casino or flick channels to the latest scandal of politicians and bordellos and lies – you will see the blonde girls, dead-eyed, who bring in the crooks and villains, the murderers, robbers and rapists, who make up the Chaos which is my legacy.
>
> Next time you see those young women anywhere, remember, one of them could be Muriel . . . or Ella . . . or it could be you![23]

The blonde girls, dead eyed, are young women, or women striving to appear young, who have discovered that to be treated as an object, not as a person, is to be robbed of your human self, your sense of existence as a person in your own right (if the word wasn't so overloaded with misleading religious connotations I would call this essence of an individual 'the soul'), and that to live selfishly, protecting and rewarding yourself at the expense of others is to cut yourself off from the love and closeness which can restore and sustain your human self.

To be for ever young is to be selfish, and to be selfish is to be for ever lonely.

Many people, while wisely refraining from becoming totally absorbed in their appearance, decide to act as young as they feel instead of as old as their years. However, to carry out their intentions they must have sufficient self-confidence to ignore their young critics. My friend Nan, in her sixties as tall, slim, long-legged as she has always been, told me that when her daughters were in their teens and she in her early forties she would buy herself a pair of jeans, the most useful and exciting garment ever invented. Then she would see the disapproval on her daughters' faces and abandon the garment 'while it was barely warm'. Still not wishing to embarrass her daughters, Nan always wears well-cut trousers.

Middle-aged men do not escape criticism for wanting to remain young. When George Harrison decided to go back on the road again in concert the *Independent on Sunday* conducted a survey where people were asked, 'Are you ever too old to rock and roll?' Michael Hurll, producer of *Top of the Pops*, said, 'It's a bit like asking should you shoot the old spaniel who lies in front of the fire and smells a bit? Of course not. You can't put old rock stars down. Anyway it's the old veterans who can fill these 70,000 seater stadiums. I took my teenage sons to see Pink Floyd, with thousands of other old hippies like me, and they were amazed.' Wendy May of the Locomotion Club said, 'The sight of ageing rockers makes me go *bleeugh*. It's really sad to see Mick Jagger and the rest of the band looking like everyone's grandad, surrounded by sixteen-year-old girls. Everybody should grow old gracefully.' Eve, a schoolgirl of fourteen, said, 'George who? I do recognize the name from somewhere. Give me a clue.'[24]

Young people often say they feel embarrassed when their elders fail to act in ways which young people, and society, see as appropriate for their age, but such embarrassment is a cover for fear. When we are young we don't want our elders to be young alongside us. We want them to be older and wiser than we are, to watch over us and create structure and certainty in a chaotic, chancy world. We want them to be firmly *there* so we can react against them and so be able to define ourselves, even if it is only in terms of 'not like them'.

Children and adolescents want their parents to be old, but not so old that they cannot provide the security needed. Those post-menopausal women who are using various medical techniques to enable them to give birth, and men who decide to leave their settling down and raising a family to their fifties and older, are doing their children no kindness. Marek Kohn's father was fifty when he was born.

I never felt that the half-century gap dominated my upbringing, nor my childhood relationship with him. But the awareness of it was a constant, sometimes perplexing and sometimes frightening.

Above all, I feared his death. Of course children often fear the death of their parents, but his age gave my anxieties a specific formulation. With the innocent presumption of childhood, I hoped to strike a bargain with God. I used to pray that my father would live until I was at least twelve, an age that seemed on the verge of adulthood: by then, I thought, I would be able to cope with it.[25]

Most of us have to face our parents' death when we are in our thirties and forties, sometimes fifties. This is always a momentous event. No matter how old and frail our parents might be, when they do die we discover that we have been harbouring the belief that our parents would live for ever. As children we saw them as a fixture in the ever changing universe. No matter how dreadful they might have been to us their sheer fixity gave us security. Now they are gone the universe is in flux. Now they are gone there is no generation between us and death. If our parents can die, so can we.

It was this discovery, so a friend in her thirties told me, which led her and her husband to have a child. They had been putting off starting a family because they both had exciting careers and felt that they had plenty of time. Now the reality of death was upon them they knew that time was short.

Having a child is proof that you existed. The existence of your children ensures that you are knitted into the warp and woof of history. Death, especially the death of our parents, reveals how ephemeral we are.

Yet it is in our middle years that we see, and actually assume, the reality of being responsible for ourselves and for other people. In Hindu life this is shown very clearly. There a boy is a boy until he marries. Families seeking wives for their sons will place in newspapers advertisements which read, 'Boy, 34, seeks educated, homely girl . . .' ('Homely' means 'able to make a home', not 'plain'.) Once a boy marries he becomes a householder, a position of great authority and responsibility, and one which he holds until all his children are themselves married. With that it becomes the responsibility of his sons to look after him and his wife. Now the parents are free. They can stay with their children and support, advise and harass them, or they can seek spiritual advancement by reading holy books, following a guru, or going on pilgrimages to holy places.

No such pattern for middle and old age exists in Western society. Whether you have children or not, whether you wish to pursue a contemplative life or be as actively involved in life as ever, turn sixty and you become

A LIVING FOSSIL

The official psychology which portrays the old in terms of deficiency and personal deterioration is the psychology written by people who are not themselves old. Like children, the elderly are not given a voice in defining their condition.[26]

The fact that until recently the over-sixties were rare fossils did not make them valuable fossils. They had little power, except what they might exert over their families. The public attitude to them was, and still is, that they were poor dears who need looking after. The charity DGAA (The Distressed Gentlefolk's Aid Association) recently ran an advertisement in the national papers for an organization called Homelife. It features a little white-haired old lady. Her head is bent and she looks up supplicatingly. Around her sloping shoulders is an arm and hand so large that the gesture seems more concerned with power and control than with support. The text states,

Homelife will be her guardian when she has nowhere else to turn.

Fortunately, Homelife provides help and advice just when needed. Run by the Charity, DGAA, Homelife helps young and old people who have been forced into reduced circumstances. Our contribution often takes the form of regular or temporary payments enabling people to remain independent in the comfort of their own home.

Homelife's work doesn't end there. In thirteen residential care and nursing homes around the country we look after elderly people who are frail or infirm and no longer able to look after themselves.

Please help us to help them by making a donation to Homelife.

Together we can continue to be her guardian.[27]

This advertisement shows how the old have good done to them whether they want it or not. There is no suggestion that, even though we become frail and infirm, we still want to make our own decisions and have these decisions respected and implemented by those who offer us help. Instead, the implication of this advertisement is, as ever, that younger people know best and that the old ought to be grateful.

But change is on the way. The Baby Boomers are now middle-aged. Soon they will be old. The *Guardian* reported:

By the year 2020 some 36 per cent of the EC population will be over the age of sixty, and 20 per cent will be more than 65 years old.

It is also calculated that by 2050, more than 30 per cent of the population will be over the age of 80, while in the next 30 years the number of workers contributing to the benefits of each retired person will fall from three to two.[28]

Meanwhile, in the USA, according to the *International Herald Tribune*:

The needs of the baby boom generation threaten to engulf the US health care and retirement systems as the size of the elder population soars over the next 40 years, according to a private study published Friday.

The number of Americans 65 and older will hit 65 million by the year 2030, compared to 30 million senior citizens today, The Population Reference Bureau said in a report, 'The Baby Boom – Entering Midlife'.

Baby boomers in the next 20 years 'will set the agenda for the nation's public policy choices in education, work-family policies, retirement programmes, and health care,' said the authors, Leon Bouvier and Carol De Vita . . .

By 2030 there will be more Americans over the age of 65 than under the age of 18, according to demographers' estimates.

That reduces the number of younger working people available to support the growing numbers of retirees.

'The baby boomers are going to put quite a squeeze on our social institutions,' Ms De Vita said at a news conference. 'That's why the 1990s are such an important decade.'[29]

Matthew Gwyther in the *Independent on Sunday* wrote:

The Baby Boom of the 1950s and 1960s was ended by a combination of The Pill and by large numbers of women entering the workforce. About 62 per cent of married women in the UK now go out to work, part or full time. The figure was 10 per cent in the 1930s and 20 per cent in the 1950s.

As a result, what demographers refer to as our Period Total Fertility Rate (PTFR) has settled down to a miserable 1.8 children per family. Europe, North America, Australasia, Japan and most of the East European countries except Russia, Poland and Romania, have 'below replacement' fertility. An average of 2.1 is required for long-term population replacement. In some parts of northern Italy people are so lacking in reproductive enthusiasm that the rate is down to 0.9 – meaning fewer than one child per family, one of the lowest rates in world history.

The dearth of youth is not simply an employment problem. Young people are consumers as well, often with large amounts of disposable income. The hard facts for those selling in youth markets are quite unpromising. The numbers of 15 to 19 year olds declined abruptly from 3.8 million in 1987 to 3.2 million last year. The decline will continue during the 1990s, and 1996 will be the blackest year when the number falls to 3.1 million. (This reflects the nadir of British women's fertility which occurred in 1977.) Thereafter the numbers will start to rise again.[30]

Advertisers are beginning to realize that they must change the way they address the middle-aged and elderly. Martin Walker in the USA recorded:

I may not be quite the weight I was when I joined the *Guardian*, and it may have become impossible to comb my hair in the way which conceals the thinner bits, but the reality of advancing age only hit home when watching TV the other day. It was a commercial for Levi jeans.

'Forget about cholesterol,' it said, showing a slim-hipped and dashing chap in the prime of his years. 'It's your jeans that have been cutting off your circulation.'

They were advertising the new style of jeans, rather more generously cut, designed for that generation which made blue jeans into an international youth uniform back in the 1960s. This is also the generation which is not quite the weight we all were back then . . .

American advertisers have woken up to the fact that the baby boom may have lost its youth, but retains its dominance of the consumer market. This bulge of post-war babies is passing through the demographic charts like a good meal passes through the body of a snake. Two-thirds of jeans buyers, sustaining a US market worth $7 billion a year are now over the age of 25. According to the latest census, there are 78 million of us baby boomer consumers who were born between 1946 and 1964. And forget the Yuppies. We are known in the market as Grumpies – grown-up mature professionals.

We Grumpies are being targeted today just as hard as we were in the days when all shirts and trousers were slim-fit. The brand loyalties that were established in the days when the jeans flared out are being repeated in these cruel days when the flare starts at the hips . . .

My wife tells me that the lingerie and swimwear stores are now featuring discreet girdles. They have comforting names like hips-slips and thigh slimmers, and many of them feature that little skirt flaring over the thighs that I vaguely recall from the British beaches in the 1950s.

Remember the jogging craze? Forget it. We Grumpies can't make that grade any more. Sales of running shoes have been stalled at around $600 million since 1986. Guess where the growth is? Sales of walking shoes have soared from $300 million to $1.5 billion a year over the past five years.

And Nike sports shoes has a new model – not some dewy-eyed athlete but the 44-year-old Nolan Ryan. The text of the ads celebrates us Grumpies: 'People who forget to retire and never get old. People who realized it's easier to keep going if you never stop' . . .

Then there is the ad for the new Varilux spectacles – bifocals for our fading eyesight. 'Erase the line between youth and middle age,' says the slogan. If only we could. Grumpies of the world unite – we don't even have our waistlines to lose.[31]

Meanwhile, Bob Tyrrell of the Henley Centre has taken a very close interest in those who are becoming the next generation of middle-aged, that is, those who fall into the demographer's 45–54 bracket. 'They've had a charmed life,' he says. 'They are very self-centred and used to being centre-stage. They avoided conscription, enjoyed the permissive society pre-Aids and got into jobs before the rise in unemployment. They drove the social revolution.

'In Britain and America the adults have been behaving like kids for the last 30 years and now they are the inheritance generation, benefiting from their parents principally through property left to them.'

The Henley Centre estimates that the value of inherited property will rise between 1990 and 2000 from an annual £7.19bn to £10.60bn. They had sex, drugs and rock'n'roll – now they're getting their parents' houses to boot . . .

Reading the tea leaves of his longer-term research, Bob Tyrrell foresees problems ahead. Yet again it will be the iconoclastic children of the sixties making the changes, refusing to behave like the generation they are following. He sees a far more confident and influential new cohort, not all despondent at being the inhabitants of an 'empty nest' once their children have departed. 'We had the age where we all wanted to be young, when youth is where it's all at,' he says. 'We all want to be fit and healthy, certainly – and the majority of middle-aged people now are – but maybe not so busy and energetic. I can see virtues like sobriety, wisdom and reflection on the rise. Our research shows that it's already starting.[32]

Perhaps the Baby Boomers are forcing a change of attitude. Kate Saunders said to me, 'Forty used to be the end for women. Now it's getting later. It's fifty.'

If fifty is the finish no wonder the advertisers still feel they can patronize the over-fifties.

Mike Laming, managing director of Development Business, a consultancy which specialises in identifying opportunities among elderly consumers, says, 'There is a growing temptation to package products for the elderly but this can lead to rebellion. That resistance lowers when something physically becomes a need in later years.'

Laming divides the over-45s into five phases: Retirement Aware, Wind-Down, Lifestyle Adjustment, Leisure Years and Inactive, the last of which begins at around 75. About half way through Phase Three comments like 'Don't label us' and 'We don't need special products' are being replaced by 'When you get older you sometimes need special things.'[33]

Does 'inactive' mean 'dead', or has Mike Laming forgotten that, even if we do not move around, we still think?

Curiously, no matter how many 'special things' we need to overcome the infirmities of our ageing bodies, inside we still feel the same person we have always been, just like David Christie-Murray.

> I am a most unhappy fellow
> My hair is thin, my teeth are yellow,
> My stomach, in distended sag,
> Looks like a half-full leather bag.
> But all these things I could abide
> If I didn't feel so young inside.[34]

Sometimes it is only our contemporaries who recognize this.

Sometimes we say to others, or perhaps just to ourselves, 'I feel old.' However, 'I feel old' has two very different meanings.

We always know ourselves both as a body and as a person. We can say, 'I feel old' and mean, 'My body feels old,' or we can say, 'I feel old' meaning 'I have lived a long time.'

'My body feels old' involves remembering when your body could do things which it now refuses to do. This is always sad, for it always involves loss, and sometimes it is frightening because you know that you are caught up in a process which you feel will get worse.

However, it is foolish in the extreme to wallow in sadness and fear. It is important to remember that everything changes all the time and that variety is the spice of life. How boring it would be if you went on doing the same things year after year after year. It is much wiser to enjoy what you are doing than to mourn what you are not. My thirty-two-year-old friend Harri swims two or three laps in the time I swim one, but I swim for as long as she does – twenty to thirty minutes – and slow swimming is very conducive to thought. Much of this book was written while I was swimming.

It is foolish, too, to assume that an ageing process will necessarily run its course no matter what you do. Joints and muscles that are regularly exercised stiffen much more slowly than those that are kept still. Hearts, lungs, blood vessels, muscles and the immune system benefit enormously from relaxation and meditation.

It is often tempting to say, 'I'm too old' in order to avoid doing something that you don't want to do. This is always unwise. If you keep telling people that you are too old they will come to think that you are much older than you are, and they won't bother to ask you to do the things you like doing.

Then there is saying, 'I feel old' when you mean, 'I have lived for a long time.'

Feeling that you have lived for a long time does not mean that you feel like an old *person*, even though you might feel like an old *body*. Feeling that you have lived for a long time is like watching a very long film, and, at those points where the story is uneventful, or repetitious, or disappointing, or lacking in subtlety because you with your great store of experience can see through the pretences of the *dramatis personae*, you become aware of just how long this film has been going on. You can feel a sense of weariness and boredom, and wonder how you can raise sufficient enthusiasm to continue watching the film.

This is not a new experience peculiar to growing old. I have been experiencing this feeling for as long as I can remember. I used to feel like that when I was five and Mother would take me with her to have afternoon tea with Auntie Hazel.

Auntie Hazel lived in a house where the doors were always closed and the blinds and curtains drawn against the sun. Outside was a garden consisting of concrete paths, a clothes line, and close-cropped spiky grass. The house was filled with ornaments which small hands were forbidden to touch. I was required to sit still and eat my fairy cake and drink my milk nicely while Auntie Hazel and Mother talked. Their conversation was never interesting. Each afternoon was the same as every other afternoon, and each afternoon lasted several aeons.

There are some advantages to getting older. As a child I was trapped in boredom. Now, at the first hint of boredom, I am up and away.

I guess what I fear most is not illness, infirmity, pain and death, but being trapped back in that boredom. It can happen so easily – and often does – to anyone who has passed sixty.

First, you have an accident or get ill. You have always looked after yourself very responsibly – known when to call a doctor, how much rest you should have, how much help you need. But now you discover that apparently you are no longer capable of making these decisions. Your family take you over and make your decisions for you. This is what happened to Fanny Pye in Nina Bawden's book *Family Money*. Home from hospital after being mugged on a London street, she lies in bed and hears her son and housekeeper talking about her: 'It was as if she had suddenly been thrust back into an artificial and terrifying childhood in which all adults were in league with one another, talking over her head and sealing her fate without ever consulting her.'[35]

Being in charge of your life is an essential part of self-confidence. When that control is wrested from you, your self-confidence dwindles.

Suppose then your family, your doctor, or the social services decide that you must go into hospital. You have turned sixty. You are put on a geriatric ward. It might never have occurred to you that you were geriatric,[36] and now there you are among

all those old dears. The staff regard you as an old dear too.

Old dears have few but simple needs. You might have needed glasses for decades, but now you don't. The staff, now in charge of your possessions, lose your glasses. You ask the staff to look for them, and they say they'll do this when they have time, but the staff are very busy people and you really shouldn't trouble them. Not long ago you would have stood up for yourself and demanded your glasses, but now you don't feel confident enough to risk a confrontation. So you stop asking for your glasses, and stumble around in a blurred world. You can't read or watch television, and the outside world becomes distant and unknowable. You no longer feel connected to it, and, as you can't escape into the other worlds that books, newspapers and television provide, the ward becomes your world.

The staff know that, just as you don't need your glasses, you don't need your teeth and your hearing aid. You swallow the pap the hospital serves, and no longer enjoy the taste and texture of food, or the pleasurable anticipation of a good meal. Unable to hear clearly what people say, you answer them as best you can. You sense, though you do not hear, that they are saying to one another, 'He's going senile, poor dear.'

The staff know that there are only two things which old dears need. The first is sleep. No matter that as we get older we need less sleep, and what sleep we do need is often best taken in relatively short naps. You as an old dear must sleep *all night*. No staying up late having a natter with your friends, or even just lying there in the dark thinking. You have to sleep (and not be a bother to the staff), and if you can't sleep the doctor will give you 'a little something' to help you sleep. So now you wake up each morning fuddled by the drug, your brain feeling like cotton wool. As your brain succumbs to the addictive properties of the sedative, your memory becomes uncertain and unreliable. 'Poor dear,' the staff say. 'She's becoming increasingly confused.'

The other thing which the staff know the old dears need are regular bowel movements. What old dears definitely don't need is privacy. You might remember the pain and humiliation of the proprietary interest your mother took in your bowels when you were little, and you might, once you had managed to exclude her from the bathroom, have kept all matters to do with bodily functions strictly to yourself. Now strangers not only enquire and demand answers about how your bowels are functioning, but they enter bathrooms and toilets without knocking, they pull curtains aside, and abandon you in situations of shame and humiliation, exposed for all the world to see. They say, 'He doesn't notice,' or 'We need to keep an eye on her.'

Old dears, so the staff know, need to be got up out of bed. You can stay in bed only when you are very, very ill, or extremely infirm, and when you are asleep at night. At other times you sit in your chair. These chairs are arranged at regular intervals around the walls of the sitting-room, while the television flickers in the corner, or are set in school-room rows with the television in front. The function of the television is not as a source of interest and entertainment, for the staff know that the old dears have lost interest in everything and do not need to be entertained. The function of the television is to suggest to visitors that the old dears are getting the stimulation that misguided geriatricians and psychologists say they need. These foolish people say that old people in their chairs should be arranged in groups so they can talk to one another, or at least see one another. Staff know that the old dears don't need this. After all, if you can't see or hear properly, can't enunciate clearly, and have trouble remembering, you're not much of a conversationalist.

If, as you are sitting there, you feel lonely and sad, and you despair that death alone can rescue you from this hell, you must make sure that you keep these feelings to yourself. If you don't, if you let fall a tear, or refuse to eat, or turn your face to the wall, a psychiatrist will be called. He and the staff know that, as Richard Burton said in his *Anatomy of Melancholy*, 'Melancholy is a necessary and inseparable accident to all old and decrepit persons.'[37] The psychiatrist will give you pills which make you biddable but which will fuddle your mind even more. Since your depression is undoubtedly endogenous, without any external cause – after all, you have everything you could possibly need – the psychiatrist might order electroconvulsive therapy for you, and thus deplete your store of memories. Neither the pills nor the electric current will answer your questions, 'What am I doing here?', 'What will become of me?'

It is no wonder that half of the post-menopausal women who fracture a hip die from complications of blood clots, pneumonia and infections within twelve months of the accident,[38] and so many old men kill themselves.[39]

Fearing this fate, many of the over-sixties try to fight back.

The traditional way of fighting back is to make a will. Then, whenever one of your possible beneficiaries seems likely to displease you, you can threaten to cut them out of your will. If the beneficiary persists in this wicked behaviour you can demonstrate that you have indeed done so.

My mother used to do this by tearing up her will and putting the pieces in the toilet bowl shortly before I went to the bathroom. (In my adult life I frequently displeased her by my relationship with 'that man', as she called him: my husband.) It happened so often that I suspected she kept a supply of will forms – each a distinctive blue – just for these emergencies. I was never told of being restored to her will, so being thrown out again had a rapidly diminishing effect. I assumed I was permanently excluded from the will and was greatly surprised to discover, when I had been living in England for ten years, that my mother and sister wanted me to use some of the inheritance due to me on Mother's death to visit her in Australia. I wonder now whether, had I never doubted that I had a place in her will and, by inference, her affection, I would have so easily left Australia and made my home in England. At the time I left home I felt that I had no ties anywhere. Mother's short-term revenge certainly had long-term consequences.

It was not that my mother did not know what havoc a will can cause in a family. Her father had made his will in the late 1940s. He left war bonds, then each worth a tidy sum, to his four daughters and oldest son, and his home to my Uncle Jack, his younger son. The home consisted of an old wooden bungalow, a garden and a paddock, part of a defunct mining community where a few homes were still scattered through the bush. The property was worth no more than the bonds that each of the other children were to receive.

All would have been well had Grandad died soon after. But he went on living, a tough old Scot determined to make a profit on the pension he got from the mine. The years went by, inflation went up, and the suburbs of the city of Newcastle spread westward, absorbing the old mining communities. The value of the bonds went down, and the value of the home went up. Despite the suggestions and then pleadings of his children,

Grandad refused to change his will. It was the only power he had left. He had been a harsh, authoritarian father with a ferocious temper. Once his children had grown up and escaped his power they had their revenge on him by treating him with contempt. The only power he had left was his will. He did not see, or if he did see he did not care, that his legacy to his children was anger, bitterness, envy and a profound sense of injustice. I witnessed what happened in the family and resolved never to get involved in such turmoil.

Power which is maintained by threat can never be enjoyed because the powerful person always has to stay in a position of vigilance. The kind of power which can be enjoyed is that which gives us freedom of choice and action. If you want that kind of power as you get older you need to take care of your health. But even that can create problems.

Hormone Replacement Therapy has been available to women for twenty-one years, and many women and doctors swear by it for creating vigour and strong bones; but, according to Ruth Hughes, there is one thing they never tell you about HRT.

'I'm quite sure that the benefits of HRT to me have been at the expense of my husband. I'm just as keen on sex now as I was in my twenties, and he just isn't potent any more. We struggle to achieve a weak erection and the whole point of the love-making now is to see if he can maintain it for any length of time, let alone ejaculate. It makes me feel very sad. I know I sound like one of those magazines, but I want him hard and to really fill me. And for the first time in our marriage he doesn't satisfy me any more.'

Julia, a fifty-one-year-old librarian, began taking HRT five years ago when her sudden migraines and joint pains were traced back to the menopause. HRT has become well established as a potent antidote to the hot flushes, night sweats, depression and other symptoms that, for many women, make this 'natural process' a nightmare. Long-term benefits include protection against bone thinning and heart attacks, two major causes of illness and death in women over fifty. Users enthusiastically report new energy, increased self-assertiveness and a fresh sense of purpose. It can also restore a flagging sex drive, as it did for Julia.

From this sprang a popular myth of HRT as 'the miracle treatment', the ultimate wonder drug for women. Through HRT, in tabloid parlance, for the first time in history, women could 'beat the menopause'.

Yet, like Julia's husband, Leslie, a fifty-four-year-old self employed builder, not everyone is happy with the changes therapy can produce. Many women find that their nearest and dearest do not welcome a middle-aged mum turning into a hang-gliding superwoman.

Even grown-up children can find it disturbing when a mother refuses to dwindle into little-old-ladyhood, especially if she emerges with an unabashed sexuality. Julia's daughters, age twenty-three and twenty-five, started giving her 'hints like twin sets and lavender water', and now meet their boyfriends in the pub instead of bringing them home.

'My son was even harder on me,' says Jenny, a divorcee of fifty-three. 'When I treated myself to a new wardrobe, he wanted me to take it all back to have the hems let down' . . .

Julia's husband also resents her periods interrupting their sex life, saying, 'I'd have thought you'd have finished with all that messy business by now.'

Others object that HRT is 'flying in the face of nature' or 'science gone mad'. Traditional biological determinists seem to have the greatest difficulty in accepting this intervention in women's biology. 'Nature designed middle-aged men and women to run down at the same time,' explains Roger, a plant biologist. 'Now women have a drug that can kick them back ten or twenty years, it destroys the balance. And given that men are already going to suffer more heart attacks and die earlier, it's hard to see the sense of it' . . .

Until male HRT is widespread, men may have grounds

for feeling that women have been given the power to turn
the tables on nature and on them.

Does this explain some of the hostility to HRT, the
fear that it will fill the world with, in Roger's words, 'ram-
paging women stuffed with storming hormones'? 'You can
adore Tina Turner and still be glad she isn't your wife!'
he says. Novels and films may portray the desirable older
woman, but an equally strong and much older tradition
shows her as a terrifying hag raging out of control: Lilith,
Medusa, the Hindu goddess Kali, Hurricane Betsy . . .

Now that women seem to have access to slowing down
some of the effects of ageing, is it surprising that deep
fears are unleashed? 'What about the future?' asks John,
ex-husband of Jenny. 'They're creating a breed of monsters. There'll be all these ferocious seventy- to ninety-year-
old women abseiling down Everest – whatever is society
going to do with them?'[40]

A woman over fifty, taking HRT or not, who wants to get
on with her own life, doing the things that interest her, making
up for the years when she put her family's needs before her
own, can cause her children great confusion and grief because
she does not behave in the way they expect. Her children, wanting the best for their children, believe that 'the best' includes
having a proper granny. Her children want her to dote on their
children because that is their reward for being good parents,
and is proof that their children are uniquely wonderful. When
the woman refuses to be a proper granny-type granny, her children become very angry.

Two friends of mine, who shall be nameless because they
don't want to upset their daughters, told me, 'My grandchildren
are nice and I'm pleased to see them. But I don't want to be
just an appendage to their lives. I have my life to live.'

At the time when women are being told they ought to be
proper grandmothers they are also being told they should lead
lives of extraordinary activity. The media abounds with stories
of feats performed by eighty- or ninety-year-old men and

women which youngsters of twenty would find hard. But, as Ann Karpf shows, all is not well.

Post-menopausal you might be, but post-aerobics? Never. Increasingly old people are depicted not as dentured cronies but leotarded achievers. But ageism hasn't gone away; it's had a face-lift.

If old people are now less likely to be invariably portrayed as passive victims, the new stereotype has stepped in smartly to take its place. Now the increasingly popular visual images of the old are on safari or climbing mountains; they effortlessly lap Olympic sized pools, run marathons, complete Open University degrees, master Swahili. The Help the Aged 'golden oldie' awards celebrate their achievements (in 1990 the eighty-nine-year old man who delivered meals-on-wheels twice-weekly, the septuagenarian jogger-for-charity). *Good Housekeeping* applauds the hundred-year-old woman punctilious about applying her make-up each morning. The *Observer* colour supplement snaps a clutch of hale ninety-year-olds still working and travelling who 'give the lie to the notion that you're past it at ninety.'

At first these new images seemed refreshing and liberating. It was a relief to know that you didn't have to swap denim for Crimplene when the free bus pass arrived. The threshold of 'old' visibly shifted, and the early images of the later Joan Collins and Jane Fonda seemed to totally redefine the life span; at the age when our foremothers were spent and sagging, these women were lithe and sizzling, effervescing with sex. But something wasn't right. The new way of valuing older people was to highlight their youthfulness. These older people were being celebrated for looking and acting young. Ageing had become a social crime.

In some ways this new stereotype of the 'young old' is even more oppressive than the 'old old' one was. Celebrities with the Hormone Replacement Therapy smiles and marathon-running pensioners may inspire some, but to others they represent an unattainable aspiration. And like the previous stereotypes, the new ones still lump old people together as a category rather than acknowledging their differences.

There's a seemingly charming story about the American feminist Gloria Steinem. On her fiftieth birthday an admirer came up and told her that she didn't look fifty. 'This is what fifty looks like,' she retorted. I used to like that story until it struck me that she was wrong: no, this is what some fifty-year-olds look like.

Those who've had materially or emotionally harder lives, who were widowed young, or brought up kids alone, those whose genetic inheritance didn't include infinitely elastic skin or unshrinking bones, whose faces are mapped with past exertion and present fatigue don't look like Gloria Steinem. But they shouldn't be punished for it.

The new images of ageing have brought their own ghastly truisms. Ladies and Gentlemen, You Are Only As Old As You Feel. They keep saying that. But what if you feel old?

If you feel old and have had enough, if life seems less inviting and more depleting, we'd rather not know. Just as we like our disabled people smiling and exceptional (the blind mountain-climber, the deaf musician) so we want the oldies who have bags of energy, who've 'never felt better', who are endlessly self-regenerating and 'amazing for their age', not those who merely show it. (The revolution will have occurred when 'you look your age' is a compliment.) We have reached a pitch that instead of admiring and learning from those who feel they've had enough and are ready to die, we're forever trying to jolly them up and yank them back to life.[41]

The old are a problem for the young when they insist on reminding the young that death will come. They are also a problem for the young when they fail to know their place. 'Their place' is defined quite simply.

1. The old should strive to be healthy and competent to look after themselves, thus not being a bother to their children.
2. Once the old become incapable of looking after themselves they should immediately become grateful and obedient, and die soon after.
3. The old should never embarrass the young.
   Here is a young man being embarrassed by his father.

Somewhere there's an enormous book. Its cover is decorated with exquisite gilt, its pages embossed with, well, even more exquisite guilt. This, after all, is the book of Family Law. Here it is written: a parent's place is in the wrong. They must always telephone you just as you are about to begin the dirtiest part of the evening's entertainment (*coitus interruptus inparentis*). Your mother must always treat your antics as a baby as though they have forever been in the public domain.

Here it is also written: a father must not look better than his son. There's no law stopping him from being a bit of all right in his youth. Indeed it can help things along if there's a good slice of family mythology about the old man's exploits in days past. But as the years wear on they should have the good manners to age properly, and that means badly. Their hair should recede, belly start to droop towards their toes. Their skin should turn translucent, the colour of sweating veal. And under no circumstances should fathers develop any sense of style.

My father has reneged on all this, damn his eyes. More to the point, damn his pony tail. Yes, his pony tail. As he slips gently into his 63rd year he has taken to wearing his hair pulled back, tied with a delicate band. It is a gentle flourish of white and dark grey which neatly complements the white beard he sports. His chiselled features have remained intact, in fact, improved. He has re-invented himself as a dandy, in mustard waistcoat and cravat. Sounds appalling? It isn't. The bastard actually carries it off . . .

The problem here is not simply jealousy, but a more

general feeling that he's misread the essential ground rules of fatherhood. Perhaps it represents a vein of conservatism in me. As long as we keep fathers looking and acting like fathers it gives us a chance to go out and re-invent the world. If our dads behave like us what's there to play for? . . .

For most people, the problem is one of familiarity. However hard you try to run away from it, one morning you get up, look in the mirror and, slam, there he is grinning at you. It's your dad, a little younger perhaps, maybe even a little more svelte, but, regardless, it's him.

It becomes ever more obvious when you lose your rag. One moment you're simply sounding off; the next you're listening to yourself being your own father when he used to shout at you about the state of your room.

Fine. I get all that. I'm almost resigned to it. But while I have received recognizable parts of him, I seem to have mislaid the good bits. The up-side to this is that I have, in my father, what social workers call a *positive role model*. Instead of being convinced that late middle age is a resting place for the burnt-out and uptight I can now consider it a fertile garden of glamour. Unfortunately, father/son relationships being what they are, it will inevitably force me to rebel. I will end my days dressed in three shades of brown rayon, wearing black plastic slip-ons and a stripey tie to breakfast, even on Sundays.[42]

For some embarrassment with the old turns to anger. In an article which presumably was meant to be funny but signally failed to achieve any wit, Chris Davis advised *Guardian* readers to 'Shove yer granny off a bus.' He wrote,

This country is becoming overrun by old people . . . Due to advances in medical science, improved nutrition and lack of a headstrong German government for forty years, the country is teeming with people too old for their own good. In yesteryear the occasional elderly nuisance could be shunted off to the south coast and forgotten about.

Unfortunately, some fool decided to give them reduced rail fares, so now they keep coming back ... Old people have an amazing propensity for complaining. At the age of sixty-five it suddenly dawns on them that society is a piece of shit, and they spend their remaining years (usually twenty-five of them) on an incessant tour de force of whining.[43]

One young man expressed his anger with the old even more directly. Paul Thomas, aged eighteen, wrote to the *Independent*,

I feel compelled to reply to the letter from Lord Young on society's bias in favour of youth. A grandfather in his eighties with cancer and a grandmother of the same age who suffers with dementia provide me not only with evidence of the existence of 'older people' but also with the absurdity of such an existence. They are not enjoying life to the full, they are simply waiting to die. The same appears to be true of the majority of 'older people' and yet their political power is increasing rather than decreasing.

Meanwhile youth has no power whatsoever. Decisions about the future are thought too complicated and delicate to even consult those who will be affected most – those too young to vote. World leaders go to war knowing that they will be dead before the consequences of such actions are felt.

Why is it assumed you have to be old to be right? Is it any wonder that many youngsters attempt suicide, while more commit it unknowingly by means of alcohol, tobacco and Ecstasy?

Whilst we are grateful for our exposure in the media in the realms of sport, music and beauty, we have to suspect that it is merely a means to stop us from demanding more of a say in serious matters. I am quite happy to lose the media to those old enough to need the distraction, in exchange for a chance of a world government by the young for the good of everybody.[44]

I remember feeling like Paul when I was eighteen. I guess Paul has difficulties with his parents as I had with mine. By the time I was eighteen, in 1949, I was discovering that the world was not going to be put to rights as we had been promised the Second World War would achieve. Paul would have had a better education than I had and be very well informed about the mess his elders have made of the world. Both of us, forty-odd years apart, thought, 'How dare they do this to me!'

Now I am part of the group whom Paul hates. When I first read his letter I was frightened for him, and wanted to warn him about hubris, overreaching yourself and bringing down the wrath of the gods. However, the old are always saying to the young, 'You'll be old one day and then you'll know how it feels.' The young never listen.

Thus history goes on repeating itself.

When I was a child during the Second World War I believed the propaganda put out by our government. This was that the great democratic nations of Australia, Britain, Russia and the USA would defeat the wicked, totalitarian triumvirate of Germany, Italy and Japan, and in the universal peace, justice and freedom would reign supreme. Time showed me that wars continue, and justice and freedom remain rare commodities.

The television producer Yasmin Pasha, born in 1962, told me, 'When I was a child I thought that everything about women and inequality and all that would be put right by the time I was grown up.' Now she finds that nothing has changed.

Calvin, as you can see, had the same problem.

Let's see if we can change the future for something better. In this chapter I could have gone on and on about how life becomes increasingly dreadful with each passing decade. How could we change this?

Suppose we begin by listing all the inescapable deficits of growing older. These are the things which, one way or another, happen to all of us, if we live long enough.

Waning sexual potency	Illness and infirmity
Menopause	Death
Loss of youthful beauty	

Calvin and Hobbes

I ASKED DAD IF HE WANTED TO SEE SOME NEW YEAR'S RESOLUTIONS I WROTE. HE SAID HE'D BE GLAD TO, AND HE WAS PLEASED TO SEE I WAS TAKING AN INTEREST IN SELF-IMPROVEMENT. I TOLD HIM THE RESOLUTIONS WEREN'T FOR *ME*, THEY WERE FOR *HIM.*

THAT'S WHY WE'RE OUTSIDE NOW.

I *WONDERED* WHAT THE RUSH WAS.

HERE ANOTHER YEAR HAS GONE BY AND EVERYTHING'S STILL THE SAME! THERE'S STILL POLLUTION AND WAR AND STUPIDITY AND GREED! THINGS HAVEN'T CHANGED!

I'M GETTING DISILLUSIONED WITH THESE NEW YEARS.

THEY DON'T SEEM VERY NEW AT ALL. EACH NEW YEAR IS JUST LIKE THE **OLD** YEAR!

THE PROBLEM WITH THE FUTURE IS THAT IT KEEPS TURNING INTO THE PRESENT.

I SAY WHAT KIND OF FUTURE *IS* THIS?! I THOUGHT THINGS WERE SUPPOSED TO IMPROVE! I THOUGHT THE FUTURE WAS SUPPOSED TO BE **BETTER!**

Now let's look at what we could do to render each of these deficits easier to bear.

Such ameliorations are much more readily available to those of us who live in the developed world. To mark the twentieth anniversary of the World Health Organization's programme on human reproduction a report was issued which showed that:

A baby girl born in the richest nations in 1990 can expect to live to the age of 81, marrying in her twenties and having two children, with annual health care expenditure on her coming to the equivalent of $1,000 (£500). One in eight babies across the world falls into this category.

By comparison one in seven babies make up the most deprived, born in the poorest countries, where a baby girl can expect to live perhaps 43 years, with a one-in-three chance of dying before her fifth birthday. She will marry in her teens and have ten or more children. Her country has less than US$1 a year to spend on her health.[45]

Nothing in life happens in isolation. Everything is in contact with everything else. Thus the inevitable physical consequences of growing old do not just happen. As they unfold they respond to their environment. Good health care makes an enormous difference. So does how these physical consequences are interpreted by the person experiencing them. If you have good health care and positive attitudes your encounters with the inevitable physical consequences will be very different from the encounters you have when you have poor health care, and when you despise and fear every aspect of ageing.

I have listed *loss of sexual potency* as the first of the inescapable consequences, but there is no clear pattern of this in our lives. Certainly in our teens and twenties sexual urges are many and fierce, but excitement and novelty as well as curiosity play a large part in this. The desire to be desirable or powerful keeps us coming back for more, as does good sex.

A woman's loss of sexual potency has more to do with bad, boring sex than with any ageing process. Conflicts between what a man regards as society's demands that he be seen as potent and his feelings of inadequacy and resentment have a greater incapacitating effect on a man's potency than does any ageing process.

The media consistently presents sex to us as the most desirable and exciting of all activities, but what many, perhaps most of us discover is that we outgrow the desire to have lots of exciting sexual partners. We find that a single relationship with a lover who is also a best friend is much more satisfying, and this relationship leads us into other interests, like children, or gardening, which absorb much of that energy and *joie de vivre* which used to go down the narrow channel of sex.

Thus, if we are lucky in our sexual partners, and wise, however our sexual potency changes over our life, it is integrated into the pattern of our lives. No two people are the same. For some people sex remains important to their dying day, and for others it does not.

For women the question of the waning of sexual potency is usually linked to the menopause. Germaine Greer insists that women lose interest in sex after the menopause, or if they don't they ought to. She also insists that every woman has a very difficult time in the menopause.

The truth is that the fifth climacteric is hard for every woman, but some are able to deal with it unaided, and others are not . . . When it comes to having a 'positive image' of the menopause the mind begins to boggle. It is hard to feel positive about vasomotor disturbance, painful intercourse and ageing; if saying that you reckon you can handle it is regarded as the expression of a positive attitude, the notion of positivity that is being invoked would seem to be paler than pallid. The truth seems to be that the question itself instructs the 'coping response'; women who appear to be coping best may in fact not be facing the situation at all. They may be sparing their partners and family from facing it too. Though such gallant behaviour will be perceived as positive, it is actually anything but that.[46]

When I was fifty-one I passed through the menopause without as much as a hot flush. I was not being gallant or protecting my family or denying reality. I was simply getting on with my life when an event, which, apart for the nine months when I was pregnant, had occurred every month since I was eleven, ceased to happen. I wasn't surprised. Menstruation had never caused me any problems, so why should the menopause?

I hadn't considered what had happened to me in my fiftieth and fifty-first year until I read Germaine's book and paused to remember those two years, and realized that that was a very good time for me. My work was going well, I had an increasing lecture programme and was travelling extensively in Britain and the USA, and, best of all, I was working on my second book, *The Construction of Life and Death* (now called *The Courage to Live*). I was reading widely in mysticism and philosophy. I had read Ernst Cassirer's *Philosophy of Symbolic Forms*,[47] and suddenly that which I had been struggling to see became crystal clear. In the midst of this I wrote a novel. It was a very bad, unpublishable novel, but it had a wonderful freeing effect on my writing, which shows in *The Courage to Live*. In the first half of that book the writing is far more academic and impersonal than in the second half.

I am telling you all this not to impress you with my industry but to show you that I didn't have time for a hot flush, much less for a charade of pretending that I wasn't a victim of 'vasomotor disturbance'. My health was good because I had been doing yoga for several years and I had a wonderful GP who understood my struggle to breathe properly and who gave me some real help. I enjoyed my life enormously. So why should the process of bodily changes cause me any problems?

I am not the only woman who has had this experience. Many women go through the menopause without difficulty. My friend Ofra Ayalon, Professor of Psychology at Haifa University, told me that from forty-five onwards were (and are) the best years of her life. These are certainly very busy years, as she had developed her bibliotherapy, the magic art of story-telling which helps children and adults to cope with trauma. Ofra writes books and travels the world to teach. She said, 'Getting older can be wonderful. No need to climb to the top of the mountain any more, and no dragons to kill any more. Now I walk down the easy slope and look at the view. No need to please anyone any more.'

Of course there are many women who do have difficulties, just as there are many women who struggle with menstrual difficulties. The medical profession is notoriously ignorant and dismissive of the physical problems that women can have. A woman needs to value herself greatly to be able to persist until she finds a doctor who takes her problems seriously and does something useful to help her. Many women lack such self-confidence, and so struggle on month after month, year after year, not wanting 'to trouble the doctor again'. The menopause compounds her problems, and occurs when other problems arise – children leaving home, parents dying, work coming to an end – which need loads of self-confidence to deal with.

The menopause is a time to cosset yourself and to take stock, not to dread.

What does arouse constant dread is the loss of youthful beauty. Perhaps it is just as well that when we're young we don't realize how beautiful we are. In our teens and twenties we peer into the mirror and see spots, or a crooked nose, or short legs. We don't see that lovely glow and freshness which older people see on the young, and mourn, and envy. Young, we inspect ourselves and see the first wrinkle, the first grey hair.

When something is inevitable usually it is best not to fight it, but to go along with it and try as best you can to turn it to your advantage. If we thought of our appearance in terms of change rather than loss we would see that we do not lose our beauty. Our beauty simply changes.

Here again the media does us a monstrous injury. The media presents us with one set of images and says, 'This is beauty', as if beauty can only be young and slim. Yet the history of art shows us that what is considered to be beautiful is different in different times and places.

As individuals we differ in what we regard as beautiful. A friend told me that she has a hobby of questioning her male friends about which women they regard as beautiful. She has discovered that many men find young women who don't smile very attractive. The men believe that if they can induce the unsmiling woman to smile this is proof of their winning ways or sexual prowess. This information solved a problem about which I have often puzzled. Why do the glossy magazines carry so many pictures of young women who look to me so disagreeably sulky?

Youthful faces and figures can be very beautiful, but they are also not very interesting. It is not until our face and body, and especially our hands, reveal aspects of the life we have lived that our own individuality shines through. If those arbiters of taste who work in the media understood this, and showed in the images used by the media the immense range of interesting beauty across all ages (and not just the occasional few arty black and white photographs) they would make us all much happier people.

At least in the rich industrialized countries there should be no reason for us to fear illness and infirmity. So much is known now about how to be healthy and avoid illness that there should be nothing to prevent most of us from having a healthy old age.

If all the people involved in the care of the elderly who become frail or ill understood that, no matter how incapacitated our body and brain might become, we still want to be given the dignity and respect of being treated as a person in our own right, then we need not fear becoming frail and ill.

We might also discover that some aspects of ageing which look quite terrible to us when we are young actually have advantages. I had a lesson about this on one occasion when I arrived at Newark airport in the USA. There was a long queue of foreigners waiting to get through immigration. I was standing beside an Englishwoman who must have been in her late seventies and was quite tiny, a really little woman. We started talking. The queue was moving so slowly, it was one of those places where the English actually talk to one another.

Always on my travels, whenever I saw someone in a wheelchair being wheeled on to the plane and off again I would think, 'I don't ever want to travel like that.' So I was surprised when this woman said to me, 'You know, I should have got a wheelchair.' I said, 'What do you want a wheelchair for?' She said, 'Oh, you get through all of this. Always get a wheelchair. They always take you to the head of the queue.'

I'd never thought of that. When we got through immigration we found there was an enormously long series of corridors to walk along before we got to the baggage carousel. Each of us was carrying a travelling bag and a bag of duty free goods. We saw a young woman coming towards us pushing an empty wheelchair. My elderly companion stopped her, and with such a sweet smile she said, 'If that's free, would you mind taking me?' So off she went in the wheelchair while I struggled on behind.

Just one more problem to face. Death.

Death requires thought. Some people are so frightened of dying that they spend their lives trying not to think about it. They can never be successful because, even if they steadfastly refrain from any encounter with the media, there are daily reminders of the brevity of life. Refusing to think about death, they lose the enthusiasm for life which a recognition of death brings. Because they are always watching out for an event which might remind them of death, they find many more reminders of death than do those people who have recognized that one day they will die.

We discover death early in our life, usually when we are no more than four or five. Then we have to decide which meaning to give to death.[48]

There are only two meanings we can give to death. Either death means the end of my identity or a doorway to another life.

We choose a meaning, and immediately the purpose of our life is fixed. If we choose to see death as the end of our identity, we have to strive to make this, our only life, satisfactory. There is a multitude of ways we can interpret 'satisfactory', but whichever we choose, we need to feel that our life is satisfactory if we are to live comfortably with ourselves and face our death with some modicum of equanimity.

If we choose to see death as a doorway to another life we

have to decide whether there is a chance that this other life
could be better than this one. Most people who choose death
as a doorway decide that this is so. Then they have to decide
whether everybody is entitled to a better life. Usually the answer
is no. Certain standards are set for entry into this other life.
Hence, if we see death as a doorway to another life, we have
to live this life in terms of the next. To live comfortably with
ourselves and face our death with some modicum of equanimity
we need to feel that we are meeting the standards of the next
life.

We need to think about these matters throughout our life
because the conclusions we draw from our experiences alter our
understanding of life and death. Many people report how a
close encounter with death lessens their fear of death and height-
ens their appreciation of life. Many old people welcome death
as an appropriate end to a satisfactory life. Even my mother,
who had always found the entire universe unsatisfactory, could
say in her eighties, 'I had a good life.'

There is another benefit which death brings, as my dear friend
Ann Hocking pointed out to me. She said, 'Life can do awful
things to you but death can get you only once.'[49] Life has done
some terrible things to Ann.

So, with some wisdom and forethought, the inevitable deficits of growing old can be ameliorated.

Why don't we simply deal with the deficits of getting older
as practically and as sensibly as we can, and the rest of the time
enjoy whatever age we are at for the benefits it brings? Youth
might have strength and vigour but increasing age brings experience and wisdom, and what a comfort and power that can be!

The reason that we cannot do this, the reason we dread
growing old, does not lie in our bodies and the patterns of our
bodily life. The reason lies in how we interpret our lives and
how we act upon our interpretations. The reason is simple.

The young hate the old, and the old hate the young.

Why?

CHAPTER 3

Youth and age: a mutual antipathy

THE HISTORY of childhood is a history of cruelty.

But isn't childhood just the dearest, sweetest time of our lives?

No. That's just being sentimental.

And an adult who is sentimental about childhood is an adult who is cruel to children.

Being sentimental means ignoring what a child actually is, what each particular child is thinking, feeling, needing, wanting; and imposing on that child our own needs, wishes, fantasies.

By sentimentalizing the notion of childhood we are cruel to the child.

Adults are experts in being cruel to children. They know how to do it because it was done to them.

Children have been treated cruelly in every age and every culture. The form of the cruelty is different in every age and every culture but, whatever is done, children are treated as objects of no importance, humiliated, shamed, scorned and tortured.

And then they grow up – and do the same to other children. As the Bible says, the sins of the fathers are visited on the children.[1]

More accurately this verse would be, 'The sins that are visited on the children, the children, now adult, visit on the children.'

Let's look at our history, and in doing so remember that the history of our species is continuous. Our bodies die but our ideas go rolling on.

Probably you've never met your great-great-grandparents and you never experienced directly the society they lived in, but among your beliefs, attitudes and opinions are ideas which are a legacy from them. These ideas might be just as your great-great-grandparents held them, or they might have been modified as they were handed down from your great-great-grandparents to your great-grandparents, from them to your grandparents, to your parents and so to you. For instance, perhaps the pride you take in your nationality could be a legacy from your great-great-grandfather. You might express it differently because what is a politically correct expression at one time is not politically correct in another, but the kernel of that belief could have travelled over time to you.

However, ideas aren't things. You don't inherit ideas in the way you can inherit a necklace. If you have inherited your great-great-grandmother's necklace, the piece of jewellery you hold in your hand is almost exactly the same object that she once held in her hand. But ideas aren't things. They are simply the constructions we make. Ideas are our interpretations of what happens to us. We don't get ideas from other people. What we get are our interpretations of other people's ideas. Our interpretations of other people's ideas can be very similar to other people's ideas, or they can be very different. You and your great-great-grandfather might have interpreted patriotism in very similar ways, but understood, say, the sense of personal worth and acceptability in very different ways.

Our written histories, both the official version in history books and the personal histories recorded in letters and diaries, tell more about what happened than how the people involved felt about what happened. Yet how we feel about what happens to us – that is, how we interpret what happens to us – is far more important, because it is *our interpretations* which determine how we act. What matters is not what happens to us but how we feel about what happens to us.

We are free to make whatever interpretations we choose, and so every event can be interpreted in an infinite number of ways. Hence you and your great-great-grandfather probably interpreted the events in your lives in very different ways. However, you and your great-great-grandfather, and every other person who has ever lived or ever will live, always need to make interpretations which enable each of you to achieve three things.

1. Interpretations which enable you to survive as a body, that is, to avoid dying. For instance, you might interpret another person's behaviour as, 'That person intends to kill me. I shall need to defend myself.'

2. Interpretations which enable you to survive as a person, that is, to continue to exist as 'I'. For instance, you might interpret another person's behaviour as, 'That person is trying to humiliate me. I refuse to be humiliated.'

3. Interpretations which enable you to maintain some kind of relationship with other people whom you both fear and need. For instance, you might interpret another person's behaviour as, 'I like him but I don't trust him. I'll be friendly but I won't let him get close to me.'

Now let's look at the history of childhood in terms of how children might have created these interpretations.

It has never been easy for children to interpret what happened to them in terms of healthy survival, a positive sense of self, and secure, trusting relationships because, as Lloyd de Mause wrote in his *History of Childhood*, 'The story of childhood is a nightmare from which we have only recently begun to awaken. The further back in history one goes, the lower the level of child care, and the more likely children are to be killed, abandoned, beaten, terrorized, and sexually abused.'[2] It is impossible in the space of this chapter to give a full account of the cruelty children have suffered and are suffering. It would take many books to do that, and they would be very painful to write and to read.

For most of the history of our species, and in the vast poverty-stricken regions of our world today, children have had little opportunity to develop interpretations which enabled them to survive as a body because so many children died and are dying a short time after birth. In industrialized countries it was well into this century before parents could limit the number of their children to no more than three and be confident that all were likely to survive to adult life. In previous centuries, as in the Third World today, parents had large numbers of children in the hope that at least one would survive and be able to look after them in their old age.

The large numbers of children who died meant that even those children who were born into societies much more warmly disposed to children than European society has been must, in their early years, have found their parents somewhat detached from them. The loss of someone we love is always a threat to our sense of identity. We can defend ourselves against this threat by refusing to become attached to someone we are likely to lose. So parents, even the potentially most loving of parents, have always practised withholding their love until they feel that the child's survival is reasonably secure.

However, from the moment of our birth, we need our parent's love to confirm our sense of self. Thus, when our parents withhold their love in the first months of our lives we don't interpret their behaviour in the words 'My parents don't love me', but we do form this interpretation in terms of a sense of coldness, emptiness, longing and disjunction.

Often in our species' history the lives of everyone, adults and children, were in danger. Traditionally, if a tribe was facing famine it was the children who were left to starve. They were, and are, sacrificed to save the adults because the adults could have more children and because they had the skills necessary for the tribe's survival.

Julie Flint, visiting an emergency feeding centre in Kurtun Warey, a bush village a hundred miles south of the Somali capital of Mogadishu, wrote,

There were 341 starving children at the emergency feeding centre opened five days earlier by the French charity, Médecins sans Frontiers. When we left two hours later there were 339 – most of them sitting, like living dead, in front of food they were not eating.

Some were unable to. Others had been ordered to bring the food away with them for the rest of the family. 'When the refugees first arrive here, many children are told to come to the feeding centres, but not to eat,' said Patrick Bongrain of the charity. 'Many children tell us: I have to go back with the food or my mother will beat me.'[3]

In the development and practice of their skills the adults used the logic of scientific thinking. Every society and culture developed a technology related to the people's needs and the conditions of their environment. However, to try to understand those matters over which they could exercise no skill – like the vagaries of the weather – they had to resort to myth and metaphor. So gods were invented to explain flood and drought and plagues of insects, and the gods, being powerful and prone to act in mysterious ways, were conceived of as being like parents as seen through a child's eyes. Gods are always seen as your father or mother, and never as your baby brother over whom you have power.

All children know that some self-sacrifice by the child can often dispel a parent's anger and win a reward. Staying at home and helping your parents instead of going out to play can avert a beating and win a cuddle at bedtime. A similar sacrifice might avert a god's wrath. So the adults sacrificed the children to the gods.

> Child sacrifice was practised by the Irish Celts, the Gauls, the Scandinavians, the Egyptians, the Phoenicians, the Moabites, the Ammonites, and, in certain periods, the Israelites. Thousands of bones of sacrificed children have been dug up by archaeologists, often with inscriptions identifying the victims as first-born sons of noble families, reaching in time all the way back to Jericho of 7000 BC. Sealing children in walls, foundations of buildings, and bridges to strengthen the structure was also common from the building of the walls of Jericho to as late as 1843 in Germany. To this day, when children play 'London Bridge is Falling Down', they are acting out a sacrifice to a river goddess when they catch the child at the end of the game.[4]

The form of the sacrifice changed over the centuries but the practice remains as popular as ever. Very young children might not be sacrificed so frequently now,[5] but young men in their millions have been and are being persuaded that *Dulce et decorum est pro patria mori*.[6] Whether you are sacrificed to propitiate a god or to preserve your country's trade advantages, there is no interpretation you can create which does not harm you. If you believe that the adults are telling you the truth about the necessity of your sacrifice you are then torn between your duty and your truth, which is 'I want to live my life.' If you see that the adults are lying to you for their own interest you are angry, but helpless, for you cannot escape their power. All you can do is vow revenge. If you can't do anything else, you can hate the old.

If you are sacrificed to the gods or for your country you might, at least, have a moment of glory and significance in your life, but what of all those unknown children who were sacrificed secretly? They were unwanted, so their parents disposed of them. They were left in some desolate place to die of exposure or to be eaten by wild animals. Even today there are newspaper reports of Chinese and Indian parents exposing their unwanted baby daughters.[7]

Other parents, perhaps with some vestige of concern for the life they had created, abandoned their children in places where they might be found and survive with what the historian John Boswell called 'the kindness of strangers'.[8]

> While collecting information about early Christian sexual mores for a previous study, I came across the argument by several prominent theologians of the early church that men should not visit brothels or have recourse to prostitutes because in doing so they might unwittingly commit incest with a child they had abandoned . . . At first I was stunned by how peculiar and oblique an argument this was against prostitution; but in the end I found even more surprising the implication that the writers' contemporaries abandoned children so commonly that a given father was likely to encounter his own child in a brothel. Was this possible?[9]

And indeed it was so. He found that

> Children were abandoned throughout Europe from Hellenistic antiquity to the end of the Middle Ages in great

numbers, by parents of every social standing, in a great variety of circumstances . . . Parents abandoned their offspring in desperation when they were unable to support them, due to poverty or disaster; in shame, when they were unwilling to keep them because of their physical condition or ancestry (e.g., illegitimate or incestuous); in self-interest or in the interests of another child, when inheritance or domestic resources would be compromised by another mouth; in hope, when they believed that someone of greater means or higher standing might find them and bring them up; in resignation, when a child was of an unwelcome gender or ominous auspices; or in callousness, if they simply could not be bothered with parenthood.[10]

Some families who took in abandoned children did bring these children up as their own, but generally the children were consigned to slavery, as in ancient Rome, or later to various forms of serfdom. By the early Middle Ages another form of abandonment had developed: oblation, where a child was given to a monastery or church. 'Although children left at churches were regularly sold, and those donated to monasteries subjected to a kind of servitude, both of these means were conscientious responses to a difficult situation.'[11]

Abandoning a child to the kindness of strangers or to the kindness of the Church was not considered to be a deplorable act.

At no point did European society as a whole entertain serious sanctions against the practice. Most ethical systems, in fact, either tolerated it or regulated it. Ancient and early Christian moralists sometimes reproached parents for exposing their offspring, but rarely because the act itself was reprehensible; it was usually condemned as a token of irresponsible sexuality, or as a dereliction of a wider duty to state or family. Almost no ancient writers, in law, narrative or literature, blamed individual parents for exposing children.[12]

How would the child concerned have interpreted such abandonment? Some may have been able to see it as a stroke of good fortune when they found themselves with people who cared for them, but most would have felt rejected, angry and bitter. Nowadays, when children's voices are heard, they tell of how keenly they feel rejected when a parent puts them into care, or into a boarding school, or when one parent divorces the other, or even when one parent dies, and how they blame themselves for what has happened. 'If I'd been really good my parents would not have abandoned me.' That little slave in Rome, bound to his master for life, or the little girl paraded as a virgin bride in a brothel must have felt rejected, envious of the siblings who had not been so rejected, and angry with parents who had acted so cruelly. Such children would have felt that there was something intrinsically wrong with them for their parents to reject them so utterly and finally, and so they would have come to hate themselves. *When we hate ourselves the hate we feel for ourselves is exactly matched by the hate we feel for others*. No wonder the Roman circus could draw crowds to watch such bloody deaths, and the various rulers down the centuries could find a populace so ready to go to war.

It was not just the abandoned children, now adult, in the population who were the source of hate necessary for the incessant wars of the Middle Ages. Barbara Tuchman, writing about the most calamitous fourteenth century, commented:

> On the whole, babies and young children appear to have been left to survive or die without concern in the first five or six years. What psychological effect this may have had on character, and possibly on history, can only be conjectured. Possibly the relative emotional blankness of a medieval infancy may account for the casual attitude toward life and suffering of the medieval man . . . If children survived to age seven, their recognized life began, more or less as miniature adults. Childhood was already over.[13]

But surely, in the ancient world and in the Middle Ages there must have been some people who cared about children? Lloyd de Mause examined this question.

One imagines that there must be all kinds of places to look to find this missing empathetic faculty in the past. The first place to look, of course, is the Bible; certainly here one should find empathy towards children's needs, for isn't Jesus always pictured holding little children? Yet when one actually reads each of the over two thousand references to children listed in the *Complete Concordance to the Bible*, these gentle images are missing. You find lots on child sacrifice, on stoning children, on beating them, on their strict obedience, on their love for their parents, and on their role as carriers of the family name, but not a single one that reveals any empathy with their needs. Even the well-known saying, 'Suffer little children, and forbid them not, to come unto me' turns out to be the customary Near Eastern practice of exorcising by laying on of hands, which many holy men did to remove the evil inherent in children: 'Then there were brought unto him little children, that he should put his hands on them, and pray . . . he laid his hands on them, and departed hence.' (Mat. 19. 13.)[14]

In her monumental study *Thou Shalt Not Be Aware*[15], Alice Miller pointed out that while the Bible abounds in stories of children being sacrificed for their parents, there is no story about a parent being sacrificed for a child.

'Christianity,' wrote John Boswell, 'may well have increased the rate of abandonment, both by insisting more rigidly than any other moral system on the absolute necessity of procreative purpose in all human sexual acts, and by providing, through churches and monasteries, regular and relatively humane modes of abandoning infants nearly everywhere on the continent.'[16]

By the late Middle Ages so many children were being abandoned that a further provision for such babies gradually developed.

[With] the rise of the foundling homes sometime in the early thirteenth century, within a century or two nearly all major European cities had such hospices, which neatly gathered all of the troubling and messy aspects of child

abandonment away from view, off the streets, under institutional supervision. Behind their walls officials dealt with
society's loose ends, and neither the parents who abandoned them nor their fellow citizens had to devote any
further thought or care to the children. Even the foundling
homes did not have to care for them for long. The majority
of children died within a few years of admission in most
areas of Europe from the time of the emergence of the
foundling homes until the eighteenth century; in some
places and times the mortality rate exceeded ninety percent
. . . Abandonment now became an even greater mystery,
hidden from the public behind institutional walls from
which few emerged, walls that afforded little opportunity
for adoption or triumph over natal adversity. The strangers
no longer had to be kind to pick up the children: now
they were paid to rescue them. But because it was their
job, they remained strangers; and the children themselves,
reared apart from society, apart from families, without
lineage either natural or adopted, either died among
strangers or entered society as strangers.[17]

Such strangers are still in our midst. I remember the girls
from the local orphanage who attended my primary school.
They all wore a uniform – a tunic, blouse, sturdy shoes and hat
– while the rest of us wore dresses and cardigans our mothers
had made. The orphans walked to and from school two by two
in a line all together, while the rest of us came and left in no
particular order with our friends or parents. I remember staring
at these orphans the way I stared at anything strange. I don't
remember ever speaking to them. They would be in their fifties,
sixties, seventies now. I hope they have done better than most
of the young people leaving what is called 'care' in Britain.
Survival rates are certainly better than those of the foundling
hospitals, but children in care receive an inferior education and
on turning eighteen are cast out into the community where no
provision is made for them to get jobs and a place to live.
Many of the homeless teenagers in British cities are abandoned
children, abandoned by their families and by the State.[18]

To be a stranger in your own country is a chilling experience. Being excluded from what is rightly yours creates pain and anger against the perpetrators of this exclusion, a rage against the old.

I have already noted that most of the children in our history, and not just those who were abandoned, suffered because their parents often failed to become attached to them so as to protect themselves from loss. Attachment between a mother and child is a mutual process. The baby turns to the mother as a sunflower turns to the sun, but if the mother is not there the baby turns to whatever face is regularly present and becomes attached to that person. This is what happened to a vast number of babies throughout history. The person they became attached to was their wet-nurse.

Sometimes the wet-nurse was the only means of the baby's survival when the mother had died, or had no milk. However, breast-feeding was seen as a menial task no lady of quality would undertake, and so babies down the centuries, if they survived, formed their first attachment to someone outside the family, or, where the wet-nurse gave them little attention, formed no attachment at all.

Our first attachment is the prototype for all the attachments that follow. The child who fails to form an attachment fails to learn a vital skill, and grows up unable to form relationships. It is through our early attachment that we learn the skill of living in groups. We want the love and approval of the object of our first attachment, and when that object shows disappointment in us or anger with us we discover shame and guilt and develop a conscience, all necessary if we are to live with other people. Behind those conscienceless loners whose stories of havoc and destruction fill our history books are the shadowy figures of the absent mother and the negligent wet-nurse.

If the wet-nurse was not negligent, if she cared for her little charge and met the baby's need for attachment, two problems were immediately created for the child. First, at some time the child would be handed back to his family. He would suffer loss, and find it hard to become attached to those who had initially rejected him. What could the child do with the rage he felt at losing the person most important to him? Hate the old.

Second, in his attachment to the wet-nurse a prototype was created which the child in later life would find hard to replicate. In our first attachment we form images of love, comfort, excitement and satisfaction which in other guises in adult life become the images which stir our sexual feelings. Why do we fall in love with one person rather than another? Because in the way we interpret the appearance and behaviour of that person we see very subtly and obliquely our earliest images of desire.

Wet-nurses were rarely of the same social class as their charges. This brought great problems for the babies in their adult life. They might never find anyone in their social circle who awakened their images of desire, or they found themselves drawn to people who were excluded from their social circle. What can you do when you experience strong sexual impulses towards a person whom your community condemns as inferior and evil? If you honestly acknowledge your feelings you become very angry with your family and the leaders of your community. That can be dangerous. What many people in this situation do is to turn their love into hate. They hate those aspects of themselves which derive from their first love, and they persecute the object of their love. This is part of the hatred which fuels apartheid. Many Afrikaaner babies formed their first attachment to their black nanny.

However, down the centuries most babies, even when they had the most loving of mothers and/or wet-nurses, suffered a special impediment in forming an attachment.

The process of forming an attachment is a very active one. The new-born baby arrives in the world ready to start a conversation with any friendly face. Research studies of babies conversing with their mothers show how a tiny baby will interact with its mother, often initiating a conversation and prompting a special response from her. Mothers who take the time to engage in these face-to-face dialogues become very knowledgeable about their baby's conversational style and content, and respond appropriately. Thus the bond between mother and baby is of the same order as a good friendship. The essence of a good friendship is not just support, liking and love – though these are important – but an ongoing conversation.

To have a good conversation we need to be able to see one another's face. Telephone conversations are never entirely satisfactory, and neither are letters. We need, too, to be able to wave our arms about and wriggle our bodies so as to convey more than our words. However, you can't do this if your arms are strapped to your sides and your head and body are tightly wrapped in a long cotton strip so that only your eyes, nose and mouth are uncovered and you are quite unable to move. You are, in a word, swaddled.

Here I intended to give a few brief facts about when and where infants were swaddled. Lloyd de Mause said, 'Almost all nations swaddled',[19] and 'Swaddling in England and America was on its way out by the end of the eighteenth century, and in France and Germany by the nineteenth.'[20] To set the scene I wanted to give a few more details about how widespread the custom was and why it died out. So I decided to pop along to the London Library to see what the *Encyclopedia Britannica* said.

The *Encyclopedia Britannica* said nothing. The London Library was being reconstructed and the other encyclopedias were out of reach, so I searched the dictionary. They all gave simple definitions of swaddling and showed that the word has long been in use. Dr Samuel Johnson drew an analogy between swaddling cloths and winding sheets – beginning and ending life wrapped in a sheet. I searched the library's subject index, but the only reference I could find proved to be one to an author whose surname was Swaddling.

So I took myself off to Sheffield City Library. There each of the subject indexes went from Swabia to Sweden without a swaddling in between. I searched the index of any history book whose title suggested an interest in ordinary life. Not a single mention of swaddling. I searched both sections of the *Encyclopedia Britannica*, the Micropedia for Ready Reference, and the Macropedia for Knowledge in Depth, *Collier's Encyclopedia*, *Everyman's Encyclopedia*, the *Macmillan Family Encyclopedia*, *Encyclopedia Americana*, the *Great Soviet Encyclopedia*, the *Encyclopedia Judaica*, and the *New Catholic Encyclopedia*. Not a mention.

I am sure that had I requested a computer search I would have been given references to research studies by social historians and anthropologists concerned with certain abstruse aspects of life in different cultures. However, that would not answer the question why a practice so common in our history and still used by various societies today is not included in the body of general knowledge. Are not the customs followed in the upbringing of children important? Or is there some kind of censorship operating here?

Anyway, in another part of the library I found the *International Standard Bible Encyclopedia*, and there, at last, was an entry on swaddling. It read:

After an infant was born, the umbilical cord was cut and tied, and then the baby was washed and rubbed with salt and oil, and wrapped in strips of cloth.[21]

This encyclopedia featured swaddling because the baby Jesus was swaddled.

And she brought forth her firstborn son, and wrapped him in swaddling clothes, and laid him in a manger; because there was no room for them in the inn.[22]

Is there any other sentence in the whole of the world's literature that has brought forth more sentimentality? Think of all those little children singing 'Away in a Manger'!

The enemies of sentimentality are the questions, 'What exactly happened?' and 'What does that actually mean?'

In the *Bible Encyclopedia* the authors do not attempt to answer the second question. After all, if swaddling was good enough for Jesus it should be good enough for every baby. They answered the first question by saying, 'These strips kept the newborn child warm and also ensured that the child's limbs would grow straight.'[23]

This is what people generally understand about swaddling. I have been asking people what they know about swaddling, and most, when they recover from their surprise at this question, talk about keeping the baby warm and secure. Swaddling is indeed considered to be sweet and gentle, just what a baby needs.

But Ofra Ayalon didn't say that. She said, 'Swaddling is child abuse.'[24]

What does Lloyd de Mause say?

'Tying the child up in various restraints was a near-universal practice. *Swaddling was the central fact of the infant's earliest years.*'[25] (My italics.)

The reason given for swaddling a child was that 'If it were left free it would scratch its eyes out, tear its ears off, break its legs, distort its bones, be terrified at the sight of its own limbs, and even crawl on all fours like an animal.'[26]

This is how Lloyd de Mause described swaddling:

Traditional swaddling is much the same in every country and age; it 'consists in entirely depriving the child of the use of its limbs, by enveloping them in an endless length bandage, so as to not unaptly resemble billets of wood; and, by which, the skin is sometimes excoriated; the flesh compressed, almost to gangrene; the circulation nearly arrested; and the child without the slightest power of motion. Its little waist is surrounded by stays . . . Its head is compressed into the form the fancy of the midwife might suggest; and its shape maintained by properly adjusted pressure.'[27]

Priscilla Robertson wrote:

The tight swaddling had often left the baby so stuck up that it was painful to change him, and this led in a vicious circle to the nurse's unwillingness to do so.

German babies were wrapped up tighter and longer than French ones, and were called *Wickelkinder*. In 1877 *Fraser's Magazine* described a German baby as 'a piteous object', pinioned and bound like a mummy in yards of bandages that were unfolded once, or at most twice a day. The child was rarely bathed. They were kept in swaddling clothes until about six months old, then often allowed to crawl on the floor with a cold potato in their fist to stop them from crying. The English author made the point that it is hard to hug a swaddled child, and that it is impossible for him to wind his arms about his mother. Even in adulthood a German girl's posture was said to be different from an English girl's because of the early swaddling. About 1908 an English visitor described the *Steckkissen*, a comparatively recent successor to the swaddling bands – a long bag that confined the legs and body but not the arms. It was lined with wadding, and nurses were told that it was dangerous to pick a baby up outside of one while his bones were still soft, so the infant lay in it day and night for eight weeks. Air, sunlight and soap were all considered equally dangerous to the child, and sleeping out of doors was not allowed.

In 1821, in Italy, Lady Morgan reported babies being wrapped up so tightly that the pressure forced blood to their heads and made their little faces purple, and she reported that when members of the enlightened middle classes questioned the practice, they were opposed by the clergy.[28]

'Swaddling,' wrote Lloyd de Mause, 'was often so complicated it took up to two hours to dress an infant.'[29] If this was so we might wonder why adults could be bothered to keep up the custom. Look how quickly disposable nappies replaced the ones that had to be washed! However, there was a reason, and it had nothing to do with what was best for babies.

Its convenience to adults was enormous – they rarely had to pay attention to infants once they were tied up. As a recent medical study of swaddling has shown, swaddled infants are extremely passive, their heart rates slow down, they cry less, they sleep far more, and in general they are so withdrawn and inert that the doctors who did the study wondered if swaddling shouldn't be tried again. The historical sources confirm this picture; doctors since antiquity agreed that 'wakefulness does not happen to children naturally or from habit, i.e., customarily, for they always sleep', and children were described as being laid for hours behind the hot oven, hung on pegs on the wall, placed in tubs, and in general, 'left, like a parcel, in every convenient corner.'[30]

Apologists for swaddling among the historians do not criticize our forefathers for believing that if babies were not swaddled they would grow up deformed, and that crawling and sleeping in the foetal position meant a 'reassertion of the child's "nature" – to wit, regression to a more animal state.'[31] There is no suggestion that perhaps these ideas might have been put to the test, and they undoubtedly would have been had concern for the child rather than convenience of the adult been the top priority. Apologists for swaddling cite the cold weather, the need for mothers to work, and the general filth of the floors of houses in past centuries as excellent reasons for swaddling. Concern for the child would have produced far earlier in our history warm, clean houses and the crèche.

Swaddling is not something belonging to the dim and distant past. In Venice recently I was in conversation with my friend Diana Leidel and the artist Angiola Churchill. Diana was telling us of a remarkable exhibition in New York of paintings by Hung Liu, a Chinese–American woman, on the theme of footbinding which showed the intense pain and humiliation suffered by those women who, as little girls, had their feet bound and crippled so as to create tiny feet, incapable of supporting a body but considered an essential attribute of a woman of high station or a courtesan. Only peasant girls did not have their feet bound.[32] Angiola said, 'That reminds me of the way the peasants in Italy swaddled their babies.'

She then told us how, when she was a child in Lombardy in the twenties, she would visit the cluster of houses where the peasants lived and there see the babies in their swaddling cloths. 'They were wet and smelly and hung on hooks out of the way so that their mothers could get on with their work.'

Angiola still had in her possession two strips of swaddling cloth which her mother had kept and used as bandages.

However, in her experience not all babies were swaddled. The peasant mothers were wet nurses to the gentry, and these babies were not swaddled and ignored but handled with more concern. (When those peasant babies were older and able to see the difference in the way the peasant and gentry babies were looked after, what conclusions would they draw about this? Would they be angry at such injustice, or say to themselves, 'I am not valuable and deserved nothing better'? Probably both, anger and self-hatred.)

However, as I learned later, the babies of the gentry in Italy in the twenties and thirties were still likely to be partly swaddled. On a private beach on the Lido, Angiola introduced me to her friend Giuliana Cammerino and asked her if she had any memories of swaddling in the thirties. Indeed she had. Her mother had been swaddled, and although when Giuliana was born her mother did not swaddle her she followed an elaborate system of layers of cloths which functioned as a nappy, and culminated, on the outside, in a large square of cloth which was pinned in such a way that the legs and hips were held tight, incapable of movement. A belt was wrapped around the baby's waist, reminiscent of the stays used in swaddling. If this is how Giuliana spent the first months of her life, it is no wonder that now she reclines on a couch or deck chair on the veranda of her beach house, looking relaxed, lovely and free in her tiny bikini!

What other long-term effects could swaddling have on babies?

To answer this question we need to be aware of what is now known about the abilities of new-born babies.

Many people still believe that babies know nothing and are incapable of remembering anything that occurred in the first six or seven years of their life. (The fact that in those early years we learn to walk, talk, feed ourselves and keep ourselves clean, all skills we remember and use for the rest of our lives, is not allowed to stand in the way of this belief.) By believing this they need not trouble themselves to take account of the baby's experience, and they need not feel guilty when they are cruel to the baby (as when they insist that a baby who is fed when hungry, or attended to when distressed will grow up 'spoilt'.)

It is now well established that in the womb babies hear

sounds, have preferences, and can make predictions, such as that certain music means pleasure, as when a pregnant mother lies down and relaxes after switching on some music. Mum resting must be much more comfortable for the baby than Mum rushing around. Babies are born knowing their mother's voice, and, nowadays in the UK, many recognize the music of the soap-opera *Neighbours*: when the television is switched on, new-born babies whose mothers have regularly watched *Neighbours* turn their heads to the source of the music.

Babies are born not only able to distinguish a face from all other sights which might occur but also preferring to look at a face rather than any other sight. Researchers simply measure the amount of time a baby looks at one thing rather than another. By the time babies are forty-eight hours old they will spend more time looking at a picture of their mother than at a picture of a woman who looks like their mother.

Nowadays many parents talk with pride and astonishment about their four-year-old who can operate the video, a task beyond the skills of many adults. Yet babies are born with the ability to operate a radio. As you know, when there is something on the radio you want to hear you switch it on, and when there is nothing you want to hear, you switch it off. If the switch is not a button to press but a dummy to suck, babies within a few days of birth will learn to turn on a recording of a human voice, and prefer this to a recording of the same pitch and intensity but not a human voice. Not long after they show that they prefer to hear their mother's voice on the recording rather than any other voice. Would that they retained this interest in their mother's voice for the rest of their life!

A six-month-old baby will notice that the mother has turned to pay attention to something and will turn in the same direction. By about fourteen months babies understand the pointing gesture and will point and check whether the mother is looking in the direction the baby expects. Left on their own babies do not point.

This research, and much more, shows that babies come into the world eager and able to make sense of the world, and to act on it and in it. What a glorious feeling it is to know that you have the power and the freedom to act! What joy! What self-confidence!

But what if you were a swaddled baby? How would you discover that your toes were attached to you and were near, while the moon was far? Hung in a corner, how would you learn to engage another person in conversation, or discover that you could act and change some part of the world? Swaddled, you were helpless.

Just how helpless and powerless the swaddled baby was is revealed in the many portraits of the infant Jesus. Although Luke described Jesus as being swaddled, he was rarely depicted so. In the Basilica di San Marco in Venice there is a tenth-century painting of the Virgin and Child, called Madonna Nico-peia, where the infant Jesus seems to be swaddled, but he is at the centre of the picture, upright directly below his mother's face, and the swaddling cloth around his head has become a halo as he beams out of the picture, a commanding, powerful golden light.

The infant Jesus depicted in the vast thirteenth-century mosaic of the central Apsis of the Basilica at Torcello wears a loose golden robe. His feet are bare, his left hand holds a scroll, his right is outstretched in a gesture of power and blessing.

In Bellini's sixteenth-century triptych of the Virgin Mary and Saints in the Basilica dei Frari in Venice the naked infant Jesus stands straight and strong on his mother's knee. Veronese's sixteenth-century *Sacre Famiglia con Santa Caterina* in the Villa di Maser shows the naked infant Jesus as a large, strong child commanding the attention of the adults around him. The infant Jesus in the fifteenth-century Piero della Francesca's Madonna of Senigallia at the ducal palace at Urbino bears a remarkable resemblance to the present Pope. Clad only in a loose robe, he sits on his mother's arm as on a throne and raises his right hand in blessing.

The infant Jesus, thus depicted, was all that the swaddled babies were not – cherished, free and powerful.

The function of church art and architecture is not simply to inspire. It is also intended to make the human observers feel small, humble and insignificant, all necessary if the observer is to be an obedient child of the Church. Those of us who were never swaddled would find it hard to imagine what memories of being trapped, immobile and frustrated would have been evoked in those people who had been swaddled, but those of us who, as babies, were never cherished would know the sadness, rage and envy the pictures of the infant Jesus might evoke. Frustration, rage, sadness, envy – all the emotions which undermine self-confidence and do not dissipate with time. Hidden, unacknowledged, they seek an outlet and object, and what more appropriate object than the old?

Swaddled babies were not only deprived of close physical comfort and social interaction with their mother for the first months of their life, they were also deprived of that active interaction with their environment which fosters the growth of intelligence. We are not born each with a specific lump of intelligence, as psychologists with their IQ tests used to think, but rather with a potential for intelligent behaviour which, for the potential to become a power, requires a rich interactive environment. It is no wonder that so many people throughout our history grow up stupid.

It seems that the practice of swaddling died out slowly, with the amount of cloths used to restrain the baby gradually becoming less. However,

> Once the infant was released from its swaddling bands, physical restraints of all kinds continued, varying by country and period. Children were sometimes tied to chairs to prevent their crawling. Right into the nineteenth century leading strings were tied to the child's clothes to control it and swing it about. Corsets and stays made of bone, wood or iron were often used for both sexes. Children were sometimes strapped into backboards and their feet put into stocks while they studied, and iron collars and other devices were used to 'improve posture'.[33]

The prevalence of such bizarre constraints inflicted on children explains why there was never any public outcry about the devices used in the eighteenth and nineteenth centuries to restrain the people deemed to be mad. Indeed, the madhouses of the eighteenth century and the asylums of the nineteenth and twentieth centuries gave many people the opportunity to do to others what had been done to them when they were children.[34]

Had I been writing this chapter some ten years ago I would have had even greater difficulty in writing about the next topic, for, if swaddling was good for the child but completely unimportant, child sexual abuse did not occur. Now some people are prepared to admit that child sexual abuse does occur. The historical record seems to suggest that it always has in one form or another.

> The child in antiquity lived his earliest years in an atmosphere of sexual abuse. Growing up in Greece and Rome often included being used sexually by older men . . . Aristotle's main objection to Plato's idea that children should be held in common was that when men had sex with boys they wouldn't know if they were their own sons, which Aristotle says would be 'most unseemly' . . .
>
> Even the Jews, who tried to stamp out adult homosexuality with severe punishments, were more lenient in the case of young boys. Despite Moses's injunction against corrupting children, the penalty for sodomy with children over 9 years of age was death by stoning, but copulation with younger children was not considered a sexual act, and was punishable only by a whipping, 'as a matter of public discipline' . . .
>
> Christianity introduced a new concept into the discussion – childhood innocence. As Clement of Alexandria said, when Christ advised people to 'become as little children' in order to enter into Heaven, one should 'not foolishly mistake his meaning. We are not little ones in the sense that we roll on the floor or crawl on the ground as snakes do.' What Christ meant was that people should become as 'uncontaminated' as children, pure, without sexual knowledge. Christians throughout the Middle Ages began to stress the idea that children were totally innocent

of all notions of pleasure and pain . . . Unfortunately, the idea that children are innocent and cannot be corrupted is a common defence by child molestors against admitting that their abuse is harming the child, so the medieval fiction that the child is innocent only makes our sources less revealing, and proves nothing about what really went on.[35]

The sentimental notion that children had no notion of pleasure or pain was a licence for adults to do whatever they liked to them without any feelings of remorse or guilt. However, children, real children and not the sentimental fictions carried in the minds of adults, showed only too clearly that they did feel pleasure and pain and understood these experiences. Adults could dismiss children's expressions of pleasure or joy as mere childish foolishness. Pain or distress they could explain away, as many still do, by saying, 'A child soon forgets.' But what could they do when real children insisted on showing that they had an awareness of and curiosity about certain parts of the body and the feelings evoked in those parts? Adults were faced with a choice. They could abandon their sentimental notions about asexual children, or they could punish those children who would not fulfil the role adult sentimentality had imposed on them. Doubtless because they as children had been punished, adults chose the second course. From the beginning of the eighteenth century

parents began severely punishing their children for masturbation, and doctors began to spread the myth that it would cause insanity, epilepsy, blindness, and death. By the nineteenth century, this campaign reached an unbelievable frenzy. Doctors and parents sometimes appeared before the child armed with knives and scissors, threatening to cut off the child's genitals; circumcision, clitoridectomy, and infibulation were sometimes used as punishment; and all sorts of restraint devices, including plaster casts and cages with spikes, were prescribed.[36]

And then there was beating. It seems that to have been a child was to have been beaten. Lloyd de Mause wrote:

The evidence which I have collected on methods of disciplining children leads me to believe that a very large percentage of the children born prior to the eighteenth century were what would be called 'battered children'. Of over two hundred statements of advice on child-rearing prior to the eighteenth century which I have examined most approved of beating children severely, and all allowed beating in varying circumstances except three, Plutarch, Palmieri, and Sadoleto . . .

Beating instruments included whips of all kinds, including cat-o'-nine-tails, shovels, canes, iron and wooden rods, bundles of sticks, the *discipline* (a whip made of small chains), and special school instruments like the flapper, which had a pear-shaped end and a round hole to raise blisters. Their comparative frequency of use may be indicated by the categories of the German schoolmaster who reckoned he had given 911,527 strokes with the stick, 124,000 lashes with the whip, 136,715 slaps with the hand, and 1,115,800 boxes on the ear. The beatings described in the sources were generally severe, involved bruising and bloodying the body, began early, and were a regular part of the child's life.[37]

The justification for this cruelty was the biblical injunction 'Spare the rod and spoil the child.' Early in the fifteenth century this became 'He that spares the Yard hates his child,' and later, 'The child whom the father loves most dear he does most punish tenderly in fear.' Children were seen as essentially evil creatures ('born in sin' according to Christian theology), and beating was the most effective way of keeping this evil under control.[38]

If beating was the only correct way of bringing up children, parents felt that they had to beat their children.

Century after century of battered children grew up and in turn battered their own children. Public protest was rare.

Even humanists and teachers who had a reputation for great gentleness, like Petrarch, Ascham, Comenius, and Pestalozzi, approved of beating children. Milton's wife complained she hated to hear the cries of his nephews when he was beating them, and Beethoven whipped his pupils with a knitting needle and sometimes bit them. Even royalty was not exempt from battering, as the childhood of Louis XIII confirms. A whip was at his father's side at table, and as early as 17 months of age, the dauphin knew enough not to cry when threatened with the whip. At 25 months regular whippings began, often on his bare skin. He had frequent nightmares about his whippings, which were administered in the morning when he awakened. When he was king he still woke at night in terror, in expectation of his morning whippings. The day of his coronation, when he was eight, he was whipped, and said, 'I would rather do without so much obeisance and honour if they wouldn't have me whipped.'[39]

In England middle- and upper-class boys had their own form of foundling hospital called a public school, and there their parents abandoned them – all for their own good, of course.

Beating was so integral to the boys' public school way of life that schools had their own vernacular terms for it; at Eton you were 'swished' and at Winchester 'tunded'. Victorian Eton had a traditional birch, like a short besom with a 3-foot handle and a 2-foot 'bush'. Senior boys had the right to 'swish'; the victim was bent over a chair while the prefect ran at him with a cane. A flogging by a master was a public ritual. The culprit was set on a block and two boys deputized as 'holders down', while the master laid in. It was a degrading and brutalizing public spectacle, when the boys would come running to enjoy another's torment . . .

Middle- and upper-class schools had an ethos of their own in regard to corporal punishment. Parents who paid directly for their children's education expected their children to be corrected and chastised as part of their social education. The severe spartan conditions in the great public schools were accepted as 'making men' of their sons; and floggings were a hallowed part of their tradition.[40]

Have times changed? The writer A. N. Wilson thinks not.

The chairman of the Headmasters' Conference has said that many people still see schools as places with 'regular beatings and long rows of beds like something out of Solzhenitsyn'. Having been 'educated' in such establishments myself I should certainly say that this was my impression of English private schools.

Mr Hobson, headmaster of Russell Harty's alma mater, Giggleswick School, adds, illogically, 'Parents know schools are not like concentration camps full of beastliness and unhappiness. Otherwise they would not send their children there.'

He overlooks the fact that a high percentage of English parents hate their children. If he ever stood in a supermarket on a Saturday and heard the way mothers address their offspring, he would realize this.

The number of parents sending their children to public schools has dramatically declined since these places tried to become more benign. The first great decline came when the Headmasters' Conference outlawed the cane.

When they began to replace the spartan dormitories with centrally heated study-bedrooms, the numbers dwindled yet further. Parents realize they can do a better job than sadistic teachers at making their children miserable, so they keep them at home.[41]

Apologists for the public school system now claim that the amount of beating allowed is minimal. Private schools in Britain are not covered by the law forbidding teachers to hit pupils. The inmates of children's homes are not protected from beatings either.

The report by Lord Williams, Q.C., into Ty Mawr [a children's home in Abergavenny] paints a depressing picture of difficult and often disturbed young men being cared for almost wholly by untrained staff with little help or guidance from their superiors at Gwent county coucil . . .

'There was an over-masculine culture at Ty Mawr. There was a degree of low-level physical violence, slapping, cuffing and knuckling, that is, striking on the head with knuckles by certain members of staff.'[42]

Where physical punishment was concerned girls fared little better.

The higher the class of a girls' private school, it is reckoned, the less likely that corporal punishment would be resorted to, but in the cheaper schools it was certainly inflicted.

Gillian Avery recalled from direct experience such a school she attended before the Second World War where in handwriting lessons 'Our hands were beaten by the headmistress if we did not make our pot-hooks correctly.'[43]

The school system in New South Wales, Australia, which I entered in 1936, strictly segregated the sexes. In the Infants School, from five to seven years, boys and girls were taught together, but after that they were taught separately, played separately, and, in the schools I attended, punished for speaking to one another in and out of school. A girl wearing the uniform of Newcastle Girls' High School (navy serge tunic, white blouse, school tie, felt hat, blazer – so suitable for a sub-tropical climate) brought disgrace to the whole school if she spoke to a boy, so the headmistress would remind us at assembly. The reason for this segregation – sex – was never mentioned. But at least in High School we weren't beaten.

In Primary School we were. We were slapped and hit with canes, rulers and blackboard pointers. In my last year at Primary School the teachers expected that I would excel in the public examination for entrance to High School. My teacher, Mrs Peebles, decided that I made too many careless errors in spelling and arithmetic, and that every time I did she would hit me with a ruler or her open hand. So, in 1942, when Singapore fell and we waited for the arrival of the conquering Japanese army, I was beaten every day at school.[44]

I was beaten often at home by my mother. My father never hit me, but he would use the threat of the razor strop which hung in the bathroom to bring me to heel. My mother's beatings made me very frightened of her, especially on those occasions when there were just the two of us in the house. Her rage would become a frenzy and, as she beat me, she would say that she intended to kill me and then herself. When I got big enough to feel that I could defend myself or escape if she did try to kill me, my rage matched my fear.

I never spoke about these beatings to any other adult because I was sure all adults would side with my mother against me. With other children there was nothing to discuss. We were all beaten. It was a fact of life, like the sun rising in the east.

If, when I was a child, someone had asked me, 'Do you love your mother?' I would have answered, 'Yes.' I faithfully bought her Christmas, birthday and Mother's Day presents, and I always kissed her hello and goodbye. But I knew then, as I know now from the evidence of other people's lives, that fear drives out love. What so many children, especially adult children, call love for their parents is merely guilt. However, it is an Absolute Law of the Universe that good children always love their parents. It's only bad children who don't. In a desperate attempt to think of themselves as good many adults refuse to recognize the cruelty which parents inflict on their children.

Social historians, Lloyd de Mause found, demonstrate this most effectively.

It is the social historian, whose job it is to dig out the reality of social conditions in the past, who defends himself most vigorously against the facts he turns up. When one social historian finds widespread infanticide, he declares it 'admirable and humane'. When another describes mothers who regularly beat their infants with sticks while still in the cradle, she comments, without a shred of evidence, that 'if her discipline was stern, it was even and just and leavened with kindness.' When a third finds mothers who dunk their infants into ice water each morning to 'strengthen them', and the children die from the practice, she says that 'they were not intentionally cruel' but simply 'had read Rousseau and Locke'. No practice in the past seems anything but benign to the social historian. When Laslett finds parents regularly sending their children, at age seven, to other homes as servants, while taking in other children to serve them, he says it was actually kindness, for it 'shows that parents may have been unwilling to submit children of their own to the discipline of work at home.' After admitting that severe whipping of young children with various instruments 'at school and at home seems to have been as common in the seventeenth century as it was later', William Sloan feels compelled to add that 'children, then as later, sometimes deserve whipping'. When Philippe Ariès comes up with so much evidence of open sexual molesting of children that he admits that 'playing with children's privy parts forms part of a widespread tradition,' he goes on to describe a 'traditional' scene where a stranger throws himself on a little boy while riding in a train, 'his hand brutally rummaging inside the child's fly' while the father smiles, and concludes: 'All that was involved was a game whose scabrous nature we should beware of exaggerating.'

Masses of evidence are hidden, distorted, softened or ignored. The child's early years are played down, formal educational content is endlessly examined, and emotional content is avoided by stressing child legislation and avoiding the home. And if the nature of the author's book is such that the ubiquity of unpleasant facts cannot be ignored, the theory is invented that 'good parents leave no traces in the records'. When, for instance, Alan Valentine examines 600 years of letters from fathers to sons, and of 126 fathers is unable to find one who isn't insensitive, moralistic, and thoroughly self-centred, he concludes: 'doubtless an infinite number of fathers have written to their sons letters which would warm and lift our hearts, if only we could find them. The happiest of fathers leave no history, and it is the men who are not at their best with their children who are likely to write the heart-rending letters which survive.' Likewise, Anna Burr, covering 250 autobiographies, notes that there are no memories of happy childhood, but carefully avoids drawing any conclusions.[45]

Although there is ample evidence from those countries where beating children is illegal, and from families where the parents never hit their children, that children do not require beating in order to become good citizens, a great many adults believe that it is right and proper for an adult to beat a child. Many such adults hide behind words. Often when I am talking about the effects on children of being beaten someone will say, 'I don't beat my children. When they need it I hit them – a slap around the legs with my hand or a wooden spoon.' Such a person forgets that what might be nothing but some physical exertion on the part of the adult – a hit or a slap – is to the recipient, the child, a beating.

Many adults cannot think clearly about this issue because they will not allow themselves to remember the cruelty that they suffered at the hands of their own parents. If they do remember the beatings and other punishments they received they tell themselves what their parents told them – that it was for their own good. ('This hurts me more than it hurts you' is a much used parental lie.)

Just how confused many adults are can be seen in a comparison of how parents teach their children how to cross the road safely and how to be unaggressive. I have yet to see a parent teaching a child to cross the road safely by leaping out into the moving traffic or crossing against a red light. Yet many parents think that they are teaching a child to be unaggressive by hitting the child, that is, by being aggressive.

Children who are beaten for being aggressive don't learn to be unaggressive. They learn that it is all right to be aggressive so long as you are bigger than the person you want to be aggressive to. Thus children learn to bide their time, and when they are adult they can take their bad feelings out on people smaller than themselves. They can do to children what was done to them.

It is not just ordinary, unthinking people who deny the effects of beating on children. Freud did too. Jeffrey Masson, in his book *Freud: the Assault on Truth*, revealed how Freud was unable to face and reveal publicly the sexual abuse which children suffered in Viennese society. Instead, Freud called the stories of sexual abuse his patients told him fantasies, and based his theory of the Oedipus complex – indeed the whole of psychoanalysis – on this premiss.[46]

Freud was never one to let facts stand in the way of a good theory. He did not regard as fantasies the stories patients told him of being beaten as a child. He simply dismissed them as being screens behind which a deep truth was hidden, a truth unknown to his patients but which he would reveal.

Before I give an example of this I'd like to remind you of what it's like to be seven. At that age we are still trying to work out which are the situations we can change by thought alone and which situations won't change no matter what we think, that is, the difference between fantasy and reality. At seven we still make mistakes.

When I was six I used to play with Fay who was a year older than me and lived across the road. One afternoon, when I was playing with Fay and her brother at their home while their parents were out, Fay decided that she would make us a big pot of tea. After she had poured milk into three cups and filled them with tea she discovered that there was no milk left in the jug. She knew that her parents would expect there to be milk in the jug, so she tipped some of the milky tea from our cups into the milk jug. At six I thought that this really wasn't the solution, but I wasn't entirely sure. I remember peering into the milk jug just to check whether the tea had become milk. It hadn't.

I don't know how Fay's parents reacted when they found tea in the milk jug, but I do know what happened to my friend Jeannie Maclean who tried a similar ploy when she was seven.

At a workshop on self-confidence I asked the people there to recall an incident in their childhood from which they had drawn the conclusion they were in some way bad and unacceptable. Jeannie told the story how she had been playing in her room with a knife which her mother had forbidden her to touch. The knife slipped and cut her rather deeply. Then she heard her mother calling her for tea. She made a rough bandage out of a handkerchief and went downstairs. She slipped into the dining-room and sat at the table with her cut and bleeding hand tucked under her bottom. She thought that if she ate with her other hand her mother would not notice. But her mother did notice, and punished Jeannie severely.

Surely Freud would have understood the difficulties a seven-year-old has in interpreting the world! After all, he had six children of his own. See what he said about another seven-year-old. This is one of the stories he told under the heading 'Infantile Mental Life: two lies told by children'.[47]

> A girl of seven (in her second year at school) had asked her father for money to buy colours for painting Easter eggs. The father had refused, saying he had no money. Shortly afterwards the girl asked again for some money for a contribution towards a wreath for the funeral of the late reigning princess. Each of the school children was to bring fifty pfennigs. The father gave her ten marks; she paid her contribution, put nine marks on her father's writing table, and with the remaining fifty pfennigs bought paints, which she hid in her toy-cupboard.
>
> At dinner the father asked suspiciously what she had done with the missing pfennigs, and whether she had not bought colours with them. She denied it; but her brother, who was two years older, and together with whom she had planned to paint the eggs, betrayed her; the colours were found in the cupboard. The father, very angry, handed the culprit over to her mother for punishment, which was severely administered. Afterwards the mother herself was overwhelmed when she saw the child's extreme despair. She caressed the little girl after punishing her, and took her for a walk to console her. But the effects of the experience, described by the patient herself as the 'turning-point' of her life, proved to be immitigable. She had hitherto been a wild, self-confident child; thenceforth she became timid and vacillating.[48]

Did Freud question

1 Why the little girl's father had not understood that his daughter had behaved like a typical seven-year-old?
2 Why the father got so angry at the loss of such a small sum?
3 Why the father ordered the mother to carry out the punishment?

4 Why the mother obeyed?

5 Why the mother was overwhelmed by what she had done?

6 How the little girl felt about her father's rage and injustice, and her mother's betrayal, violence and attempts at reparation?

7 How frequently her father had punished her and her brother?

8 Had she lied about the money in the hope of avoiding punishment?

9 Had she lied about the money in the hope that all the money might now somehow be on his desk?

No, Freud did not.

Instead he considered the question of money. In adult life the girl had great difficulty in accepting money from other people, and this came, according to Freud, not so much from the beating as from the fact that when she was three she had been responsible for the nursemaid's being dismissed by her mother. The nursemaid was having an affair with a doctor and giving the little girl money not to tell. However, the mother saw this money and all was revealed.

From this Freud concluded:

To take money from anyone had thus early come to mean for her the yielding of the body, the erotic relation. To take money from her father was equivalent to a declaration of love. The phantasy that her father was her lover was so seductive that the childish desire for colours for the Easter eggs was easily, by its aid, indulged in spite of the prohibition. But she could not confess to the appropriation of the money; she was obliged to disavow it, because the motive of the deed, unknown to herself, could not be confessed. The father's chastisement was thus a refusal of the tenderness offered him, a humiliation, and so it broke her spirit . . .

It will scarcely be necessary, for the psycho-analyst, to insist upon the fact that in this child's little experience we are confronted with one of those extremely common cases of persistence of early anal erotism in the later erotic life.[49]

May I draw your attention to Freud's words 'this child's little experience'. None of these experiences was little to the child. This way of talking about his patients is typical of what became the tradition in psychoanalysis of belittling and denigrating the terrible experiences children have, and the suffering of those people who are still trapped in those experiences.

Perhaps it could be argued that the reason Freud did not pay attention to the beatings his patients had endured was that when something is ubiquitous we often fail to see it. I am for ever trying to explain to people that what we are doing all the time is creating meaning. Because they do it all the time, many people aren't aware of what they are always doing. Similarly, people notice acts of cruelty which are unusual, especially when the victims are strangers. Stories of children being forced to take part in satanic rituals always create a great fuss, but no one comments when a child in a supermarket is slapped, shouted at and humiliated by his parents.

Moreover, parents have rights. Children do not.

The idea that children are people in their own right, not merely objects owned by their parents, has never been popular not even today. If children could be useful to the parents, if they would be insurance for the parents' old age, or another pair of hands, they were valued, but only as objects. Lionel Rose, writing about child oppression in Britain between 1860 and 1913, said,

> Admittedly Victorian factory laws and correctional legisla-
> tion, with the advent of industrial schools and reforma-
> tories, were a recognition that children needed special
> treatment, but in social matters they were treated as objects
> rather than subjects. In large poor families their value was
> primarily economic, and in domestic workshops parents
> could be harder and more ruthless than a large factory
> employer . . .
>
> Victorians saw the child as the chattel of the parents

... John Gorst (a former Conservative Education Minister) could still say in 1913: 'The independent rights of children are scarcely recognized or acknowledged by the governing classes. It has become customary to regard them as mere appendages of their parents; the idea that a child has any legal right of its own is startling and unacceptable.'[50]

The sentimental notion that the childhood years are 'the happiest years of your life', a time of golden afternoons filled with blissful play, is very far from the truth. Children have always worked. In peasant societies infants start working as soon as they can walk. Until the creation of the public school upper-class boys were sent to other families to serve that family, while girls were trained in household skills and their marriages arranged. When children did go to school, they worked, not played.

Up until the Industrial Revolution of the eighteenth century Britain was not a wealthy power. However, wealth accumulated with the slave trade (and many of the slaves were children), and the families who made money out of selling slaves invested that money in mines and factories which employed children in the cruellest of conditions.[51]

Children still work. Some countries have laws to limit the amount and kind of work they do, but the economy of most countries, especially those of the Third World, still depends on the work done by children.[52]

Working at a job, or minding younger children, or meeting adult responsibilities has for children a long-term deleterious effect. As children we can look forward to adult life only if we can regard what adults do as exciting, interesting and important. Children who discover that adult life is hard, and that adult responsibilities are wearisome and imprisoning are reluctant to assume those responsibilities when they become adult. Some such children become dilettantes and refuse to take part in any form of adult life. Some appear to take on the responsibilities of adult life by marrying and having children, but prove to be irresponsible parents and spouses. Others assume the responsibilities of marriage and children, but only with bitterness and regret. They make the lives of their family a misery. But how can you become a mature adult when you have never been allowed to be a child?

The notion that the child is the possession of the parents has not disappeared from our society. Parents might no longer send their children out to work as soon as they are big enough to perform small tasks, but many parents still impose on their children a task which the children must fulfil. They must be Good Children, a Credit to Their Parents. They must fulfil the parents' failed ambitions. They must always be Happy Children, and never cause the parent any pain or doubt. Pulling coal trucks was, in one way, much easier. At least you knew when your job was done. Being a Credit to Your Parents is a never-ending task.

One of the greatest advances made this century is the recognition of the importance of play for children. Through play children learn about themselves and the world. They experiment with different roles and explore alternative futures. Through play they can resolve some of the issues in their lives. Play develops creative intelligence.

Children who are not allowed to play are stunted, deprived children. There are many such children, even in those societies which are rich in play materials and play opportunities. The best kind of play for a child is that where the child chooses the materials and what to do with them. Much of the best kind of play is where the child appears to the observer to be doing nothing much at all. The action of the play is in the child's internal world.

Some parents disapprove greatly of this kind of play, for in it the child is beyond the parent's control. Such parents seek to deprive the child of all such play and instead try to organize every minute of the child's day. Such children may grow up with some useful skills, like being able to ride a horse or play tennis, and have many social acquaintances, but their creative intelligence might be even more stunted than the child who herded goats or wove cloth. At least the little herdsman or weaver might not be chided with 'After all I've done for you.'

It is very difficult to be grateful for something you didn't want.

Parents who organize every moment of their child's life do not say that they are trying to limit the child's freedom to think. Their reason, they say, is the excellent one of not wasting time. In this they maintain the education system whereby children are moulded into the shape the parents and society want.

When in the nineteenth century children were allowed to have some schooling the aim of this education was not to develop each child's own individual talents but to drill the children in the skills needed in the workforce. The current educational reforms by the Conservative government bear a remarkable resemblance to the Revised Code introduced in 1862, known to teachers as 'Payment by Results'.[53]

The educational system aimed also at making it clear to children that their place in the hierarchy of society was absolutely fixed.[54] Working-class children were deprived of the vision of life as an array of possibilities, and instead given the cold comfort that if they lived lives of obedience they would earn respect.

Not that children of the upper classes fared much better. They were separated from their parents, cast into the care of nannies whose beliefs about the importance of plain food, cold rooms, cold baths and regular bowel movements created a regime of cruelty.[55] Yet, with no other adult to protect them, the children were very dependent on their nannies.

Lionel Rose described how many nannies had

a fund of macabre old wives' tales and superstitions, which they regaled and even deliberately frightened the children with. Children's heads were filled with fears and fantasies, compounded by the morbid surroundings of nursery life, and Magdalen King-Hall has remarked: 'One is struck, when reading Victorian memoirs, by the many obscure terrors that seemed to have haunted the children of that period.' The threat to one impressionable girl that the chimney sweep would take her away if she was naughty was enough to scare her every time she saw one, and the same girl was frightened of the shadows on the staircase of the great house she lived in. King-Hall cites the memoirs of Lady Sybil Lubbock whose upbringing in the 1880s was riddled with fears of 'the eye of God', burglars, penny-for-the-guy urchins, mad dogs and gypsy women. Deprived of the company of their own parents, children picked up many fanciful notions from contact with ignorant and superstitious servants.[56]

Nannies and servants inspired such fears in their charges so as to keep the children in order, thus continuing a long tradition. Lloyd de Mause wrote:

Most ancients agreed that it was good to have images of witches constantly before children, to let t¹.em feel the terror of waiting up at night for ghosts to steal them away, eat them, tear them to pieces, and suck their blood or their bone marrow. By medieval times, of course, witches and devils took the front stage, with the occasional Jew thrown in as a cutter of babies' throats . . . After the Reformation, God himself who 'holds you over the pit of hell, much as one holds a spider, or some loathsome insect, over the fire,' was a major bogeyman used to terrify children, and tracts were written in baby talk describing the tortures God had in store for children in Hell . . . When religion was no longer the focus of the terrorizing campaign figures closer to home were used: the werewolf will gulp you down, Blue Beard will chop you up, Boney (Bonaparte) will eat your flesh, the black man or the chimney sweep will steal you away at night . . . In Germany until recently there would appear in shops before Christmas time stacks of stick brooms, tied in the middle, and making a stiff brush at both ends. These were used to beat children; during the first week in December, adults would dress up in terrifying costumes and pretend to be a messenger of Christ, called *Pelz-nickel*, who would punish children and tell them whether they would get Christmas presents or not.[57]

Looking at the outcome of the cruelty inflicted on children down the ages, Lloyd de Mause commented:

It goes without saying that the effects on the child in the past of such severe physical and sexual abuse as I have described were immense ... The first is the enormous number of nightmares and hallucinations by children which I have found in the sources. Although written records by adults which indicate anything at all about a child's emotional life are rare at best, whenever discovered they usually reveal recurring nightmares and even outright hallucinations. Since antiquity, pediatric literature regularly had sections on how to cure children's 'terrible dreams', and children were sometimes beaten for having nightmares. Children lay awake nights terrorized by imaginary ghosts, demons, 'a witch on the pillow', 'a large black dog under the bed', or 'a crooked finger crawling across the room'. In addition the history of witchcraft in the West is filled with reports of children's convulsive fits, loss of hearing, or speech, loss of memory, hallucinations of devils, confession of intercourse with devils, and accusations of witchcraft against adults, including their parents.[58]

Anyone who takes the time to get to know someone who has suffered or is suffering periods of psychosis will discover that those experiences which are commonly called hallucinations are not random events, the epiphenomena of a physical illness, but integral parts of the person's meaning structure derived from the person's real lived experience.

Sometimes the delusion and hallucinations are simply resurgences of memories from earliest childhood, usually memories of being physically and/or sexually abused, or being imprisoned in some way, perhaps in a cot or cupboard, or being abandoned. The person has never been able to deal with these memories because there had never been anyone in the person's life to confirm that such events did occur. At whatever age we are, when we suffer a trauma we need someone to say to us, 'Yes, that did happen.' Otherwise we have difficulty in distinguishing our memories of the event from our feelings about the event.

One of the conspiracies which results in cruelty is that of psychiatrists and the parents of children diagnosed as schizophrenic. Together they insist that schizophrenia is a genetic illness best treated by drugs. Although the psychiatrists' own research shows that how well these adult children do depends on how their parents treat them, such psychiatrists insist that how the parents treated the children before the psychosis is quite irrelevant.[59] Such psychiatrists are simply protecting their power and prestige. Some such parents have horrible secrets to hide, as I well know, while others are loving, well-meaning parents who cannot face what all parents need to face. When we are parents of young children, no matter how hard we try, we make mistakes, often through no fault of our own, and often because we thought what we were doing was for the best.

Sometimes the mistake we make is simply the way we describe the world to our children.

When I began working as a clinical psychologist in the early sixties I could understand directly the feelings of self-hatred which my patients described. With my psychotic patients I could understand the unrealness of external reality and the fear of acting in that reality. I understood my patients' fear of other people, but I was very slow in coming to understand how so many people, not just psychiatric patients, look about them and see a terrifying world, a much more terrifying world than I see.

I realized that I had something very important to thank my parents and teachers for. When they wanted to frighten me into obedience they used aspects of the real world – a slap, a harsh word. They did not evoke ogres and witches, or an all-seeing and punishing God, or a divine plan of a Just World where all pleasure is balanced by pain. Unfortunately, peopling their child's world with fantasy figures and describing the world as being at the mercy of unseen, powerful forces are what most parents do. They do it to their children because that is what their parents did to them.

The world has always been filled with people whose fear of the world is far in excess of what the world can do to them. It is bad enough to be frightened of dying of cancer or, in a war, by a sniper's bullet, but if you believe that if you commit a sin cancer or a bullet will be your punishment, then your fear of cancer or a bullet is far in excess of the fear of the real possibility that you will die in that way. Moreover, if cancer or a bullet is the punishment you believe you deserve, you won't take the best precautions to preserve yourself. Good children always accept their punishment.

The world has always been filled with frightened people. Fear and hate go hand in hand. The world has always been filled with people who hate.

Has this fear and hate become less in our present time?

What a question to ask!

On the day I was writing this the *Guardian* carried the following editorial.

Vedrana Glavaj, aged 3; Roki Sulejmanovic, aged 14 months. They are only two of the hundreds of children who have died so far in Bosnia. But we know their names because they were shot, very visibly, on Saturday evening in the bus seeking to evacuate them from Sarajevo. We do not know the name of the six-year-old girl seen in the morgue of Kossovo Hospital, also in Sarajevo. She was decapitated by a mortar blast during a Serbian bombardment on Friday when the Bosnian army attempted to break out. Nor do we know the names of the nine children in Velika Kladusa, a town in north-western Bihac province under Serbian blockade, who have died in an epidemic of gastroenteritis. Thousands more anonymous children are at daily risk of death from violence or disease. Their mothers and fathers, of course, know their names – but only if they are still alive.[60]

If you look in your newspaper the day you read this page you will be able to find several paragraphs to match that one.

Meanwhile, the children of Somalia and Mozambique die of starvation. Meanwhile, as Amnesty International reported:

Every day, somewhere in the world, children face arrest, detention and death, because of their ideas, beliefs or origins, sex, language or religion.

Many children are held as political prisoners by governments, cut off from family and outside support, tortured and even killed.

● Some are held in reprisal for the activities of adults.

● Some suffer physical or mental torture to force confessions from the family.

● Some are refugees seeking asylum from the threat of persecution or death.

● Some are forcibly adopted by strangers.

● Some 'disappear' never to be seen again.

In over 50 countries, children's basic human rights are violated.[61]

Meanwhile, in the name of ancestral values, little black girls, and not just tribal children in Africa, suffer genital mutilation.[62]

Meanwhile, children are born the victims of Aids and drug abuse.

Meanwhile, most children in the Third World live in poverty, while in Britain one quarter of all children live in poverty, whereas in 1979 only ten per cent of children did.[63]

Meanwhile, children continue to be physically and sexually abused, and killed. Shelterless children in Brazil are killed by the forces of law and order, while in Britain the age group most likely to be murdered are children under one.[64]

Meanwhile children continue to be treated with humiliation and contempt.

They are still treated as objects of no value. Their points of view, their needs and wishes, are regarded as being of no importance. Any adult who tries to follow a system of education which takes into account the child's point of view is denigrated and often prevented from teaching in this way.

For instance, over the last ten years or more many teachers in Britain have recognized that their pupils include many who belong to religions other than Christianity and many whose parents have chosen not to teach them any religious beliefs. Accordingly, teachers have developed religious education syllabuses which examine the ideas and practices common to most religions. Such teaching promotes tolerance and a wide general knowledge. The present Conservative government plans to abolish such teaching, and in this has the support of the influential tabloid the *Daily Mail*. The paper's editorial comment, under the heading 'Christian mission in the classroom', stated:

> Britain's schools are required by law to provide religious education. Their syllabuses should reflect the Christian tradition of our nation though taking account of other faiths.
>
> In practice two thirds of the 117 education authorities in England and Wales have so far failed to produce such a syllabus. In far too many cases what is taught under the heading of religious education is a multi-faith mishmash in which Jesus, the Bible and the Ten Commandments hardly appear.
>
> This unappetising cocktail springs from a child-centred approach to education in which pupils are expected to choose whatever beliefs suit them from a cursory course in comparative religion as if all were equally valid.
>
> This is not what is needed today.
>
> The decline of parental authority and the decay of organized religion make the role of the school in teaching elementary morals more important than ever.
>
> Secretary John Patten is right to crusade for a reinstatement of Christian beliefs in the classroom. The worry remains about the people who are called upon to carry it out.[65]

Note that *child-centred* equals *bad*.

I tried to find out who wrote this editorial, but was told by a spokesman for the *Daily Mail* that it was an expression of the views of the paper. So the *Daily Mail* certainly cannot be criticized for being child-centred. However, presumably this editorial was written by one man (there aren't many women in senior positions at the *Daily Mail*) and discussed and agreed upon by one or two others. It is likely that this group of editors went to schools where they were beaten. It is also unlikely that they were ever the recipients of child-centred education. Have they all forgotten how, as children, they wished that the adults who were educating them would take account of their point of view?

Many adults do forget their childhood suffering, and so they become unaware of what the children around them are suffering.

Christians in the Middle Ages said that children were innocent and so did not feel pain, and, accordingly, doctors down the centuries have interpreted this to mean that children suffering illness and injury did not need painkillers. They created a medical theory to support this belief. Nerves carry a myelin sheath which, so the theory went, was necessary for the transmission of pain. Since myelin sheaths are incomplete in young children, doctors deduced that young children did not feel pain. It is known now that myelization is not necessary for the transmission of pain, yet many children in pain do not receive help.

In one study, 25 children undergoing surgery received only 24 doses of painkiller, while 18 adults received 871 doses. Another study of pain treatment after open heart surgery showed that all 50 adults received pain relief, but 24 per cent of the 50 children received nothing.[66]

Likewise the mental pain of children is ignored.

Adults find it hard to accept that any child could become depressed enough to take his own life, let alone make the decision to do so. The consensus is extended to the health professions, where psychiatrists and doctors were taught that child suicide was so rare as to be virtually non-existent. 'Until recently there has been an overwhelming consensus that children do not suffer from depression and it has not yet filtered through to the public that this is a problem,' said Dr Ian Goodyer, head of developmental psychiatry at Cambridge University.

In recent years, a succession of gloomy headlines has documented a rise in suicides among older adolescents and young men and women: suicides among men under 25 have doubled in 10 years and almost a third of those who called Samaritans for the first time were under 25.

However, a number of studies pointing to a disturbingly high incidence of attempted suicide among under-16s has received less attention. A new survey by Samaritans has provided the most shocking hint yet of the size of the problem.

Samaritan youth workers spoke to more than 3,000 teenagers, mostly between 13 and 16, in London schools over the past year. In confidential questionnaires issued after the talks, 40 per cent of the children said they had at some time tried to take their own life . . .

According to Di Stubbs of Samaritans, all the organization's branches have received calls from children under 10. Recognized suicide attempts among under-12s remain rare, but suicidal thoughts, threats, and actions have been recorded in up to a third of children between six and 12 referred to psychiatric clinics . . .

In all, hospitals deal with more than 5,000 under-16s who have attempted to kill themselves every year . . .

'I was struck when working with them just what a despairing group they were,' said Dr Eric Taylor, consultant child psychiatrist at the Institute of Psychiatry, London. 'There is a reluctance in adults appreciating very intense distress in young people, though it's hard to ignore it if you walk into a casualty department.'

Many attempters come from broken homes and, though the link is not always made, a high proportion have been sexually or physically abused. 'The majority of young people who set about attempting or committing suicide are reflecting experiences in which they have felt abused themselves,' said Peter Wilson, a psychotherapist and chairman of Young Minds which campaigns for help for emotionally disturbed children . . .

Even those admitted to hospital slip through the counselling net. 'They're not easy to engage into psychiatric treatment,' Dr Taylor said. 'You can engage about half but even to get that many you need to have a system of responding quickly.'

That is not enough, according to Mr Wilson. 'The annoying thing is that most people will agree that children matter, but when it comes to providing facilities for the more vulnerable child you find that there is an absolute deafness.'[67]

Since children do not feel pain, they can be used as pawns in adults' games. Witness an advertisement in a recent Moscow newspaper.

A woman will give birth to a beautiful, healthy child and sell it to attentive, caring foreign parents.[68]

Even though adults insist that children do not feel pain and forget any injury done to them, many adults get distressed when their children persist in behaving as if they are in pain. Lloyd de Mause observed:

Mothers who sent their infants to wet-nurses for three years were genuinely distressed that their children then didn't want to return to them, yet they had no capacity to locate the reason. A hundred generations of mothers tied up their infants in swaddling bands and impassively watched them scream in protest because they lacked the psychic mechanism necessary to empathize with them.[69]

Lacking empathy, or preferring to trust experts' advice rather than their own feelings, mothers in more recent times have waited, listening to their baby's screams, and watching the hands of the clock creep to the appointed time when the baby could be fed.[70] Mothers who nowadays feed on demand are often chided by older women who should remember the agony for mother and baby of the strict four-hourly feeds.

However, for one of these older women to be able to say to a young mother, 'You are right. I didn't feed my babies when they were hungry, and I was wrong to do that,' she would have had to have had the courage to recognize what she had done and to take responsibility for it. This is what many parents are unable to do.

Yet, until we parents recognize and take responsibility for what we do in bringing up our children adults will continue to treat children cruelly.

And the black tide of hatred will continue to roll on from one generation to the next, from the young to the old and the old to the young. This black tide has rolled all through history, and it continues to roll. As children we suffer, and learn to hate the old. We fear to become old because we fear to become the object of this hatred by the young. Yet, as we go from babyhood to childhood and onwards, we learn to hate the young. We see them taking what we think is rightly ours, and we envy and hate them. Moreover, we deflect on to the young some of the hatred we have for the old.

It's no use saying, 'People are wicked. They must change.' The Church has been saying that for ever (though not about the way adults treat children) and people have not reformed. To change we have to see what we do, and then go on to understand why.

To understand why we need to be aware that

♦ Underlying everything we do is our need to hold ourselves together as a person. We need to survive not just as a body but as a person.

♦ We can, and often do, hold two contrary beliefs simultaneously. When we are thinking, 'I must be bad, otherwise my good parents wouldn't punish me', we are also thinking, 'How dare they do this to me!' *Guilt and vengeful pride go hand in hand.*

The need to survive as a person and the ability to hold two contrary beliefs simultaneously become our motives in not seeing what we do. We can be cruel to others when we feel that we cannot hold ourselves together. For instance, mothers, feeling overwhelmed by the many demands on them, turn their fear into rage against their children. We can be cruel when we want to lie about our contrary beliefs. Witness the adult children who, while talking about how inadequate and guilty they feel about being unable to look after their aged parent, consign that parent to an appalling nursing home.

This is why, when our species first appeared, the second generation of human beings didn't say of their parents, 'That's no way to bring up children!' and proceed to bring up their children in understanding and kindness. Cain certainly didn't learn from his parents not to be cruel.

Of course nowadays there are many parents who strive to see their children as persons in their own right, and act in the child's interests, not their own. This is happening not just among educated, middle-class parents. I write for the mass market magazine *Chat*, and get many letters from mothers who are trying to do just this, and seem to be doing it well.

But it isn't easy to be a kind, understanding parent.

The sight of a parent being kind and understanding to a child creates punitive envy in many adults. Whenever I write something in *Chat* pointing out the deleterious effects on children of beating I get letters from readers calling me a 'do-gooder' or a 'woolly-minded "expert"' who is destroying the morals of the nation. At twenty-seven, when I became a mother, I had a theory that if I met the needs of my son Edward as well as I possibly could for the first few years of his life he would acquire an inner strength and certainty that would enable him to meet and overcome the difficulties he was sure to encounter later in life. Whenever my then husband Ted saw me putting this theory into practice he would shake his head and say, 'You're only making a rod for your own back.' If I didn't beat my child, my child would beat me! He never explained just how this would come about. He just spoke in the terms of an older person who knows all about inevitable doom and disaster.

Edward is now thirty-five, and I can report that Ted was wrong and I was right.

When I was married I would make no response to Ted's dire warnings. I didn't have the self-confidence to argue and defend myself. Not like my friend Candida Lacey. She told me this wonderful story about herself and her two-year-old daughter Eve, illustrating just how difficult it is to be a young mother who tries to understand her child.

Eve was being angelic in the optician's waiting-room. She

sat next to me, engrossed in one of the children's books. Fine. Until it was time to go. She adamantly refused to put the book back on the table. For a full five minutes I tried to reason with her – we could go home and look at her books, other children would like to see this book, and so on. No use. Eventually, I picked her up and walked towards the door. That did it. Major tantrum with a child kicking and screaming under my arm. This continued down the street. When we got to the car I put her on the pavement while I unlocked the door. At this point some two-year-olds would merely stand and whimper. Not Eve. She hurled herself to the ground, beating her fists in the air, her face twisted with rage and streaked with tears. Sitting on the pavement beside her I tried to keep calm and calm her. It didn't work. It was getting late. And dark. I picked her up and tried to put her in the car seat. She stiffened and screamed. Her small body refused to bend into the sitting position. It was impossible to manoeuvre the straps of the car seat over her flailing arms.

'Eve, stop it! Sit down!'

I shouted as much to make myself heard as in anger.

'How dare you treat a child like that! Look at her, she's terrified, poor little mite!'

I looked over my shoulder to see a woman, probably in her late fifties, wringing her hands and jumping from one foot to the other. Eve took advantage of my momentary lapse of concentration to lunge forwards. I caught her, then tried again to make her sit in the seat.

'Sit down! Now!'

'Oh, this is terrible! I'm going to report you for such cruelty.'

The agitated spectator had taken out a pad and pencil and was writing down the number of the licence plate. Now I was furious. I took Eve out of the car and turned to the woman:

'I'll save you the trouble of that. I'll give you my name and address. I want a social worker here, *right now*. Maybe she will be able to *help* me.'

Silence. Both she and Eve looked at me, startled. Eve went limp. She shuddered and then clung around my neck, sobbing softly. My accuser looked slightly ashamed.

'They can be difficult at that age, can't they?' she murmured confidingly, before disappearing into the darkness.[71]

This is an example of how the old sentimentalize very young children while ignoring the reality of the situation of the children and their young parents. The suffering, or supposed suffering, of little children is often sentimentalized by the old in order to justify their persecution of the young. Maggie O'Kane wrote:

The killing in eastern Bosnia is more like a pigeon shoot than a war. With their mortars and rockets, the Serbs are picking off villages and towns. Their leaders – Radovan Karadzic and Slobodan Milosevic – have been insisting for months that if they do not take over these villages and drive out the Muslims, then Serbs will become second class citizens in an Islamic Bosnian state. [*This, incidentally, is an example of trying to preserve the sense of being a person by being cruel to others.*]

At base camp at the bottom of the hill, Savka, a fat, kind woman of sixty, offers Turkish delight sweets. Wrapped in a billowing black skirt and a brown headscarf, she stayed with her boys on the front line. She settles on the bench and tells of how she used to tend the fields with her Muslim neighbours – but now the Muslims are sending crucified, headless Serbian children in batches of four down the river Drina.

Further back from the front lines, the children still have their heads and in this less perilous Serbian-secured territory nice motherly women resembling Savka say the Muslims did not crucify the children, but just cut their throats.

Now we understand one of the reasons why thousands of Bosnian women are in hot sweaty trains, begging for asylum in Europe. It is because of stories about the children.[72]

Sentimentality and cruelty go hand in hand. Usually mothers whose child is having a temper tantrum in a public place are aware that the adults in the vicinity are saying to themselves if not to one another, 'If that child was mine I'd give it a good hiding.'

Such adults are demonstrating, through their hatred of the young, how they dealt with the hatred of the old they brought from their childhood.

There are four main ways in which we can deal with this hatred inside us. We can say,

1 I remember what happened to me and I shall treat my children differently.
2 I don't remember my childhood, so I'll bring my children up in the way that other people do.
3 I was beaten as a child and it didn't do me any harm.
4 Now I've got power I'm not going to let it go.

Let's look at each of these in turn.

1 I remember what happened to me and I shall treat my children differently.

The much-loved agony aunt Claire Rayner, in an interview with Corinna Honan in the *Daily Mail*, spoke of the great cruelty her parents had inflicted on her as a child. Beating was only part of this cruelty. Claire said,

'Neither my mother nor my father ever told me they loved me. I don't remember them ever kissing or hugging me. I was hit by my mother more than by my father. Real beating with a belt, anything she could get her hands on. I remember being beaten with saucepans. I can track a scar right along my skull from one. She could not control her temper. If things didn't go her way, God help you. Everybody hit you in those days. I was an evacuee to a lot of different people during the war, and everybody had permission to beat you up.'

Corinna asked Claire whether she had beaten her own children.

No, she never beat them, she says. She beat the table with her fists instead. Or threw plates at the floor. She thinks she probably reinvented herself at nineteen, as the total opposite to her parents; hard-working, unconditionally loving and tolerant.

'I am so *vehemently* opposed to physical punishment for children. Either you deal with a past like mine and see what was bad and consciously avoid it and make use of it, or you buy it all and let it just emerge as a repetition. People *can* break the chains. You can change the pattern, but you can't do it without thinking about it. I managed to on my own, which is the luck of the draw.'[73]

One way of dealing with the hatred and the pain is to talk about it and write it. Claire has done just this. But the cost to her has been great.

After the birth of each of her three babies she became profoundly depressed. If, as a little girl, your parents have convinced you that you are totally despicable and unlovable, when you later become pregnant you can feel that anything you produce from inside you must be bad, and when you do produce something wonderful you are sure that you don't deserve this gift, and that you're incapable of looking after it properly. Turning against yourself in this way, you become depressed.[74]

Claire survived these depressions and learned from them, but she remains vulnerable to criticism. She has yet to adopt the attitude which those of us who know her feel she should, namely, 'Anyone who doesn't like me is a fool, and I'm not going to waste time on fools.'

Claire remembered her childhood, stayed with the pain, and tried to learn from it. There is no end to such learning. Unfortunately, some people resolve to remember their childhood but they do not learn from it. They want to feel the pain they suffered, but deny their hatred. They think of themselves as being sensitive, caring and unaggressive.

They often feel overwhelmed by the wickedness of the world, and so they suffer great fear, especially of other people's aggression. To deny their own hatred of the old they have to deny their own aggression. They cannot let themselves see that, even though we might live in a society where it is not necessary to kill people in order to survive, we have to defend ourselves as a person against other people. We refuse to accept the meanings which other people seek to impose on us, and we seek to impose our meaning on other people. Deciding that your child should go to bed now, and not three hours later, is an example of imposing your meaning on another person. Trying to persuade other people that you are not aggressive is itself an act of aggression.

When such people become parents they find it very difficult to deal with their children's aggression. They punish their children through guilt and shame for being aggressive, and they fail to help their children develop a wide range of flexible skills in dealing with anger and aggression, both their own and other people's. They love their children dearly, and in many ways they give their children great care, but in showing themselves to be so frightened of the world and thus suggesting to their children that they too should be frightened, and by refusing to acknowledge their hatred of the old and the aggression inherent in all of us, they fail their children, and so are cruel.

And so the black tide rolls on.

2 I don't remember my childhood, but I bring up my children in the way other people do.

I used to be surprised at the number of people I met who did not remember their childhood. Some people told me that they remembered nothing of their life before they were twelve, or even fifteen. Others remembered highlights – like holidays, or their favourite pop group. Now I am no longer surprised by this. One way to deal with the hatred and the pain is to forget it, and that means forgetting the circumstances which gave rise to the hatred and the pain. (In a kind of collective amnesia swaddling has been forgotten.)

Forgetting your childhood undermines your sense of being a person. How can you answer the question 'Who am I?' if you have forgotten where you came from and what happened along the way.

What happens when you have children? Forgetting your childhood means that you haven't thought about your parents' child-raising methods and worked out some improvements. So you have to look around you and see what other parents do.

What do you see? You see the three major methods – the slap, the bribe, and the guilt. They are used in no particular pattern, just whatever appeals to the parent at the time. Sometimes these methods make the child do what the parent wants, and sometimes they do not. However, all three methods have the same long-term outcome. Self-hatred and hatred of the old.

THE SLAP

I have already said much about beating. Leonard Michaels in his very short story 'The Hand' said it all much better.

> I smacked my little boy. My anger was powerful. Like justice. Then I discovered no feeling in the hand. I said, 'Listen, I want to explain the complexities to you.' I spoke with seriousness and care, particularly of fathers. He asked, when I finished, if I wanted him to forgive me. I said yes. He said no. Like trumps.[75]

THE BRIBE

An afternoon in Marchmont Street in London. A five-year-old girl asks her mother for something. I don't hear what. The mother isn't paying much attention. She says, 'Not now. This evening perhaps. If you're good.'

There are three possible endings to this story.

♦ The little girl behaves as her mother wants all afternoon and evening, when her mother gives her her reward. The little girl is pleased, but draws the conclusion that, since her mother won't give her what she wants simply because she wants it, her mother doesn't love her as the person she is but only when she is good. In short, the only love she can get is cupboard love.

Result. Self-hatred.

♦ The little girl behaves as her mother wants, but the mother forgets the promise she made. If reminded by the little girl, she denies it.

Result. A sense of injustice. Hatred of the old.

♦ The little girl fails to behave as her mother wants, and her mother punishes her by withdrawing the reward.

Result. Guilt at failure. Anger at injustice. Self-hatred. Hatred of the old.

GUILT

'After all I've done for you.'

Best summed up in Roger McGough's poem.

> I was forever hearing about the sacrifices
> My parents made.
> Little ones almost daily
> Big ones when required.
>
> Having me meant sacrifices. Going without.
> And then to cap it all, the Scholarship:
> School uniforms, violin lessons,
> Elocution, extra tuition.
>
> 'If it's not one thing it's another.
> I hope you're worth it.' But was I?
> The dictionary confirmed my doubts:
> '*Sacrifice*, a ritual killing of a person
> or animal with the intention of pleasing a deity.'
>
> Sacrifice. No, I wasn't worth it.
> All that blood for a few O-levels.[76]

And so the black tide rolls on.

3   I was beaten as a child and it never did me any harm.

We all have the most wonderful defence which enables us to survive physical pain. We can separate ourselves from the pain and not feel it. In the dentist's chair we can imagine ourselves somewhere else, and not feel the drill.

Women who as children were sexually abused can describe how they could escape from the pain and degradation by leaving their bodies to suffer, and situating themselves somewhere else in the room.[77] Boys who are thrashed frequently can take pride in what pain they can endure, and boast to their friends, 'It didn't hurt.'

It is a very useful defence to have in a very cruel world.

But defences are expensive. There is always a price to pay.

This defence is, in effect, a lie which we tell ourselves. We don't really leave our bodies. We just tell ourselves that we do.

Telling lies to ourselves to stop the pain is far more dangerous than taking drugs to stop the pain. Sure, 'It's not hurting' or 'I'm somewhere else' said on a rare occasion won't harm us, just as taking the occasional Valium tablet won't harm us. It is when we go on and on telling ourselves lies that we harm ourselves far more than if we go on and on taking Valium.

The person that we know ourselves to be is made up of all the conclusions we have drawn from our experiences, all our attitudes, beliefs and opinions, and all the feelings, images and memories that are an integral part of these conclusions, attitudes, beliefs and opinions. All of this creates a meaning structure. A person *is* a meaning structure. You are your meaning structure.

Whenever you feel yourself falling apart, it is your meaning structure falling apart. This happens when you discover that an important part of your meaning structure does not fit with reality. Perhaps you thought that someone you love loves you, and you find that you are wrong. Perhaps you thought your job was secure, and you found that you were wrong. When you realize that you have made a serious error of judgement you question every other judgement you have ever made, and you feel your meaning structure start to crumble. You feel yourself start to crumble, shatter, disappear. You feel absolute terror.

You have to do something to hold yourself together.

When we are small children and being treated cruelly by the adults on whom we depend we feel this terror as well as the pain of the cruelty. We have to do something to hold ourselves together.

What most of us do is decide that the adult is right to treat us in this way. We are bad and deserve to be punished. However, if the cruelty goes on and on we have to do something more to stop ourselves from being overwhelmed by the pain and by our feelings of utter helplessness.

Whenever we feel helpless our meaning structure comes

under threat. We need to feel that we, our meaning structure, can act on the world. Free choice and free action makes our meaning structure secure. If we have no choice and no free action, our meaning structure starts to fall apart. This is why people are greatly affected by being imprisoned and deprived of all free choice and action.

Adult prisoners who understand the importance of free choice and action create in their daily routine some area where they have control and choice. The hostages returning from the Lebanon described how they had set themselves a routine of exercise, or played games, or carried out mental tasks. Small children try to establish and maintain some areas of free choice and control, and know their importance (hence the temper tantrums when an area is lost), but they are much more in the power of their parents than prisoners are in the power of their guards. So they have to resort to other methods to hold themselves together.

One method is to create a split in your meaning structure.

While our brain remains intact everything that goes into our meaning structure stays there. Everything that goes into our meaning structure changes because our meaning structure is constantly changing as we draw new conclusions and modify the old ones. A memory is never an exact action-replay but a new and changing construction. We pay attention to some parts of our meaning structure, and ignore other parts because we have no immediate need for them. There are parts we do not want to pay attention to. Being able to say to yourself at three in the morning, 'I'm not going to think about that now' is a very useful skill, but saying to yourself, 'That didn't happen', when all the time you know it did, is not. The first is simply a matter of directing your conscious thought. The second is attempting to divide your meaning structure into different sections by putting up a partition.

The partition most commonly used is the one which aims to separate off and then hide the pain and humiliation we have suffered or are suffering. The partition has to be supported by a lie.

The truth 'I am suffering' has to be hidden behind the lie 'I am not suffering'.

In the short term and in the present this can be an essential survival tactic. However, if the suffering and the lie go on and on, if what is hidden is not present suffering but past suffering, we do ourselves damage.

To know ourselves and to grow in wisdom, courage and confidence we need to know and experience our meaning structure as being all of one piece. Splitting ourselves, we become lesser beings.

One of the many ironies of human life is that we are born social creatures. We need other people as much as we need air, food and water. Yet we are for ever alone in our own meaning structure. The only way we can enter another person's meaning structure is through our imagination. We have to make the imaginative leap of empathy. The essence of our humanness is our capacity for empathy. Without empathy we are no more than a biological computer, each operating in its own little world.

We are born with a capacity for empathy. Babies, once they become involved in their conversation with their mother, are able to empathize with their mother. They have no notion of why she might be happy or sad, but they can feel her feeling and respond appropriately. They will share her joy, or seek to comfort her when she is sad. (Some mothers, needing to be looked after, let their babies mother them, thus forcing the babies to take on adult responsibilities so early in life.)

Our capacity for empathy seems to arise out of our capacity to suffer – to feel pain, loss and loneliness. Empathy is our natural antidote to pain, loss and loneliness, because through empathy we can comfort and be comforted.

However, if we deny our suffering we lose our capacity for empathy.

Losing our capacity for empathy, we become less of the human being we might have been. We become less than human.

Children who are subjected to extensive and repeated cruelty often resort to the defence of partitioning off their experience of suffering and denying its existence. Some of them, later in life, take down the partition, suffer the pain, and become whole. Such people are the exception. Most people who learned to deny their suffering in childhood continue to deny it. Not feeling their own pain, unable to empathize with anyone else's pain, they become cruel. The world offers them many outlets for their cruelty.

The history of childhood is the history of cruelty and suffering because the adults lacked empathy, and they lacked empathy because, as children, they suffered and, to preserve themselves, they became indifferent to the pain.

The person who says, 'I was beaten as a child and it never did me any harm,' says this, not in shame or excuse, but in high-minded virtue. 'I suffered and thus became a better person, so you must suffer.' Thus adults can not only be cruel to children, they can feel virtuous while doing so.

In doing this they can turn their hatred of the old on to the young.

They can also turn their hatred of the old on to their enemies and treat them cruelly.

Enemies have always had an essential function in the organization of our society. We need to live in groups, but groups always pose the problem of what we shall do with our anger and aggression which can tear a group apart. Enemies provide the answer.[78]

We define our group as good. Together we are clean, unselfish, kind, responsible, and unaggressive. Our enemies are bad. They are dirty, greedy, cruel, irresponsible and aggressive. We can project all our unacceptable feelings – our greed, envy, anger and aggression – on to our enemies and feel virtuous in hating them.

The more harshly children are brought up, the more they have need for enemies, for they have more hatred to express. Enemies get handed down from one generation to another like the family jewels. There is a feeling of great virtue in hating your parents' enemies with the hatred brought from childhood for the old. What would happen to racism if we didn't do this?

And if our enemies fall into our hands, what shall we do? There is never a shortage of soldiers, concentration camp guards and torturers. Torturers are much needed. At present torture is practised by one government in three.[79]

When you read about the bizarre methods that torturers use, do you ever wonder how the torturer ever thought of such things? The answer is that torturers simply elaborate upon what was done to them as children.[80]

And so the black tide rolls on.

4 Now I've got power I'm not going to let it go.

When you're a child and suffering, you can comfort yourself with the thought that one day you'll be grown up and have the power and prestige which the adult, who is inflicting pain on you, has. It is a good way of holding yourself together and giving yourself hope. But if, as you grow up, you do not come to understand yourself, your intention to use your power as an adult to meet your own ends can bring disaster.

In our society the post-retirement old do not have much power and prestige, so those people who have promised themselves that they would use adult power for their own benefit have to make the most of that power when they are young adults. As children their needs were not met, so in adult life they decide to meet their own needs. They might hold down a job, marry, have children, but they act with all the foresight and planning of a two-year-old: 'I want it and I want it now.' They create havoc in their lives and in the lives of those around them. They might pride themselves on being kind and loving to their children, but through their selfishness, lack of under-standing, and lack of foresight, they inflict great cruelty on them. I could illustrate this with dozens of stories about people I have known who lavished love and understanding on their small children, and then took that all away because they wanted to use their adult power to meet their own needs, not their children's.

In societies where the old do have power the way that power is used reveals very clearly the hatred the old have for the young. The young in such societies have to be more circumspect in expressing their hatred.

Much sentimental tosh is expended about societies where the old are in power. Young people are supposed to respect and revere the old, and hang on their every word of wisdom. When Angiola, Giuliana and I were talking on the Lido about swaddling, Angiola said to Giuliana, 'Surely Italian women have nothing to fear about growing old. They're at the centre of their family, the matriarch, all that love and respect from the family.' Giuliana shook her head, 'That's nothing but sentimentality.'

If the young in these societies really did love, respect and revere the old, surely, when social circumstances change and the structure which gave the old their power and position no longer exists, the young would continue to care for the old? Do they indeed! They toss out the old and treat them with all the hatred and disrespect that the young show for the old in our society.

Africa used to be one of the world's best places to grow old. Advanced age was regarded as a blessing and the elderly revered as sacred, the crucial link between the living and the ancestors, the holders of wisdom and culture.

Expressions for the elderly in West African languages often mean 'he or she who knows' or 'he or she who has vision'. Talk of the Western practice of placing ageing relatives in nursing homes makes most Africans shudder with horror. The duty of the young is spelled out in a Ghanaian proverb: 'If your elders take care of you while cutting your teeth, you must in turn take care of them while they are losing theirs.'

But today, as with so much of African society, times are changing – and for the elderly, radically so. The growing influence of Western-style education, free market economics and accelerated migration is putting Africa's traditional extended families under strain and people's ability to care for the elderly in jeopardy.

'During our childhood in Ghana, we stayed in the family house, so we helped the aged, we did everything for them,' said Veronica Ayisi, a fifty-five-year-old volunteer for Help Age Ghana. 'But now, because of "civilization", all their children have travelled, some have married and gone away, and there is no one to help them' . . .

Part of the blame lies with Africa's gradual integration into the world economy. Rising foreign debts and flagging economies are forcing states to impose structural adjustment programmes in an effort to please foreign creditors and to attract investment. As a result unemployment and prices have soared.

'The salaries people are getting do not keep them going nor their own immediate family,' said Nana Apt, a professor of sociology at the University of Ghana and president of the African Gerontological Society. 'So that now it becomes easier for children to say, "Look, I can't help the elderly", because they themselves cannot cope.'[81]

Similar arguments are advanced to explain why those immigrants from the Indian subcontinent who arrived in Britain in the fifties and sixties and who now are growing old are not being looked after by their families. Houses in Britain, it is said, are too small for an extended family, even if the family could afford to support their elderly relative. In a television documentary entitled *Who Cares*, the narrator, Saeed Jaffrey, said:

For centuries the extended family has been the basis of Indian society. People have been brought up to expect that their children will look after them when they grow old. But not in Britain. Here more and more older people are being abandoned by the very children for whom, in coming here, they sacrificed so much.[82]

When members of a family love one another they order their priorities so that as far as possible they can stay together. Margaret Forster's novel *Have the Men Had Enough?* is a fictional account of how she and her husband, Hunter Davies, and their children kept his mother living with them as she sank further and further into dementia.[83] Their experience is not unusual, for in some families love for the old overrides the hate. However, when families are kept together only by bonds of law and duty, as soon as these bonds cease to exist, the family flies apart.

The old stay in power in those countries where there is still a myth operating that the state must be ruled by a powerful father-figure. According to Charles Glass, a journalist who has travelled widely in the Middle East and who was once a hostage in Lebanon, the US government assumed that

> it could dominate the revolution [in Iran] through young, US-educated technocrats, just as it had dominated the Shah's Iran. To the analysts' surprise, *their* young men failed to control the revolution, and other young men, devoted to an old man, occupied their embassy.
>
> Young revolutionaries did not inherit the Peacock Throne, and the prospect of today's young malcontents banding together to overthrow Rafsanjani and his theocrats is inconsistent with Iranian myth. The Iranian novelist Reza Baraheni, who had been tortured by the Shah's secret police, sensed this long before Khomeini flew back from exile in Paris to Mehrabad Airport: 'In most of the major stories of the past and present, the father of the family, the head of the tribe, the father of society, the father of history, the king, in other words, the old man, wins, and the young men and women of the family and society are defeated; they lose the battle without exception. The authority of the tradition of the fathers is with us all the time. In fact, our history is the history of infanticide.'[84]

China has always been dominated by the myth of the Son of Heaven. The change from the Emperor to Chairman Mao was not a great change. The Son of Heaven could not be unseated, and neither could his representatives, the powerful old. In China there is no retiring age for the old. No matter how many brilliant papers young academics and scientists publish, no matter that their professors do not publish at all, the young cannot make any advance until the old ahead of them die. The old will not give way to the young, as the story of Deng Yingchao, born 4 February 1904, died 11 July 1992, shows.

> Her boyfriend was arrested by warlord police when she was only 16. She demanded to see the police chief and take his place. She was Number One in the Awakening Society – a group of patriotic Chinese students agitating

for democracy. Her boyfriend was Number Five (they drew positions by lot) known much later as Premier Zhou En-Lai.

Deng Yingchao, who has died aged 88, survived the warlords, and with Zhou went to study in Paris, forming a Communist Group which antedated the Chinese Communist Party. They returned to China for marriage and the revolution. This long and placid partnership became an essential part of the Premier Zhou myth. The couple who stayed together struggled for socialism together.

On the Long March Deng gathered wild fungus to make soup when Zhou fell ill. She herself was then carried on a stretcher for hundreds of miles, suffering from TB. Edgar Snow, author of *Red Star Over China*, found her recuperating in Beijing incognito, trapped by the Japanese occupation, and smuggled her out as his amah.

In recent years the Chinese press has quoted Deng's advice to the new generation: 'Young men and women should subordinate their own marriage and lifestyle to political demands and what benefits the revolution.' Post-1949 politics might have long been less stormy if Mao Zedong and his wife Jiang Qing had behaved like the austere Zhou couple.

Perhaps Deng carried subordination to the revolution, alias Premier Zhou, rather too far. The daughter of an impoverished landlord in Henan province, she lost the fiery spark which the 1919 student movement had kindled.

After the communist victory, Deng (unlike Jiang Qing) kept out of frontline politics, only joining the Party's Central Committee in 1969. She was active in social issues and became a well-liked Auntie figure among the leadership and their children.

She watched her husband die of cancer and overwork without denouncing the Gang of Four who hastened his death. She remained loyal to the Party even when it was wrong.

In mid-May 1989 Deng joined a gathering of the Party elders to decide what to do about Tiananmen Square. They agreed there was 'no way to retreat' and yield to the students' demands. 'If we did,' they concluded, 'we would fall from power.' The rest, martial law and tanks, is now history.

Did Deng recall her passionate involvement in the Awakening Society 70 years before? As the elders die, it is becoming a familiar tale. Another ageing revolutionary has wound down her final years opposing a new revolution.[85]

And so the black tide rolls on.

Where do you stand in that black tide?

If you fear growing old, how much of that fear is a response to the hatred you feel for the old and to the hatred you suspect is, or will be, directed at you by the young?

If you are frightened of growing old, it is not a solution to say, 'I don't hate anyone,' for even if you are the kindest, most loving person who has ever graced this earth, you can still be hated for what other people see you representing.

It is very easy to feel benign about the entire world when life is going along well for you. But when it isn't – when your home is burgled, or the law treats you unjustly, or someone else gets what was rightly yours, or when someone close to you betrays you – you do feel rage and hatred. Sometimes this rage and hatred seem entirely justified, and sometimes they seem excessive and directed not solely at the perpetrators of your injury. There's nothing like a present injury for tapping into the well of childhood hatred.

That needs to be addressed.

However, there is something else which adds to our fear of growing old.

Perhaps the greatest cruelty adults inflict on children is that they stop them developing the intelligence whereby we can understand ourselves. (Just how they do this I have described in detail in my book *Wanting Everything*.)

And so we grow up stupid. Sure, we can programme computers, put a man on the moon, cure some cancers, operate a car, a washing machine, a fax, a telephone, sure, we can do lots of complex things, but at living our lives competently and happily we are such failures. In understanding ourselves we are so very stupid. And so we fear to grow old, for, as the years pass, the chickens we hatched prove to be vultures. As the years pass, our vultures come home to roost.

CHAPTER 4

Laying eggs and hatching vultures

MY FATHER always said, 'You only get back what you give away.'

What he meant was that if you're nice to people they'll be nice to you, and if you're nasty to them, they'll be nasty to you. It's not a bad rule to follow, but it doesn't always work out. You can be as nice as you possibly can be to some people, and they treat you terribly, while others can be most forgiving of the nasty things you've done to them.

The trouble is that we don't always know what it is we give away.

We act, and other people interpret our actions.

Other people respond to our actions, not in terms of what we did, but in terms of how they interpret what we did.

As self-sacrificing parents doing the very best for our children, we can think that our children understand and appreciate this, but they don't. As lovers we can feel that our partners must understand how we feel without a word being spoken, but they don't. As friends and colleagues we can feel that our friends and colleagues must see things in the way that we do, but they don't.

Each of us is always in the business of interpreting what happens and creating meaning. No two people ever create exactly the same meaning. If we don't realize this and act on it, our chickens turn into vultures.

One woman told me that she did not realize this until fairly late in her life when the vultures who came home to roost were too big to be ignored. She said, 'I used to just live. What happened to me mattered, but my reaction to other people didn't mean a thing. I didn't consider how other people felt. When someone told me I was selfish I was very surprised. I didn't think I was because I did so much for other people, all the time. Then when I looked at it, I realized that I didn't care how other people felt, and that's where the selfish attitude came in.'

Unfortunately, if in childhood we do not discover that other people see things differently from us and that it is very important to us that we find out just how other people see things, we do not develop the skills necessary to do this. The skills of empathy and sensitive questioning and listening are like the skills of speaking more than one language or appreciating music. The earlier we start, the more skilful we are, and the more the skill becomes an integral part of our being.

So, the first step in turning our chickens into vultures is to believe that: *Everybody interprets everything in the same way as I do, and anyone who doesn't is either mad or bad.*

The next step is to believe: *I'm going to live for ever.*

When we are young we know intellectually that one day we will die, but in our hearts we do not believe it. My friend Alan Brien told me, 'I was in the RAF when I was seventeen and three quarters, and it looks to me now like I don't believe anybody should be allowed to go and even buy a packet of cigarettes at that age, but it seemed to be okay to me. I thought I was immortal. I thought nothing would happen to me, and I thought everything would go my way, and by the time I was forty, if ever that came, we would have a socialist commonwealth and all problems would be solved. I think that this is part of youth and one shouldn't take it away from them. Though I do say, "Look at history and learn from history and see those things."'

As time passes and we go from seventeen to twenty-seven, from twenty-seven to thirty-seven, from thirty-seven to forty-seven, the evidence that people die continues to mount. Many people resort to magical thinking to maintain their belief that they will live for ever. A married couple I know (they're friends so I won't name them) refuse to make a will even though they have a business, a house, and children to consider. 'If you make a will,' they say, 'it means you're going to die.' My argument that not making a will simply makes lawyers rich cuts no ice with them.

Talking to Fay Weldon, I established that, although on the one hand she feels that death has no terror for her, she believes that she can't die while she's obligated to complete some work. She said, 'I can't die. I've got all these contracts. If I'm writing something it's all right, but, if I'm between two things and I make a journey or I fly, I'm much more nervous because I can't see any reason why I should be preserved. Whereas if I'm writing something I sense it is all organized, the entire cosmos is organized. I'm thankful that there's no way that this aircraft is going to crash.'

Some people do eventually realize the inevitability of death. My friend Una Gault told me, 'Up till when I was thirty I had an image of time stretching ahead of me, limitless. Then suddenly I started calculating, "I've spent a third of my life. What have I done with a third of my life? What's the other two-thirds going to be like?"'

Believing that you will live for ever fits closely with the third step in turning chickens into vultures. It is the belief that *our acts have no consequences or very limited consequences*. It is the refusal to see that the consequences of every action we perform spread outward in a vast, never-ending network of consequences. We live in a world where everything is connected to everything else.

The playwright Edward Albee said, 'All my plays are about people missing the boat, closing down too young, coming to the end of their lives with regret at things not done, as opposed to things done. I find that most people spend too much time living as if they're never going to die. They skid through their lives. Sleep through them sometimes.'[1]

Even though we say to ourselves, 'The world is as it is and people just move around in it: I've got endless time: What I do doesn't matter', we know, at some level, that we are lying to ourselves.

We are frightened of growing old because we know that sooner or later we are going to wake up in the early hours of the morning with the dread thought, 'What is going to become of me?'

In that black hour we might recognize the lie we were taught as children to believe:

IF YOU'RE GOOD, NOTHING BAD CAN HAPPEN TO YOU

How very comforting it is to think that we live in a cosmos where everything that happens is part of a Grand Plan. Some physicists tell us that a plan exists, though they can't quite agree on what the plan is, whereas the theologians of whatever religion we might name have always known what the plan is.

Their plan is quite simple. We live in a Just World where goodness is rewarded and badness is punished.

Of course, no two religions agree on what is good and what is bad, what the rewards and punishments are, and who administers them and how. Within each religion people argue about these matters. Nevertheless, the message of all religions is the same. If you're good, you're safe. If you're bad, you're in danger.

There are many people who would say that they have no religious belief, yet they still like to believe that we live in a Just World where, somehow, we will be compensated for all our losses, suffering and disappointments, provided, of course, we deserve such compensation. They say, 'There must be something more. If there wasn't, all this would be meaningless.'

What they reveal in saying this is the profound injury they suffered in childhood. They came into the world able to live in the present, to be curious about and enjoy what they encountered, not needing to justify the present in terms of the past and the future. Then they were cast out of Paradise. They became self-conscious, ashamed and guilty. Nothing the world could offer would assure them of their worth and assuage their shame and guilt. The world thereafter disappointed them, and so they were left longing for something which lay outside the world and in an unknown future. A sad way to live.

Many children are presented with a belief in the Just World

in the form of 'Wish upon a star and your dream will come true.' This is the dogma of Disneyland. My friend Diana Leidel told me, 'One of my mother's guiding principles was, "If you keep wishing and hoping for something good to happen it will happen". I don't think that served her in any good stead. As long as I continued to believe that, it didn't serve me in any good stead either. One day I realized that it was perfectly ridiculous.'

Of course Diana's wishes had to be approved by her mother. 'She wanted to be good to everyone at all costs. She made a real distinction between being good and being bad. The best thing I could do would be to be a good girl. Not necessarily to be intelligent or clever or resourceful but to be good.'

It's sad when your wishes don't come true. It can be sad when they do. There is a Bosnian joke which goes, 'Mujo is fishing, and catches a goldfish. In return for saving its life, it grants him one wish. He wishes to become a prince. The next morning his wife wakes him up. "Get up Ferdinand, we are going to Sarajevo."'[2]

Babies are born without any concept of good and bad. They come into the world with a very clear notion of pleasant and unpleasant, but not good and bad. This is why adults down the centuries have found it so easy to define children as being inherently wicked, and thus justify their cruel treatment of children.

However, children learn very quickly to see themselves and their world in terms of the categories of good and bad. 'Am I good enough?' becomes their basic quest, and everything they do is in the framework of this question.

Here, again, is one of those situations where, because something is ubiquitous, we fail to see it. Traditionally, psychiatrists, psychologists and psychoanalysts, being themselves absorbed with the question 'Am I good enough?', fail to see that unsatisfactory answers to this question lead us to behave in ways which are called mad. The more we see ourselves as being bad and unacceptable, the more frightened we become, and, in the desperate attempt to hold ourselves together, the more we have to resort to those defences which psychiatrists call mental illnesses.[3] So psychiatrists look for faulty genes and adverse biochemical changes, psychologists for negative reinforcements and dysfunctional cognitions, and psychoanalysts for unconscious impulses. They fail to notice that the question which absorbs their patients is not 'How can I be well?' or 'How can I be happy?' but 'How can I be good?' They turn the quest for goodness into a symptom called 'low self-esteem'.

Failing to realize this, they do not then go on and examine how each patient defines 'good' and 'bad', the workings of the Just World, and the implications of these. There are many different interpretations of the Just World.

Definitions of 'good' rarely include 'being myself and accepting who I am'. Definitions of 'good' usually imply a standard and a regrettable or sinful falling away from that standard. Children are not expected to work out their own definitions but to accept those imposed on them by the adults around them.

Louise Anike, in her book *Older Women: Ready or Not*, set out the definition of 'good' which, despite the work of the Women's Movement, is still the one which is presented to most young girls and which most women believe they ought to follow and feel guilty when they don't.

When I was born, it seems to me, a Contract was drawn up in which parents and the society in which they lived colluded on the terms and conditions and clauses on the way I should live.

The Contract clauses were:

This is a female baby, therefore she will grow to be (preferably) beautiful and well-formed (meaning slender); she will be obedient and dutiful; she will be intelligent enough to be socially at ease; she will be passive and conform to the relevant morality and mores, and also uphold them; she will be secondary to her brother(s); she will receive just enough education to enable her to earn her own living until she is married or, at least, converse reasonably and be literate; she will be malleable and acquiescent though virtuous, and upon entering the state of marriage she will be a virgin; in her marriage she will be a good caring dutiful, loyal wife who respects her husband, taking unto herself his political, social and religious views; she will never by thought or deed be sexually unfaithful to her husband no matter what type of man he will prove to be and no matter if he is unfaithful; she will have children whom she will nurture and cherish for so long as they live; she will perform all household duties competently, as well as perform miracles daily with her housekeeping money and feel fulfilled with her home, her husband and her children; she will also be obliged to be of service and productive all the days of her life in whatsoever form it is asked of her; if she be widowed, she will preferably remain unmarried out of loyalty to his memory and speak only in good terms of her life with him.

If she does all these things, she will be deemed to be a good woman.

To be a good woman is the highest accolade possible to women.[4]

I wondered whether it would be possible to define 'a good man' in such a universal way. I asked two of my friends, Craig Newnes, a psychologist, and Mike Fishwick, my editor, for their definitions of 'a good man'. I chose them because, having known them both for a long time, I have seen each of them go through a period in their life where they had to think about what constitutes goodness for a man. Not that they would have thought about it in those terms. They had to think about it in terms of whether, as intelligent, well-educated, creative, attractive men, they would continue to enjoy all the options those qualities afford a man, or whether they would take on the responsibilities and limitations of being a husband and father.

Craig wrote,

In the early 1950s, as now, being a good man meant different things to different people. If you were white and working-class it could mean volunteering, as your father had done, rather than being conscripted. If you were upper-class it would mean doing much the same things, to serve king, country and the status quo. Just occasionally, if you were bright and middle-class, or socialist, it would mean conscientiously withdrawing from Britain's military incursions into Malaya and elsewhere. If you were Jamaican it could mean abandoning your culture to find work in the promised land at the centre of the Commonwealth in order to support your family. It could mean smoking 60 cigarettes a day like John Wayne while single-handedly burying Communism; or staying at home on an African farm to help the women till the fields. By the 1960s much had changed, more men spoke out against war and those that went enthusiastically to Vietnam came back broken and ready to speak out. To some extent the idea of being good began to go out of fashion. It was still considered good to provide for a family, but was it good or bad to stand up for gay rights, to die for rock and roll like Jim Morrison and Jimi Hendrix, or smash guitars and hotel rooms like The Who? We were told the Kennedys were good men, that Martin Luther King had been a good man and Gandhi, who slept with virgins, was a good man.

Somewhere in the 1970s I dropped the idea that being good was worth aiming for. Somewhere out there being a good man still meant providing for a family, but could you do this, have an affair, work late, get drunk, and still be good? If you were honest, hard-working and true to your principles, was this good or was this merely honest, hard-working and true to your principles?

I have a strange idea now that for many of us being good is wholly irrelevant. We are tortured by guilt at not being good enough (for whom, for what), we want to be one of the boys and at one with the girls, we want to co-operate with and not exploit women, but many of us don't know how. We want to quell racism and, paradoxically, our own intolerance. If we have families we still want to provide for them and be productive in our workplaces and gardens. We want to be firm but kind with our children, and honest in our relationships. We want to stand up for our beliefs and be counted. And sometimes, in our crazier moments, we still want to die for our country and be remembered as knights of the round table.

Both Craig and Mike found what I had asked them to do a great challenge. Craig always responds quickly to challenges, and so his description of a good man reached me within few weeks of my asking him. Mike thought about the matter for many months. He often spoke to me about how hard a task it was. He took the task with him on holiday, and brought it back undone. Finally, when I told him this book was, as I spoke, rolling off my printer, he set to work, and the following arrived by fax.

It is easy to think of being a male as not much cop – that there's not much challenge in it, that men are pretty simple beings. It is easy to think that, and I do, a lot of the time. The traditional view of the 'the good man' – with allowances made for the pressures of class, one way or another – is that he stands his round, holds his drink, is good to do business with, doesn't cry, provides an income for his family, is loyal and inspires loyalty, understands power in terms of teamwork and receiving and obeying orders, and understands life in terms of a natural progression up the sundry ladders, without ever relying on Buggins's turn.

It is also very tempting to assume that the leopard doesn't change his spots – and that you should never trust someone who tells you he's a New Man. At least with the Old Man you knew where you were, and there was no danger of sneaky, well-disguised relapses. Before writing this, however, I took a look at Kipling's 'If', that great injunction to manliness which most people dislike as instinctively as they dislike Kipling. There has always been something about it, contrariwise, that appealed to me, and I think that it's because it is a recipe for survival in a public world that nowadays could certainly be addressed to women in public life: don't panic, believe in yourself, be patient, don't lie, don't hate, don't be too glam, don't be too smart, keep a steady head through ups and downs, and so on and so on. Which leads me to think that the traditional male role, that of the typically good man, developed as the one best suited to public affairs, and that what some men, including myself, are enjoying very much these days is exploring the world of domestic affairs, just as many women are discovering the world of business, politics, law, and most recently priesthood. Each of these worlds used to be closed to men and women respectively, and each has its own challenges.

What I'm not saying, of course, is that women should aspire to the ways of the traditional 'good man'. The world is changing fast, and those old ways, the ones that are all too easy to caricature, seem ever less appropriate. Actually, it's rather sad that in the cut-throat world of contemporary business there is little room for – for instance – loyalty. (Kipling was too smart for that – 'If all men count on you, but none too much!') Perhaps there never was. It's worth pointing out, though, that men are changing for sound, Marxist, technological reasons – how can union members be loyal to each other if there are no mines to go down together? – as much as the equally sound critique of feminism. As ever, it's the economics that count, and when a quick mind in front of a computer screen can provide a far better income than manly sinews, who cares what sex it is?

I have gone on rather too long, and well beyond my brief, but it's hard not to separate the question 'What is a good man?' from 'What has become of the good man?' The truth is that the new good man explores all the other things that his humanity offers to him – sharing the cooking (which is fun), sharing the children (even more fun), sharing the income provision (hooray!), sharing the housework, washing and ironing (no fun at all and the famously internecine area of conflict), and developing enough wisdom, were he made redundant, not to spend his days dressing for work and going to sit in the park for fear of admitting his failure. In the end, sexual politics aside for a second, it's about being a good person – which makes for an even more interesting discussion.

At the end of his fax Mike noted that Annie, his secretary, had told him that what he had said was middle-class and protected, and he agreed with her. That is an important point because the description Louise Anike gave of a good woman applies to women of all classes, races and creeds. However, even if men do have a wider scope than women for defining what is good, the demands which society makes of us, and the demands we make of ourselves, to be good are exceedingly great.

Even as we work anxiously at being good, our pride and our need to survive can use our strivings for their own ends. We want to be good, survive as a person, and have our own way. Surviving as a person is not altruistic, and having our own way is selfish, so we hide these wishes from others and, unwisely, from ourselves, because they are incompatible with our desire to be good. But we still try to fulfil all three desires.

Thus a father who defines 'a good man' as someone who takes care of his family, can interpret this in terms of doing for family members what they could well do for themselves, and organizing their activities so that they never have to take responsibility for any failure. While giving his family an easy time he ensures that he is powerful and in control, and, since they depend on him, they will never desert him. A mother who defines 'a good woman' as a woman who is sensitive and caring, and demonstrates this by being easily upset and worrying about the family, ensures that the family will strive never to upset or worry her, and always try to please her. While both such parents have the aim of creating a close, secure, loving family, what they create is a family of secrets, hidden resentments, and conflicts where the family members are torn between conforming to the parents' wishes, and thus undermining their own self-confidence, or trying to maintain their own sense of self in the only way left to them, by separating themselves from the family.

Many fathers and mothers, believing that they have been good parents according to their definitions, complain bitterly when their children fail to behave in the way they wanted. Some such parents comfort themselves by saying, 'I've been too good.' This is not a questioning of the belief in the Just World. It is simply a complaint that, in the functioning of a Just World, the system of justice can be tampered with by wicked, ungrateful people.

Another anxiety associated with high degrees of goodness arises from the belief that only the good die young. God wants the good ones in heaven with Him. The sinners can struggle on for longer. (So, if you're afraid of dying, sin!) My ninety-five-year-old aunt comforted herself through thirty years of lonely widowhood with, as she said to me, 'He was too good to live, Dorothy, too good to live.'

In their understanding of how a Just World system works, some people concentrate on the rewards and some on the punishments.

Certainly concentrating on the rewards encourages positive thinking. Nowadays many parents, like many psychologists, have discovered that children learn more quickly when their correct responses are rewarded rather than when their errors are punished. (This is why beating is so inefficient in producing the behaviour you want in a child.) Children educated in total and consistent behavioural methods at home and at school have their belief in the Just World greatly strengthened, and later are very shocked to discover that the rest of the world is not organized in the same way. They are likely to find, too, that such organized teaching has robbed them of much of their creativity.

In the behavioural system of teaching the adults decide what responses will be rewarded. Little allowance might be made for the differences in the way children and adults perceive the world. When my son Edward was at school he organized his room, he said, so that he could find anything immediately he wanted it. This system meant that I could never find a place in his room where I could put a foot to floor. He must have developed some creative forms of organization, for in his work he shows a remarkable talent for organization.

Children who are educated to believe that there is only one correct answer to a problem can lose, not only much of their creativity, but their appreciation of the importance of creativity.

Judith Williamson in her column 'Second Sight' gave an example of this.

I have just returned from three months' teaching at an American university, a good deal wealthier, and emotionally exhausted from trying to bridge two entirely different education systems. It was with relief that last Monday I walked through the swing doors of the large, underfunded polytechnic where for two days a week I participate in a lively intellectual environment full of bright, undersupported students and (less full of) dedicated, underpaid staff.

The last thing I wanted to receive was a letter in the painstaking copper-plate hand of an American student complaining about his grade (a 'C' or average) thus: 'To the best of my knowledge, I have performed all the tasks required . . . I have read the required readings, I have studied the course material and I believe I did just as you asked . . .'

All at once the memory of teaching at the prestigious West Coast institution flooded back as I recalled its students' endless concern to produce exactly 'what I wanted'. Since what I wanted was for them to think for themselves, we were constantly at cross purposes. They were accustomed to multiple-choice style exams and the representation of recently imparted facts; my exhaustion came from repeatedly explaining that I intended to grade them (as I do at home) on my perception of the quality and originality of their work, not just its quantity or punctuality.

But this was a notion American students found hard to comprehend, and when they did, hard to bear. On the whole (of course there were notable exceptions) they wanted watertight formulae for getting good grades, and the American system panders to this because no university-level teachers actually mark their students' work. This is done by Teaching Assistants whose payment for the task supports them through graduate school . . . The professor merely hands out a reading list and delivers a series of lectures on which the students are expected to take notes. Exams are then set to check whether students have read the course material and taken in the lectures. It is technically possible to get a series of straight As in the system with no more comprehension than a parrot.

Nevertheless, everyone is happy because everything is quantifiable and works very neatly. Students live in a world of simple tasks and clearly defined results.[5]

Even when we are not locked into a behavioural system, certain rewards can take on such a load of meaning that we live our lives trapped and fascinated by them. For many people, particularly women, food becomes such a reward. As children we are told, 'If you're good you can have an ice cream', 'If you stop crying I'll give you a chocolate.' With some rewards, like money, gold stars, and storing up treasure in heaven, you can't get too much. But with food you can. You get rewarded for not eating food. If you're thin you're attractive, and if you're attractive you'll be loved. How can you decide when you're eating something particularly delicious whether you're enjoying a reward or being sinful? No wonder so many women have problems with food!

Happiness can be seen as a reward, as I found when I visited Tahiti.

The missionaries arrived early in Tahiti, the Protestants in 1796, the Catholics in 1836. The Tahitians, now well imbued with the Christian vision of the Just World, see happiness – the enjoyment of all that their bountiful islands can offer – as their reward.

During my visit I was taken by my guide, a handsome Tahitian of twenty-eight, to see the mountains. When we set off in his jeep I made the mistake of telling him that I was a psychologist. He immediately launched into an account of his problems with his girlfriend. There they were, living in paradise, but she refused to be happy. She did not want to go camping, swimming, or visiting friends. Worst of all, she did not want to have sex. He wanted sex every day. She saw too much of her mother. Her mother had no education. This failure in education, it seemed, was her inability to recognize her subservience to a man. I thought that if he treated her with the same demanding disregard as he was treating me it was no wonder she was miserable. He had no awareness that I might have views about female subservience and that I might not, while on holiday, want to listen to his account of his troubles. If I offered a brief interpretation, like 'She's caught between her mother and you', and 'It sounds like she's depressed', he ignored it. However, the scenery was not as interesting as I had expected, so I listened.

Again and again he mentioned being happy. His girlfriend deprived him of his happiness. He wanted to be happy. Happiness was his reward. He worked because the money he made enabled him to be happy. Tahitians, he told me, do not have to work. They can live on fruits and fishing. Tahitians live each day as it comes. They wake up in the morning and if it's a good day for fishing they go fishing.

Near the end of our trip when, at last, he had exhausted his account of his troubles, I asked him about Tahitians and happiness. Tahitians, he said, expected to be happy. It seemed, from the way he spoke, that not being happy was, for Tahitians, a matter of shame.

I asked, 'What happens when Tahitians aren't happy?'

Unhappy Tahitians, he said, become violent. They get involved in fights. Murders are rare because there are no guns and knives, but sometimes people are killed by heavy blows.

To be happy, or to protest at one's unhappiness, a Tahitian needs to be young. He said, 'We own our bodies, and when we want to give them up we can. Tahitians die around sixty or sixty-five. They can't go on doing the things they like doing, so they die.'

Some people claim that they are not interested in rewards like money, fame, prestige, happiness or storing up treasure in heaven. Virtue, they say, is its own reward.

Alan Brien has the answer for that. He said, 'Virtue is its own reward is a contradiction in terms. Something cannot be its own reward because the definition of a reward is something that is given on top of the thing. If being virtuous is being its own reward, it means there is no reward for being virtuous whatsoever. Actually, the people who are getting the rewards are the people who benefit. Chances are ninety-nine to a hundred per cent that the person who gains the reward is the person who has committed the crime. You think of religion. The whole benefit of religion goes to the people who are in charge because they can put off people's complaints to after death, to another time when there is nobody around. It is so simple that you cannot believe that they can do it.'

Then there are the people who concentrate on the punishments in a Just World. Some religions specialize in this.

Derek Brown in Meerut, Uttar Pradesh, on the tenth day of Moharrum which is the most solemn in the Shia calendar, described this scene:

A score of young men, chanting rhythmically, move out of the prayer hall into the dripping humidity of Ghanta Ghar (clock tower bazaar). Their shouts grow more frenzied, and at an unseen signal, metal flashes through the hot air. Bunches of blades, attached to heavy chains, bite into naked backs and blood gushes. 'They are expressing their feelings at the martyrdom of Imam Hussein, grandson of the Prophet,' explains Ali Hyder, an elder of Meerut's small but devoted community of Shi'ite Muslims. 'Imam Hussein was the pioneer of non-violence.'

The disciples of non-violence continue their self-flagellation. Close up, it is a difficult sight to bear. The short chain is attached to a handle, and the blades – 12 or 14 of them to each chain – are short, sharp and slightly curved.

The participants show themselves no mercy, thrashing hard over one shoulder and then over the other in a frenzy of devotion. 'Yah Hussein!' they cry. The oldest is perhaps forty-five, and the youngest looks about twelve.

A few yards down the route, the rhythm changes to a slow, passionate hymn of praise to the fallen hero, martyred in southern Iraq in the seventh century AD. There

is a soft booming beat behind the voices; it comes from
hands thumping hard on chests.

Then the shrieks resume. '*Zanjeer!*' The clash of metal,
as of jailer's keys, sounds and the tightly bunched pro-
cession moves on, leaving gouts of blood on the road.[6]

The Catholic Church justifies its emphasis on suffering in
terms of learning to be obedient. Benedictine nun Dame Felic-
itas Corrigan explained:

> Through suffering alone you learn the love of God, exem-
> plified in Christ's sacrifice for us. What is Catholic faith?
> It is Christ, a person, it isn't a thing. It isn't a doctrine,
> the infallibility of the Pope. No. Christ didn't need faith,
> he was God. He didn't need hope, he was God. He didn't
> need charity, he was Love itself, to be poured out on the
> cross. He had to learn obedience through suffering. That
> is the only way to learn and the only lesson we have to
> learn.[7]

Catholic children are introduced very early in their lives to
learning obedience through suffering in such a way that fear
and joy become for them indissolubly linked. When this happens
to us suffering becomes the only way we can reach joy. We lose
our ability to experience ourselves, to know ourselves in joy, as
we did when we were babies, and we know ourselves only
through suffering. 'If I'm not suffering I feel guilty' can be said
by many millions of people educated in this way.

The Catholic Church has always produced many martyrs.
Not that Protestants have ever been averse to a bit of martyrdom. How better to prove that you are good than to demonstrate your capacity for suffering! However, the Protestant
churches have always been strong on sinners and repentance,
especially in the revivalist tradition.

This tradition has been adopted by the American self-help
book industry. Lou Miele explained this to me. Your books, he
said, are not published in the United States because you will
persist in telling people that they should give up judging them-

selves in terms of goodness and badness, accept themselves and accept that most of what happens in life happens by chance. Whereas American self-help books say, 'You are a sinner. See the error of your ways! Repent, and never sin again!' Americans expect their self-help books to make them feel guilty. They resolve to reform – to eat less, stop smoking, make their cognitions functional, not love so much. So they do – for a while – and then they sink back into their old, sinful ways. Caught in this cycle they make no profound changes because the self-help book has taught them nothing, but only confirmed what they had been taught was their essential, incorrigible nature, that they are sinners and must seek salvation. Thus the market for self-help books remains strong, unthreatened by any book which says, 'You are free.'

Living in a Just World we can never be free.

Living in social groups requires us to develop concepts of justice, fairness, guilt and responsibility. If we think of ourselves simply as people living here, trying to work out how best to organize our society and live our lives, we find the complexities of justice, fairness, guilt and responsibility very difficult. However, once we introduce the notion of a Just World, whatever that Just World might be, our attempt at understanding and living appropriately are impossibly confounded. Our belief in a Just World brings us, not security, but great misery.

Most people are immensely confused about what they are responsible for and what they are not.[8] The Australian journalist Bernadette Connole, brought up a good Catholic girl, told me, 'It's hard as a Catholic. The nuns where I went to school, although they inculcated me with a sense of social justice you also had the sense of wanting to save the world. You were made to feel guilty if children were starving in Ethiopia. It was your fault. And I still have to watch myself today. If there's a war on or if there's a famine, I think, "How can I fix that?" We Catholics have kept a lot of therapists in jobs in Sydney. We don't know how to handle guilt.'

If, as an adult in power, you want children to believe in your version of the Just World, it is imperative that you forbid the children to question the Just World in any way. Every Just

World belief contains faults in logic and is at variance with what actually happens. Being forbidden to examine the nature of the world we live in and the nature and purpose of our lives cripples our ability to think. How different our history would have been if the Church had not forbidden critical thought!

Our own personal histories would be very different too. My friend and contemporary Ann Grahame told me how the pro-scription on critical thought affected her life. I had told Ann how, when I was a child, my mother would say to me, 'Don't tell family business to a stranger!' For Mother, anyone who wasn't family was a stranger.

Ann said, 'Like you, we weren't allowed to tell our business to everyone. When people asked you how you were you said, "Very well, thank you." You'd never go into any details. We were never to ask for anything. There used to be a Mrs Peacock up the road and she didn't have any children. She was quite fond of us, me particularly. I'd go up there and do a bit of dusting. I remember she said to Mother, "Your children never ask for a thing." Later on I thought that's a bit sad really, never to ask for a drink of water or anything. I was told never to ask for anything. Mind you she used to open her lolly tin and offer us something, but we never asked. I think we were pretty obedient as far as doing the right things that mother had instilled in us like that.'

She went on, 'I've changed a bit now. I've realized that not everything you want is going to be offered to you anyway. I think I've changed in lots of ways. I think I'm still fairly indepen-dent. I still prefer to do things for myself if possible. But, if it isn't possible, I would ask for help, whereas then I thought well-mannered children never ask. The way we were brought up things were either black or white. You never did something or you always did something. There wasn't a compromise. We were a very good Methodist family. Church people think things are pretty well black and white. We weren't encouraged to think about things for yourself. It was handed to us on a plate. You do this or that.'

I asked how well she had accepted that.

'I think I accepted that because we didn't have much choice.

Mother would make you feel a bit guilty. Dad was very gentle. If you didn't want to go to church, she'd say your father would be very upset, or very hurt, if you didn't go to church. I think I was quite pleased when I started nursing and I didn't have to go. I couldn't go every Sunday I'd be working so I was quite ready at that stage not to go, and to break away a bit. Mother really liked to say what was what and rule the roost. Underneath I was a bit rebellious. I really liked to do my own thing, but you're in this bind of feeling guilty if you don't do what they want. Why should you want to go against my wishes, you're really hurting me, and really hurting Dad. Often you go along just for the peace of it. I just changed gradually. When the children were little, the oldest ones went to Sunday School. The older I got the more I thought for myself. I just drifted away. Now I don't go at all.'

While children are being taught that they live in a Just World they have plenty of opportunities to observe the absence of justice. They see adults behaving badly and not being punished. They find their own efforts to be good not recognized, much less rewarded. Unable to express their doubts about the Just World, they try to forget them, but their sense of security is undermined. When asked about her childhood the novelist Lesley Glaister said, 'On the surface I was happy but I had a fear that it was a frosting on the surface with a hole underneath.'[9]

If we accept the teaching that we must not question the existence and functioning of a Just World we become unable to question why we feel so bad about ourselves, and why we feel this badness in a particular way. Some people have just a vaguely uncomfortable feeling of being unacceptable, while some people always feel themselves to be on the point of fragmentation or disappearance. Some people dislike themselves so much they just want to be someone else. Some people locate some aspect of their appearance – large ears or some physical disability – as focus and cause of their unacceptability. Some people feel that they live in a world of competent, happy giants, amd only they are small, sad, and incompetent. Some people number their faults and cannot rest as they try to overcome them. Some people present themselves as confident and happy, and count their blessings, but secretly fear that one day they will be found out. Some people live as the Outsider lives.

She had felt an outsider since she was born it seemed. A pensive, dreamy child, she had stood contemplating whilst others grappled energetically with life's problems.

To her the answer had always seemed obvious. She was irritated by their naïvety and probably she irritated them with her dogmatic assertions, her stubbornness.

Yet she had been proved wrong. Each time rankled within her mind, flooding her with a kind of embarrassed disbelief as she recollected the moment of realization that her dogmatic comments had been proved to be only the product of her own thinking and were not in fact the truth.

Take the facts of life. How she had squashed the confidentially imparted statements of her friends. Such a thing could not be. They were crude and ignorant, misled by others' dirty tales. And yet she knew she had been so wrong.

Such moments turned her mind in upon itself, doubt filling all her thoughts. What in fact then was true? Was there in fact no God up there watching over her? Did he not punish offenders? Surely she, who was so good and obedient, would be rewarded.

Daily she had seen it was not so. The others, the misled ones, the loud mouthed boys, grubby knees above wrinkled grey stockings (how she despised them), continued to flourish. And what of the sneaks, the little girls who lied, who nipped babies and stole toy prams, running, screaming with laughter around the houses, pursued by herself, hot and distressed, they were not punished.

She awoke to the realization that those adults whose words were constantly of God's love were not as others. They led ostentatiously upright lives and were so evidently unhappy. She had hardly begun to experience life and yet she had been exhorted to deny her own needs for the sake of others.

Christ died for us, they said.

She had struggled terribly with the conflicts, constantly an outsider, reasoning within her head, trying to make sense of chaos. Whilst others threw themselves into fresh pleasures she had drawn back. She who had been repeatedly told how wrong it was to enjoy life, now found it impossible to do so.

She wondered if she had misheard the message. Were her beliefs only her own thoughts and not the true facts? Who had told her not to trust her own feelings? That anger, grief and pleasure were wrong? That we should think of others, not ourselves?

Denial, denial.

'Look, God, I am doing what you asked. I refused a second piece of chocolate cake and put the ten shillings I was given into my savings book and did not buy the tempting sweeties. Please reward me. Show me a little of your boundless love, oh God.'

She stands now, an outsider, looking out of her red brick prison upon the outside world. Still asking for a little love. All those denials and for what? For an encompassing misery that cannot be comforted. For the pain of being torn in two by past losses too easily given up.

Is it too late to change? Her head hurts with the thought of it. To change now would require drastic measures. It would mean a rebirth.

Now she begins to understand a little of what was done to her and why.

To stand alone is dangerous. To take what you want puts you in danger of challenge, of combat, and they are stronger than she is.

They run the world and fear is their ally.[10]

The 'red brick prison' might be a tidy suburban house, where the Outsider is cut off from and chooses to be cut off from other people. Or it might be the prison of depression.

At this time every year, Santa Claus checks his records to see which boys and girls have been well behaved;

To see which children have not been too difficult for Mother and father;

To see who has not been too selfish or demanding or disobedient;

To see who has been well brought up and is well mannered and pleasant and agreeable and cheerful and helpful and clever and good.

To these children he will give a gift which could become extremely useful to them in later life:

A big, thick book titled "UNDERSTANDING YOUR DEPRESSION"

Leunig

To get depressed all you need to do is hold the two beliefs which Michael Leunig illustrates here – that you are bad and unacceptable and have to work hard to be good, and that you live in a Just World (as Santa Claus here exemplifies). Then all you have to do is wait for a disaster to occur to you.

Believers in a Just World have no difficulty in dealing with disasters which occur to other people. Other people are bad and deserve what happens to them. It is when disaster happens to the believers that problems arise. The disaster can be explained only in one of two ways. Either the system of justice has not operated properly and you've been unjustly punished, or it has operated properly and you've got what you deserve.

If you choose the first you become angry, bitter and resentful. Our society is full of angry, bitter and resentful people. Some of them appear in the media, voicing their complaints about women priests, or homosexuals, or the youth of today, but all with the same implied theme, 'I've been good and I've been cheated of my rewards.'

If you choose the second you become depressed. Turning against yourself and hating yourself, you cut yourself off from other people, from your past and your future, and from the world itself. You lock yourself into the prison of depression.[11]

If we live long enough disaster is sure to strike us. Belief in a Just World where goodness is rewarded and badness is punished leads inevitably to paranoia or depression. Belief in a Just World leads to fear of growing old. Time might run out before we get our rewards and compensation. Old age might be the punishment for our sins.

I met a journalist, Andy, who was twenty-nine and who told me that he was very frightened of growing old. However, when we had time to talk about this, it was not the growing old that he feared but time passing.

Andy said, 'I don't worry about being old. I worry about time running out. Getting old is something you do, that will happen, but time running out is to my mind, it's a mark of how well you've done, how much you've done. That's what brings the worry. If I look into the future and I could see a picture of myself and I was bald and all that kind of thing, I wouldn't worry, but I'd have had to have done everything.'

I asked him what 'everything' was. He said, 'I'd like to find my destiny. I grew up thinking I was special. I still do now. There's something for me to do that'll make me stand out. Finding something that really makes you jump out of bed every morning. You just don't want to go to sleep because you're wasting time. You want to get on with this thing. So that it's easy even if it takes up twenty hours of your day.'

Did he see destiny as something he created for himself or a fate he could not avoid, part of some Grand Design?

Andy recalled someone saying, ' "You don't find your dreams, you make your dreams." I have come to believe that. I believe the other a bit now and then, because that keeps you going when the treadmill side of life really gets you down a bit. I do believe you have to make it. I don't see it as fate. You're worried that your time will run out before you find your destiny. If that happens I'm afraid I'll be bitter, and that does scare me, or, even worse, mediocre. That would scare me even more.'

The mediocre people were those who 'get it wrong when they make judgements because they use their own lives as a yardstick.' He was particularly scornful of his contemporaries at school who had gone on to secure positions in the City and the professions. Yet he envied their advantages and wanted their respect. It angered him that it was the mediocre people who would judge the worth of his creative work.

Andy was, he said, 'a kid from the film generation', and so he saw the question of destiny in terms of Hollywood. It was all about dreams. Only dreams could make life worth living. Dreams should be cherished, for anyone who throws away his dreams will perish. His fellows will scorn him. Dreams always come true. The question was how.

Hollywood gives two answers to this question. Dreams come true because you work hard and make them come true, or because happy chance and the beneficence of other people cause them to come true.

These are simply alternative versions of the Just World belief. A sort of an active and passive version. Work hard and you'll be rewarded. Simply be good and grace will come upon you.

(This is a form of the Christian argument about the relative value of good works as against faith for the gaining of salvation.)

But what if you feel that you have achieved nothing and that there is nothing about you that marks you out as special? For Andy that is when he thinks, 'I've not got the courage to do what I should do, or I haven't got the ability, or I'm not as bright as I think I am, I'm not as good with words as I think I am. There are many other better writers. Freelance work just makes you another writer. The time for doing is a certain decade in your life because the other times, they're not for doing. You set yourself up in your early years for the way it's going to be, and if you bugger it up at the beginning you're not going to get it. You're not going to kick start it later.'

When he thinks that he panics. 'I'm lying awake in a cold sweat. Panic is the mega realization that you've got one life and time can't be put back and you've blown it, that you are paying for your past actions in the future and you can't get out of it. It's a straitjacket, or a train line, there's no way off it.'

In times of terror we talk to ourselves and try to persuade ourselves that everything is going to be all right.

Andy said, 'Some days I feel optimistic. Then I say to myself, "You are special, boy, and you're going to keep that heart of a child, and you're going to use the wisdom that you have with years to look at life like a child would, and then you're going to do something with it, like writing the screenplay, or you're going to live conventionally in business but somebody in business will see your potential and say, 'I love that guy's fresh approach to life, I love the way he works with people. Despite the fact that he's not had as much experience as I want, I like him.'" I want somebody older than me to spot me, like a talent scout, and I see this great take-off career-wise because this special character I think I've got has actually paid off. Somebody's spotted it and given me the break. I alternate betweeen those two feelings, the optimism like that, and the pessimism.'

Here Andy encapsulated the dream that we all have, in one form or another. We dream that we will do something so brilliant, so original, that we will receive fame, wealth, love, and popularity, and we dream that, less energetically, we will simply be, and someone will be sufficiently perspicacious to recognize our great worth. Boys dream of being a Hero and being recognized by a Father Figure, and girls dream of being a Heroine and being recognized by Prince Charming. (For some girls Prince Charming is a woman.)

As we get older this dream takes on different forms, depending on what we encounter in our lives and how we feel about ourselves.

Andy valued being a child, and that part of him he called 'the heart of a child'. He said, 'As a child you're kind of a guardian of morals, a guardian of the things that people sacrifice when they grow older,' and, 'I know that if I give up the heart of a child then I'll be lost for ever. That's my only weapon against age.'

When he talked of what he expected from life he said, 'I don't think I'm asking a lot.'

'Who are you asking it of?' I asked.

'I'm only asking for the courage for myself to come from somewhere inside myself, and I'm asking for some parts of society to understand what I'm trying to do. I've got a friend, we both feel the same way. We feel like kids that have been allowed to stay up late in this adult world that we're in, and I kind of enjoy that. That's the bit I don't want to lose. I've got friends that are married with babies and I go around there and I think, well, I've got my flat and I have people over for dinner, but I think that when they do that they're playing house. When I do it it's okay. When these PR chaps take me somewhere on a trip and they wheel out God knows who from the industry, chief director of this, and chief research development man, I still get the giggles with the whole thing. I feel like a kid who's been allowed to stay up late. That's a defence system because I've seen pompous people at those things. I've seen adults take it seriously. I've seen adults, the light's gone out in their eyes. They're on automatic pilot. That child thing's a defence there. A big weapon for me. Also a handicap, maybe you give off an air that you're not taking things seriously, and people don't take you seriously in return, and that hurts your ego. I do want the best of both worlds. I do want to behave like a child who's allowed to stay up late but I do want to be treated like an adult. Is that impossible to get?'

A crucial part of Andy's meaning structure might be sketched as figure 1.

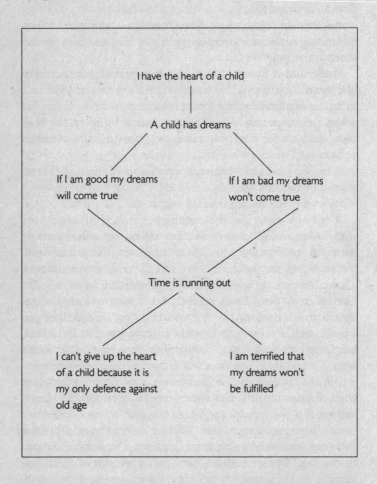

I have the heart of a child

A child has dreams

If I am good my dreams will come true

If I am bad my dreams won't come true

Time is running out

I can't give up the heart of a child because it is my only defence against old age

I am terrified that my dreams won't be fulfilled

Andy had chosen the Hollywood version of the Just World rather than the Christian one which leads to the dream 'I'll get my reward in heaven'/'God will recognize my true worth.' However, in whatever religious or moral training he had as a child, he acquired a great many rods with which to beat himself. He judged himself very harshly. I found that he brushed aside any praise or reassurance I gave him. He took little account of the fact that he was a well-liked and respected journalist, with a wide circle of friends. He had established himself in a very competitive career at a time when most graduates were finding it difficult, if not impossible, to get a job. The more he berated himself, the more he felt he had to hang on to his dream.

If he could be kinder to himself, praise his own achievements, like himself as much as his friends liked him, he would be able to let himself see that his dream is not a picture of reality but a hope, a necessary hope, but one that changes over time. If he could see that the world is neither Just nor un-Just but simply is, he would discover freedom, and realize that in such a world we can be lucky, and whether we deserve it is quite irrelevant. Then his heart of a child need no longer be trapped in the search for rewards, and could instead do what children do best – play.

If only we could all learn this.

We want our rewards to be total compensation for what we have suffered. We want to feel that now everything is all right. But of course it can't ever be all right. We lost. We suffered. That is the reality. That is our past. Nothing can put it right. The film won't be re-run so that we can have a happy ending. Our heroism, our virtue, our suffering, yes, it's part of our history, but no admiring crowds are going to gather around, telling us how wonderful, how patient, how long-suffering we were. These things happened, and there is no compensation.

We can wait, hoping that someone, somehow, somewhere will compensate us. We can wait, like beggars outside a bank, hoping that the manager will step out with a bag of gold just for us, and in the meantime we can collect, gratefully, what small coins passers-by might give us. We can stay there, trapped by our longing for what can never be. Or we can say, 'That was terrible. But it happened, and that's that. I must get on with the rest of my life.'

If I were a Kurd trying to survive on a mountainside, or a Bosnian dispossessed of home, family and country, a Somali starving, or a survivor of political torture, I might not be able to summon the courage to say this. I might, in order to survive as a person, need to put my hope in some justice lying outside the world. I trust that such a failure of courage would be understood by well-fed people whose lives are not in danger.

Those of us who are not starving, who have somewhere to live and some structure of society to belong to, should be able (provided we have the courage and honesty to try) to say, 'Bad things have happened to me. I was unlucky. There's no compensation. No reward. Tough. Now I'll get on with my life.'

That we live in a Just World is a lie which other people tell us. If we are unwise, we turn it into the most dangerous of lies, the lies we tell ourselves.

Lying to ourselves prevents us from carrying out our most important task which follows from the fact that,

The universe exists, but we can never know it directly.

This understanding can be expressed in many different ways.

We cannot see reality – only human reality.

Not even science can step outside human reality and see what reality is.

How we see the world depends on human purposes.

Different people have different rules for seeing reality.

There is no way of seeing the world which is value free.[12]

All we can ever know are the meanings about it which we create.[13] Of course we can easily create meanings which refer in no way at all to the universe. We can create fantasies, and fantasies can be useful and entertaining. We can deal in fantasy with all those desires it would be unwise to enact. However, if, in our daily life, we make no reference to what the universe is doing, we soon encounter disaster, not the least of which is when our fellows decide that we are 'out of touch with reality', that is, mad.

Our most important task is to strive, day by day, to make the meanings we create as accurate a representation of what is actually happening as we possibly can. A perfect fit of reality and our picture of it is a goal we can never reach (and even if we ever did, we could never know it), but we must strive for accuracy, otherwise we shall encounter disaster. An inaccurate representation of how many stairs we are climbing will result in a tumble: an inaccurate representation of our lover's needs will result in estrangement. There is a multitude of ways by which we can get close to reality. Being logical and scientific is only one of them. Great art gets close. Bad, pretentious art just exists in its fantasies.

If we are trying to see reality through a cracked lens, whatever picture we create will be distorted and inaccurate. Our lens is the meaning structure we have created, our self. We put cracks in that lens when we tell ourselves lies.

Creating the most accurate picture of reality that we possibly can is essential if we hope to avoid self-inflicted disasters. Lying to ourselves makes it certain that we shall have vultures to come home to roost.

We can lie to ourselves about what is happening around us. We can lie to ourselves about what is happening, has happened or will happen to us. There is an infinite number of possible lies. Here I shall talk about just five, but ones that breed a fine array of vultures.

I REALLY HAVE CHANGED

An important part of knowing ourselves is knowing which parts of our meaning structure have actually changed over the years and which parts remain the same. If we don't know this we can be surprised and shocked by our reactions in certain situations.

In our childhood we adopt, fairly uncritically, many of the attitudes and practices of our parents. In adolescence, in order to separate ourselves from our parents, we become very critical of them and reject their attitudes and practices. Many people are greatly surprised and sometimes shocked when, on becoming parents themselves, they find themselves behaving like their parents. This can be funny. It can also be tragic. I have heard many parents say, 'When I was young I vowed I'd never beat my children the way I was beaten, but I do.'

We like to tell ourselves that we have changed because we want to think of ourselves as becoming wiser, more knowledgeable, more competent. However, in childhood we adopted certain ideas because they gave us a sense of power, or made us feel secure, or enabled us to avoid personal responsibility. We do not want to give up these ideas. We can tell ourselves we have changed when in fact all we have done is to dress our old, fixed ideas in new clothes.

Throughout history there have been revolutionaries who fought for freedom. They had grown up in some totalitarian system, seen its cruelties, resolved to fight against it and establish new freedoms. If they survived and gained power for themselves, did they create this freedom for their fellows? No. They simply dressed the old totalitarianism in new clothes. The totalitarianism of Tsarist Russia was followed by the totalitarianism of Communism. Luther fought for religious freedom for himself, but once in power denied it to others. One wonderful exception to this pattern is Vaclav Havel in Czechoslovakia, but he could not hold on to freedom for all his compatriots against the power of the racist bigots in his country.

It is not simply that power corrupts. Even when they have not gained power, young revolutionaries can become old reactionaries. Solzhenitsyn showed extraordinary courage in his fight against the totalitarian system in the USSR. Yet now, from the self-imposed isolation of Vermont, Solzhenitsyn has issued a book prescribing the cure for Russia's ills. The English edition carries the title *Rebuilding Russia*, but, according to the Russian writer Tatyana Tolstaya, a more accurate translation would be 'How We Should Arrange Russia': Solzhenitsyn gives directions, not suggestions. She wrote:

Solzhenitsyn supposes that there is a single truth, that the truth is one. The combined evidence of his work suggests also that he believes that it is known to him alone ... Solzhenitsyn commands 12 (or 11½) republics to separate from Russia proper, in the name of the people. He would leave only the Ukraine, Belorussia, and the Russian part of Kazakhstan in a 'Russian union'. And what should be done if one of the 12 'big' republics doesn't want to separate? 'With the same resolve we, that is, those remaining, – will then need to proclaim our separation from them.'

'We' – the three Slavic peoples – merge into a single whole while banishing the 12 larger peoples utterly without regard to their desires. Solzhenitsyn knows perfectly well the horror of such forced separation but with Biblical cruelty he divides people into ours and not ours.[14]

Some people tell themselves they have changed when all they have done is changed from one version of the Just World belief to another.

I have met several people who grew up in families where they were taught that in the end justice triumphs, truth prevails, and that you can always trust policemen, lawyers and doctors, if not politicians. Events in their adult life showed them that this was not an accurate representation of the world. Rather than accepting this and the fact that their parents had lied to them, they leapt into the arms of the Church and proclaimed themselves saved. Some people, having been brought up with the Christian tradition of the Just World and in adulthood having come to doubt it, turned thankfully to a Just World version of Lovelock's Gaia hypothesis,[15] or found another religion. To go from Methodism to Buddhism is quite a leap, but to go from Presbyterianism to Islam is nowt but a step.

There are many therapy techniques which allow, nay, encourage people to stick with their old ideas but, by giving their old ideas new names, create the illusion of change. Because the ideas have not actually changed, the person does not change, and the therapist has a client for life.

Many psychoanalysts have made a comfortable living out of helping their patients discover that they are not intrinsically bad but came to feel that they were because of the way they were treated by their parents. Instead of helping them to discover that they should not take personally what their parents did (their parents would have treated any child born to them at that time in the same way), the psychoanalysts encourage their patients to dwell on the iniquities of their parents and use them as an excuse for the patient's bad behaviour. The patient is certainly not encouraged to realize that an explanation of why we came to do what we did is not an excuse for continuing to do it. As children we drew certain conclusions from limited evidence. As adults we have access to much more evidence, and we are free to choose to draw other conclusions.

Understanding and accepting this fact means taking responsibility for yourself, which can be very difficult. It means recognizing that you are always engaged in making decisions. Even when you say, 'I'll let someone else decide,' you have made the decision to let someone else decide. Even when you say, 'It's my parents' fault that I made a mess of my life,' you have made the decision to blame your parents rather than sort out the complex chain of events which led to your present situation. The meanings which you choose to create along the way are part of this chain of events.

The State and the Church have never been interested in helping people make the kind of discoveries which enable them to take responsibility for themselves. People who take responsibility for themselves think for themselves. They are always a threat to authoritarian institutions, and consequently have been persecuted by the State and the Church. It is not just by chance that the most widespread form of therapy at present in the USA, called Recovery and based on the philosophy of Alcoholics Anonymous, is sponsored by the government. Zoë Heller wrote:

> AA – with its description of alcoholism as a disease, its insistence on the spiritual, faith-based nature of the cure and its profound distrust of agnostic rationalism – monopolizes the available treatment for both alcohol and drug dependency throughout America. If you book into an in-patient 'detox' programme, whether at the Betty Ford Clinic or a federally funded hospital, the treatment will almost certainly be based on the religious imperatives of the 12 Steps[16] and require attendance at AA or NA meetings. If you get convicted of drunk driving, the chances are that the punishment will include six months or a year of mandatory AA. The few secular alternatives that do exist represent a tiny challenge to AA hegemony. Rational

Recovery, the biggest non-religious organization, has about 2,000 members at any given time: AA boasts one million plus.[17]

The American Psychiatric Association, in their Diagnostic and Statistical Manual of Mental Disorders, have long described every problem in life as a disorder. The DSM III-R includes various 'Personality Disorders' such as 'Dependent Personality Disorder' (someone who lacks confidence and doesn't like making decisions or being alone), 'Passive Aggressive Personality Disorder' (someone who prefers not to co-operate with authority) and 'Personality Disorder Not Otherwise Specified' (the rest of us). One major disorder is addiction (also called dependence) and now, it seems, there is no aspect of life to which we cannot become addicted. Just as therapy groups for alcoholics were deemed to be anonymous, so the other addiction groups became anonymous. There are 'Cocaine Anonymous, Emotions Anonymous, Fear of Success Anonymous, Fear of Failure Anonymous, Debtors Anonymous, Sex and Love Addicts Anonymous, Overeaters Anonymous, Bulimics/Anorexics Anonymous, Spenders Anonymous, Parents Anonymous, Child Abusers Anonymous, Shoplifters Anonymous, and Recovering Couples Anonymous.'[18] And then there is co-dependency.

This was originally a term used to describe the problems of people married to alcoholics. It was felt that they often stayed around, enduring horrible lives, and 'enabling' their spouse's addiction, because they suffered from a deficient 'sense of self'. To help deal with these particular problems, a 12 Step group called Al-Anon was established, and since then co-dependency groups for all the main addictions have grown up. Cocaine Anonymous, for example, has a Co-Anon, Sex Addicts Anonymous has a Co-Sa. Meanwhile, the definition of co-dependency has grown to embrace any sort of needy or dependent behaviour, whether connected to an addiction on not. And it has done terrific business – filling thousands of beds in clinics, selling millions of books. 'Co-dependency,' announced the report for the First National Co-Dependency Conference in 1989, 'has arrived.'

Anne Wilson Schaef, author of the best-selling *Co-dependence: Misunderstood – Mistreated*, describes co-dependency as 'a disease process whose assumptions, beliefs, and lack of spiritual awareness lead to a process of non-living which is progressive.'[19] For an ailment so deadly, it is remarkably easy to have.[20]

Recovery is a perpetual process. An addict is said to be for ever in recovery. An addict can never become a person who has recovered. To be recovered the person would have to have eradicated in some way the cause of the addiction and become responsible for himself or herself. The definitions of the cause of the addiction and the Recovery therapy preclude both of these. If you are perpetually in Recovery you can never recover the unself-conscious self-confidence with which you were born.

In order to preserve and extend their power, prestige and wealth (and remember that, as Lucy Johnstone said, 'Psychiatry is required to be the agent of society while purporting to be the agent of the individual; and its main function is not treatment but social control'[21]) American psychiatrists have defined every problematic aspect of human life as having a genetic biological cause. Do you realize that you could be born with a co-dependency gene? The day may come when doctors will be able to excise the co-dependency gene, and we'll no longer be troubled by feelings of affection and concern for people who are not sufficiently good to merit our attachment. Until such a medical breakthrough comes, it's a case of once an addict, always an addict.

The Recovery programme says, 'As you were born an addict you can never learn how to look after yourself. You must hand yourself over to a Higher Power and let that Higher Power look after you for the rest of your life.'[22]

There are some aspects of ourselves for which we are not responsible. We are not responsible for that collection of genes which came into being when our father's sperm met our mother's ovum. If that collection included a gene which says, 'Let's have another drink,' or one that says, 'Put it on your account', we are not to blame. Instead we can spend our lives bewailing our cruel fate. However, Recovery cannot countenance blaming God. You can't blame the person you depend on. Other scapegoats have to be found.

In the various Recovery groups people are expected to explore their childhoods. And what do they find there? That they were badly treated by their parents. Joy, oh joy! We can blame our parents for mistreating this poor child.

Alice Miller, who wrote so movingly and perceptively about the cruelty children suffer at the hands of their parents, now tries to prevent anyone from quoting her work, as I discovered when I was writing *Wanting Everything*.[23] She is tired of people misinterpreting her work. Alas, the damage had already been done. Recovery had discovered the 'inner child' and turned it to its own use.

Alice Miller's message was, 'Recognize that as a child you suffered. Allow yourself to mourn, because out of this can come a reconciliation of the child you once were and the adult you now are. Then you will be able to live freely and creatively.' Recovery's use of the 'inner child' has been to make it an excuse for insensitivity and self-indulgence. One chief exponent of this is John Bradshaw who, wrote Zoë Heller, in his television series and his best-selling books, stated that

> problems relating to the inner child are at the root of all dysfunction. Almost all of us are dysfunctional, he says, because almost all of us have a wounded inner child – wounded by the abuse we received from our parents. It is useless to object that you were not abused as a child. You will be accused of being 'out of touch with your feelings' or, simply, 'in denial'. Abuse is understood by the recovery movement as any parental behaviour which is 'less than nurturing' – a daddy who shouted at you when you made a mess; a mommy who didn't at all times make you feel like a very special person. Given this, the important question was not so much, 'Were you abused?' but, in

Bradshaw's words, 'What species of flawed relating did your family specialise in?'

Although the second question does acknowledge distinctions within this newly vast category of abuse, Bradshaw shows minimal interest in the question of degree. In his books, as in the recovery movement at large, there is a reluctance to hierarchize suffering. This is presented as an egalitarian position, but it functions as a profound insensitivity, helping to justify the abnegation of all civic and social concerns. Anxious to afford all pain 'equal validity'. Bradshaw blithely likens members of Adult Children of Alcoholics to 'Holocaust survivors'. Invulnerable to charges of self-indulgence, he confides that to heal his own inner child, he 'chose some things that my inner child likes. For the last few years, we always fly first class.'[24]

Changing is always a hazardous business. If you change one important part of your meaning structure, every other part must change. If you decide, say, that instead of following in every aspect of your life the precept, 'If a job's worth doing, it's worth doing well', you will in future follow the precept, 'If a job's worth doing, it's worth doing badly', because you have realized that striving for perfection wastes valuable time, then every aspect of your life will change. You will have to think about and decide which tasks are worth doing and how much time you will spend on each task. How onerous that would be!

How much better to tell the world and yourself that you have changed, and get the praise for that, and secretly not change at all.

Except it means that you go on making the same mistakes.

Creating vultures.

How even more terrible the vultures if, at the same time, you have been saying to yourself,

WHAT I DO DOESN'T HURT PEOPLE

Most of us don't consciously tell ourselves this lie. We just live our lives unthinkingly, and it is only when someone criticizes what we have done, or when someone else's pain and protest pierces our awareness, that we say to ourselves, 'What I do doesn't hurt anyone.'

However, we have already prepared the ground by accepting two lies that were told to us when we were children.

The first lie was that events have no consequences, or very limited consequences, and, if you were powerful, you could actually decide what those consequences would be.

When we were children we found that the adults talked about consequences as if there are absolute laws that A leads to B and B leads to C. Remember how they would say, 'If you work hard at school you'll get a good job,' and 'You keep behaving like that and no one will want to have anything to do with you'? If you tried to point out that lots of people worked hard at school and didn't get jobs, while others didn't work hard and did get jobs, or that your friends liked the way you behaved, you were told not to be cheeky, don't answer back, and one day you'll be sorry you didn't listen to good advice. You certainly were not given any assistance in learning how to work out the probabilities that such and such an action would have certain results. A hard-working student leaving school in 1948 had a much better chance of getting a job than an equally hard-working student leaving school in 1992. Nor were you helped to consider the network of possible consequences which stem from any action. Working hard at school might be fine in terms of future employment but not so fine in terms of going out with friends, playing sport, listening to music, reading books and so on. Instead you were taught the lie that actions had certain consequences and those consequences only.

Then there were the occasions where the adults brought, or appeared to bring, the consequences to an abrupt end. You would hear them say things like, 'I gave my son a good hiding and that was the end of it.' If you tried to extend the consequences you were in trouble. You wanted something, and your parents said no. You protested, and your parents said, 'That's enough. Not another word. That's the end of the matter.' It wasn't the end of the matter for you. You went on thinking about it, feeling aggrieved, distressed, angry, but these thoughts and feelings were not deemed by those in power over you as being consequences of their use of that power. Your thoughts and feelings were seen to have no cause and therefore no value. 'You're making a fuss over nothing.' Thus you were taught the lie that actions do not have consequences.

The other lie you were taught was that it is not necessary to take other people's feelings into account. Certainly 'what will people think' was used as a weapon to coerce you into obedience, but the implication here was that other people's feelings and perceptions were important only in terms of approval/disapproval, liking/disliking. That other people had thoughts and feelings about a vast number of matters, and that these thoughts and feelings were likely to be very different from our own, was an aspect of life which adults hid from us, and necessarily so, for if we discovered that adults were aware of and took account of other people's thoughts and feelings, we would ask, 'Why don't you take account of mine?'

The answer to that question was, 'Because you're a child and children don't matter.' Many adults hold the view that if children do have thoughts and feelings these have no lasting significance. Children, they say, do not have the capacity for profound understanding. Adults can maintain these views only by steadfastly refusing to listen to children. If we do listen we discover that children remember and children think.

For children to reveal their thoughts and feelings to an adult, that adult must be trusted by the child. Alice Ehrlich obviously trusts her father Richard Ehrlich, the food writer. He began one of his articles with this story:

> My daughter Alice, aged four, had not finished her boiled egg at breakfast. Later she grabbed a piece of toast from her sister Rebecca's plate and polished it off. Watching her eat, I opined that she was probably hungry because she hadn't finished her egg.
>
> 'I'm not hungry,' she said.
>
> 'But you must be,' I said. 'You're eating Rebecca's toast.'
> Alice insisted she was not hungry. I insisted back. Finally

she said, 'Look, you don't know if I'm hungry. You're your self. Mummy is her self. Rebecca is her self. And I'm *my* self.'

Her lesson in epistemology and ontology came back to me a few days later when my wife and I were flying to Madrid for a weekend break. I told Emma of my plans for eating *sopa de ajo* – garlic soup.

'Do you mean to tell me,' she asked, 'that you already know what you want to eat for supper?'

Since I go abroad with plans for the dishes I want to eat, I tend to assume everyone else does the same. This is the kind of logical fallacy that got me into trouble with Alice.[25]

Because Richard listens to Alice, there is a fair chance that she will listen to him. She might even take his advice about what food to eat.

At this point in the first draft of this chapter, to contrast with Alice's story I put a brief account of childhood given to me by one of my readers. Wittily, laconically, she told me how her father had, when she was little, used her casually and brutally and encouraged other men to do the same. My reader had agreed that I should include the story, but when I sent her a copy of the draft and she saw what she had written spontaneously set out in large, clear type what came back to her was 'the terror of what actually happened when my mother found out'.

My reader now feels pity for all those who injured her. Her anger is reserved for her mother. 'I wish just once she had been honest and not denied reality.'

Adults who assert that what the child knows did happen did not, do more harm than the person who inflicts pain and humiliation, for they prevent the child from carrying out the most important task, which is to create meanings which are as accurate a representation of what is actually happening as the child possibly can.

Since in carrying out this task we cannot check our meanings against an absolute reality, we have to rely on other people saying to us, 'Yes, that's what I see, too.' When people don't do that for us, when they say, 'You have got it totally wrong' and 'You are stupid and wicked to think such things,' we lose confidence in ourselves, and our world becomes frightening. In the histories of those people who earn the diagnosis of schizophrenia are always incidents where the child's accurate perceptions are denied in word and deed by the adults important to the child. One definition of schizophrenia or psychosis is 'being out of touch with reality'.

My reader's parents did not consider the long-term consequences of their behaviour on their child. Even more stupidly, they did not consider the long-term consequences to themselves. Most parents can grasp the idea that if you look after your children when they are young they might look after you when you are old. Some parents even grasp the idea that if you are kind, loving and understanding to your children, and do not terrorize them into fearing you, they will continue to love you, and in adult life be your friends. It seems to me that if you go to all that trouble and expense to raise children you might as well do it in a way which creates a relationship with someone who shares your history, and who understands, accepts and loves you.

However, to achieve such a relationship with an adult child we as parents must be able to acknowledge that everything we did with regard to our children had consequences for them, and not always the consequences we wanted. Unfortunately, many parents will not accept this responsibility. When their children are young such parents excuse their own behaviour with 'children forget' and 'it's for their own good'. Later, if their adult children want to discuss any of the events in childhood which distressed them, such parents deny that these events occurred, or become hurt and angry at such unjust accusations, or tell their children that they deserved what happened to them.

Many adults feel that their parents would react like this if they confronted them, and so they do not bother to try. Instead, they keep their distance. In a workshop on self-confidence one woman said, 'When I was fourteen my father and I had a bad row. He was yelling at me. He said I was a mistake. I should never have been born. We've never been close since then. I still see him occasionally, but it's just small talk. My mother's death didn't change anything.'

That was one fairly clear-cut incident. Most of what happens to us in childhood which affects us most profoundly is much more complex and subtle.

I was at a street party in my old home town. Sitting opposite me was a friend, Louise, who was aged sixty-eight and had lived in this street all her married life, a life not without tragedy. I remember Louise as a young mother, a slim, pretty woman. Now she had grown stout, her hair was white, a grandmotherly figure to be patronized or ignored. But her green eyes looked out under lids that folded back sharply. The kindly old grandmother appearance was an illusion. She was a lizard, very old, very wise. She listened, observed, judged, but said nothing.

Between us was a newcomer to the street, a woman in her mid-thirties, grossly overweight. Louise and her husband were soon to move to a flat near the beach. On learning this the woman proceeded to instruct Louise on how to organize the move. Louise murmured, 'That's most useful to know,' and the woman, not hearing the irony in her voice, elaborated her advice in a tone increasingly patronizing. After all, she was a much-travelled woman of the world, while Louise had lived all her married life in just one place. I watched fascinated, waiting for Louise to reveal herself, for her lizard tongue to dart out and swallow up this foolish woman.

Now the woman was telling Louise how impossible her four-year-old son Sean was. He would not do as he was told. He would scream at her, and she would scream back. (Other friends had already told me that this was so.) Sean, a beautiful boy with curly blond hair and a sturdy, manly body, was happily wandering amongst the adults, offering them potato crisps from a bowl. When he got tired of this he came over to where his mother was sitting. She ignored him. I asked him if he would like to sit on my lap. He said he would. I lifted him up, and we had a great time talking.

Sean's mother was now telling Louise how she minded two children because she needed the extra money. She said that she

was not a registered child-minder, and implied in her telling
that Louise would agree with her that the law need not be
observed. Louise's lizard eyes narrowed.

Sean jumped off my lap and, in trying to get his mother's
attention, knocked a small bowl of biscuits to the ground.

'Pick them up, Sean,' said his mother, her voice cold and
distant.

Sean obeyed instantly, kneeling at her feet, carefully placing
every scrap of biscuit in the bowl. He returned the bowl to the
table.

'Very good, Sean,' said his mother in the mechanical voice
of someone who has done a course on behaviour modification.

Sean climbed back on my lap, and we played a game with
my sticky name-tag, seeing how many places he could stick it,
on my cheek, on my ear, my nose, my glasses. He was getting
excited. I thought that a too exciting game would end in tears,
so I distracted him and hid the name tag. His older sister wan-
dered by, and he jumped off my lap to follow her.

Then he returned, and his mother, perhaps weary of talk,
perhaps at last sensing that Louise's silence did not mean acqui-
escence, and so feeling in need of comfort, called Sean to her.
He rushed to her, and she lifted his little manly body up so
they were face to face. He knelt on her thighs, but her thighs
had a huge fat stomach between them. So his legs are spread
apart, and his penis pressed tight against her yielding flesh. He
rested his head on her shoulder and she embraced him like a
lover.

What sense could Sean make of his mother's behaviour?
Would it be a sense which will allow him to outgrow his mother
in the way that children must outgrow their parents if they are
to become independent adults, capable of parenting their own
children? And, before we condemn his mother for preventing
this, we might ask what kind of parenting she had had to leave
her so insensitive and so needy.

The consequences of our parents' actions do not end with
childhood. Yet many parents do not acknowledge this. They
refuse to see that the attitudes they adopt towards their adult
children – their choice of career, their partner, their own child-

ren – have consequences. Make yourself into a querulous, critical, rejecting, demanding, ageing parent, and you ensure a miserable old age.

Even the manner of our dying has consequences for our children. Joanna Smith wrote:

> My Dad hanged himself on Father's Day. He is dead and he left no note. This is the truth and will remain so. This is now my history and that of my family for ever. This fact will not change . . .
>
> He had been a lying, cheating, womanizing, drunken, violent and very charming man . . .
>
> I wondered if there was something I could have done to make a difference in his life. And in truth I know there was not. My dad's pain and anger began long before I knew him. A time when he had not been allowed to ask for help, to say he needed love, to be. Like many of us, his pain and anger were too old for words. And now he hangs for ever in the seedy basement of a rented house where he lived alone. A sad, bitter, frustrated and angry man.
>
> I am telling you this because I want you to know about him and about me. And how sorry I am that he did not stay. And so you can understand that although I loved him, I am also furious for what he has done. My dad hanged himself on Father's Day. He is dead and he left no note and I am furious with him for this.
>
> He took away my right to tell him the things I wanted to say to him. My right to say I love you and a final goodbye. He also took away my right to hear the things he might have wanted to say to me. I am left with the feeling that his final message to me was Fuck You.
>
> I have no illness to explain his death, no accident for which I can blame fate or mechanics or even a person. I have no idea how he felt or what he thought. And I never will have. All I have is the fact of him hanging. Too much, yet nothing at all. He took away my right to prepare for his death, for this very final separation. He left me brutally,

aggressively, totally, and sometimes I find myself saying, how dare you do this to me? I feel an injustice has been done. I say, but I thought I was your favoured child. Why? Come back now. And still he hangs.

I know that although I now think of him often each day, there will come a time when I will not. When he will be someone I can talk about with fondness and humour and few tears. And until then I will keep feeling the things I feel and being true to myself and not society's image of what is acceptable for those grieving. At the moment, therefore, I feel very sad and bloody angry and I wish he'd stayed.[26]

Suicide is a selfish act. So think on this, you parents who want to make a premature exit into death. Don't kid yourself, 'They'll be better off without me.' If you don't have the courage to see life through to the end (and there are few things so certain as that life does come to an end), how can your children find the courage to face what they have to face? It's no use saying, 'They'll forget me.' We never forget our parents.

In our memory the past becomes today, and we can see, or at least speculate about, the consequences of actions many years ago. Once when I was visiting my Aunt Margaret in her nursing home we talked about my mother. 'You know, Dorothy,' Aunt Margaret said, 'when your father and mother were first married your father would call in home to see our mother and your mother wouldn't get out of the car and come in and say hello. Mother was so hurt.'

I saw the picture as clearly as if I had been there. Dad's mother had died before I was born, but I had seen her photographs. She looked very old. She died when she was sixty-three. I knew the old family home very well – a wooden bungalow, with a central hallway and front veranda running the width of the house. The hallway led to the kitchen where there was a black fuel stove and a large wooden table where the family sat. Grandma Conn always sat in her rocking chair in the kitchen. She would be there, and out the front of the house would be Dad's little two-seater car, and in it Mother, dark-haired, beautiful, was sitting tense and silent.

Dad would try ineffectually to bridge the gap between the two most important women in his life. That would have been the scene in 1923. Aunt Margaret and I recalled it in 1991. She said, 'Mother's only disappointment was when your mother wouldn't come in to have a cup of tea.' And if it hadn't happened, if my mother had got out of that car, and greeted her mother-in-law lovingly, and joined in family life, you wouldn't at this moment be reading this book, for it would never have been written.

Mother was so absorbed in her fear of other people, her need to defend herself, her righteousness, that she was oblivious of the pain she caused other people. All my books are my attempts to understand and come to terms with the pain she caused me. Had she joined family life, had she allowed me to become part of a wide family group, I might still have become a writer, but I would never have written the books that I have written.[27]

It is curious that, as much as we want our acts to have no consequences, we want our acts to have the consequences that many people know us, talk about us, and remember us after our death. We want our lives to have significance, a permanent significance, and not just be like a candle in the wind. We do so want to have our cake and eat it, not to be held responsible for what we do, but praised and loved for it just the same.

I have talked of the consequences of our actions rolling forward into the future and coming towards us from the past. The consequences also spread outwards in the present to other people. We act, and other people interpret what we do, and then act on those interpretations. We interpret the world, and other people interpret our interpretations. Sir Yehudi Menuhin, wrote Lynne Barber, 'has been revered as a great violinist for most of the twentieth century. But in recent years, he has become something more – a guru, a wise man, a musical Laurens van der Post, a priest of the order of Prince Charles. His wife calls him the Bodhisattva, the Hindu messenger of the gods. Transcending nationality, religion and politics, he speaks for a higher moral universe, above and beyond this workaday world.' His wife, Lady Menuhin, who sees to all the practical aspects of Yehudi's life, said, 'He doesn't believe in evil, which is nice for him, but not so nice for those of us who have to keep the evil away, which is there.'[28]

We have no control over how other people interpret our actions and our interpretations, so we cannot possibly limit or control the consequences of our actions. Moreover, it is not possible to act in any way which has only good consequences or only bad consequences. The economic policies of the Conservative government reduced inflation but created much unemployment. My mother might have caused me much pain, but she did make my life much more interesting. I don't long to be an ageing granny pottering about some Australian town, something which could have been my fate had she been kind to me.

The fact that the consequences of our actions have effects which are near and far, good and bad, creates endless problems in our relationships with other people, never more so than when we tell ourselves the lie,

SEX WILL SOLVE ALL MY PROBLEMS

The Catholic Church teaches that sex is for procreation only.
Would that were so!
How simple life would be!
The truth is that sex can be used to solve all known human problems.
Not that it actually solves all known human problems.
Only some of them.
Occasionally.
Actually sex creates as many problems as it solves.
Here are some alternative uses for sex.

1 WANTING TO HAVE FUN
Sex can be the greatest fun ever, provided you and your partner

like one another and agree about what activities are to be enjoyed. Sex where one person enjoys and the other endures is not fun but exploitation.

Does sex go on and on being fun? The great interest in vibrators, videos, dressing up and pornography suggests to me that many people don't find sex to be all that much fun. If you need an aid to get you going, you didn't want to go in the first place.

Under the heading 'Everything You Never Wanted to Know About Sex' the columnist Suzanne Moore wrote:

> I have had enough of carnal knowledge. OK, so I know it is my duty as a modern woman to think that sex is endlessly fascinating, that my main ambition should be advancing my sexual repertoire and that somewhere between working and looking after the kids, I should be slotting in classes on sexual massage.
>
> Women, after all, are being increasingly targeted as consumers of all things sexual, from up-market erotic literature to down-market magazines. After years of using women to sell sex to men, sex is now being sold to women. This is generally seen as a good, even vaguely feminist, thing rather than a marketing ploy. Women are taking control

of their own erotic needs; we are now in a position to ask for it – or are we? Are all these exhortations to sexual pleasure actually what we want? Are they even interesting?

Leafing through magazines such as *Women on Top*, *For Women* and *Playgirl*, one is struck not by the unlimited possibilities of desire but the tired reversal of pornography for men. Oiled pectorals replace erect nipples, unzipped jeans, suspenders, flagged by inane page three-type blurbs: 'Keith our front cover hunk, is in fact a computer boffin and specialises in tracking down technical faults. Keep an eye out for him the next time your Apple-Mac packs up! Hopefully, he'll have his tool with him.' Who writes this stuff? And why? Good sex in such magazines is cheerful stuff. Bonking, a bit of bondage, nothing fancy, nothing deep . . .

I tried *Sexual Happiness For Women, An Illustrated Practical Guide To Sexual Fulfilment*. This is sex as Mission Impossible, complete with charts, graphs, questionnaires. The idea that anything might come naturally is clearly anathema to the authors. Little is left to the imagination because this, let us not forget, is sexual therapy, sex medicalised into a dysfunction that will inevitably have a cure. Sexual healing at the expense of sexual feeling.

The argument for such guides is, of course, that we still live in appalling ignorance about sexual matters . . .

Oral histories such as Maureen Sutton's *We Didn't Know Aught*[29] in which she talks to Lincolnshire women about their experiences in the thirties, conjure up an era of astonishing ignorance but also wonderful vitality. There is talk of a honeymoon on which neither partner had a clue ('When I first married, I didn't know which end to go in, front or back, so I played it by ear') of hidden pregnancies, of sex a chore at times, a delight at others . . .

It's not that I'm suggesting a return to the misery that accompanied those times; it's just that, unlike the current glut of sexual information, there is a real sense of sex actually being sexy, funny, good and bad, as being part of life and not its whole meaning. Having fought for a long time not to be seen simply as sexual objects, how come women are now happy to be defined as sexual subjects? While I am happy that women are making all kinds of fantastic filth, having all kinds of wild times, is it still too much to want to be considered more than the sum of one's sexual parts – however well informed they might be?[30]

2 WANTING TO HAVE CHILDREN

Do you have sex to have children in order to ensure the continuation of the human race?

SO YOU & DAD DID IT TWICE THEN MUM?

Not many of us are so altruistic with regard to our species. Throughout the world and throughout history people had children for economic reasons – to provide workers and ensure the line of inheritance. Where women can choose whether they will have children, the choice to do so has to do with a sense of fulfilment. There is nothing so wondrous as a baby. But a wondrous baby will not grow into a wondrous child if the parents have loaded on to the child the expectation that the child will satisfy their longings and compensate them for their sufferings. No child can make everything right.

3 WANTING TO BE LOVING AND TO BE LOVED

It is possible to love someone, not be loved in return, and not be hurt by this, but to do this the loving person must not reach out, and loving is so much a feeling of reaching out. To love and be loved is an experience which can make the whole of our life feel worthwhile. But what misery we make for ourselves when we want it to last for ever, and forget that everything and everyone changes. What even greater misery we make for ourselves when we fall in love not with a person but with our image of that person.

Wanting fun, wanting children, and wanting to love and be loved are problems which sex can solve if, and only if, we do not lose ourselves in our fantasies, but see the other person as a whole, real person. Then the consequences of our actions will include considerable satisfaction. However, if we have sex with a fantasy, or with only part of a person, disaster will follow as the night the day. All the following uses of sex are examples of sex with a fantasy and/or with part of a person.

4   WANTING NOT TO BE LONELY

Having sex might distract us from our loneliness, but, oh, the greater loneliness afterwards.

5   WANTING COMFORT AND RELIEF FROM TENSION

In May 1992, BBC TV broadcast a dramatic series by Alick Rowe called *Friday on My Mind*[31] about a young woman who was married to an RAF fighter pilot in training to go to the Gulf. He was killed in an accident, and after the funeral she went to bed with one of his colleagues. When the first episode was broadcast a group of widows of RAF aircrew officers wrote to the *Guardian* 'to record our distaste and distress with the programme . . . This programme was offensive to widows everywhere.'[32]

How little we understand one another! The play was not about widows but about how we try to deal with pain. It was an accurate portrayal of how some people, women and men, in that state of disbelief that follows bereavement, become frozen, unable to feel anything and unable to act in a world which seems distant and unreal. Some of these people continue in that state for many months. Others know (usually without knowing that they know) that having sex can break that freeze, and let the world and the pain become real.

If they are lucky they choose a partner who understands what is happening and who sees the act as being in the same order as driving an injured friend to a casualty department. *Friday on My Mind* showed the woman, her frozen state broken, now able to act and to feel the pain. Unfortunately, chance had brought her a man whose wife did not make him feel needed, and he needed to be needed. From such a misunderstanding the dramatic consequences flowed.

We ought to have the generosity to understand that sex to comfort one another and reduce tension when we are in the extremes of pain or danger can be a wise survival technique. However, when sex as a means of reducing tension becomes routine, as when a husband uses his wife as a receptacle for discharging the tension he has acquired during the day, and thus getting a good night's sleep, it should be seen for what it is – exploitation – and not tolerated.

6   WANTING TO FEEL THAT YOU EXIST/WANTING TO FEEL THAT EXTERNAL REALITY EXISTS

When we are under tremendous stress, particularly when we have discovered that we have made a serious error of judgement, we discover that part of our experience of our existence becomes unreal. Our experience of our existence consists of two realities – the internal reality of our thoughts and feelings and the external reality of what goes on around us. For those of us who are People Persons, or extraverts,[33] it is internal reality which becomes unreal. We feel that we are disappearing. For those of us who are What Have I Achieved Today Persons, or introverts, it is external reality which becomes unreal. We feel that we are retreating into our solitary internal reality and losing our grip on our external reality which becomes increasingly strange. If you are an introvert you'll know exactly what I mean. You have always taken external reality on trust, not as given and real, but you always doubt it. If you are an extravert you would not have had this experience. Your external reality might become confusing, or frightening, but it is always real.

Extraverts maintain the reality of their internal reality, their sense of self, by keeping in their external reality many people and things to which they can relate. They maintain their existence through relationships. Introverts maintain the reality of their external reality by making efforts to act upon it and keep it under control. (Alone on a desert island, an introvert would draw up a programme of activities and get the place organized, while an extravert would make friends with the seagulls.)

Extraverts and introverts can use sex as a way of maintaining the reality of their potentially unreal reality. So-called 'highly sexed' extraverts who are constantly seeking more sexual partners are simply trying to maintain through sex their sense of existence. Introverts can use sex as a way of maintaining and controlling their contact with external reality, thus keeping it real.

Friday on My Mind showed an introvert and an extravert doing just this. The widow was an introvert who, while wanting to withdraw into her internal reality as introverts do when they are under stress, knew she was in danger of losing contact altogether with external reality. She made what she wanted to be an uncommitted contact with external reality, but one which she needed to be strong enough to penetrate her internal reality. (Our bodies inhabit both our realities. This is why sex is such a powerful experience.) Her lover was an extravert who, if he couldn't be liked, would settle for being needed. He was married to a well-organized introvert who did not reveal her needs.

(Good novelists and playwrights like Alick Rowe know all about extraverts and introverts, but, of course, write about them using their own language, not mine. They recognize how extraverts and introverts both complement and confront one another. Bad novelists and playwrights are unaware of this basic dimension of human behaviour.)

The partner of a person who tries through sex to increase a sense of reality always feels used. If you have been at the receiving end of an extravert trying to maintain an internal reality through sex, you will know just how shallow such a relationship can be. If you have been at the receiving end of an introvert trying to maintain contact with external reality and control it through sex, you will know just how lonely the sex act can be.

There is another aspect of how we experience our sense of existence which distinguishes extraverts from introverts. It is what we see as the most important purpose of our existence, the ultimate reason which underlies everything we do. Introverts and extraverts often act in the same way, but for totally different reasons. For instance, an introvert and an extravert might both work very hard. If you asked them, 'Why is it important to you to work very hard?' they might both give the same answer, 'I want a sense of achievement.' If you then asked, 'Why is it important to you that you achieve?' the extravert would answer in terms of relationships. 'If I achieve other people will like me, respect me, want me to work with them' and so on. The introvert will say, 'Achievement is what life is about.' The introvert's sense of achievement need not be in terms of fame and wealth. It can be simply the satisfaction of getting something organized, under control, completed.

Couples, both heterosexual and homosexual, are made up of an introvert and an extravert. (Some couples, I have found, insist that they are two introverts or two extraverts, but here they are looking only at what they do instead of the reasons why they do it.) At the root of all their quarrels lies the difference in what each of them regards as the ultimate purpose of life. When a couple argue about how they should spend their money, the introvert is saying, 'We must plan and organize and achieve something with our money,' and the extravert is saying, 'Can't we do things as a family?'

Opposites attract. Introverts and extraverts complement one another. If a couple understand and respect one another's totally different ways of experiencing themselves and their world, they can overcome their misunderstandings. But if they don't, they can't.

Introverts and extraverts – the conditions of our being – make sex a minefield.

7   USING SEX TO RESTORE SELF-CONFIDENCE

When we are small children we are taught that some forms of being good apply to all children – like telling the truth and being obedient – and some forms apply only to boys and others only to girls. Good boys are manly and good girls are feminine. Which gender we are becomes an important part of being good, and thus being accepted, valued and loved. As children we soon discover that our gender implies sexuality, and from this we deduce that we can prove our acceptability and worth and be loved by displaying our sexuality. All the messages we get from the media confirm this.

However, the way we were taught to be good undermined our natural self-confidence. Unless in adult life we have the sense to rediscover our natural self-confidence, we spend our lives trying to shore up the ruin of our self-confidence which our education in goodness created. Some people try to restore their self-confidence by achievement, and some by caring for others. Many people try to restore it by proving to themselves, their partners and the world at large that they are great lovers.

If you strive to look sexually attractive perhaps the world will assume that you are, but you can't be sure. Think how much time people spend discussing whether or not they think someone is sexually attractive! Some partners are very appreciative (we women are well trained in how to support a man's ego) – but can you be sure they're telling the truth? It's said that actors are only as good as their last film, but where sexuality is concerned you're only as good as the fuck you're having. Doubt sets in straight after.

8   WANTING MONEY

Sex for money, whether it is in a marriage for money, or as a highly paid courtesan, or as a prostitute or rent-boy, destroys the person. Being used is humiliating, and humiliation withers self-confidence and engenders self-disgust. Dealing with the pain by becoming numb, or denying it, reduces the capacity to be human.

Stories about happy prostitutes are just lies to hide the cruelty which prostitution is. Consider those young girls and boys in the nightclubs and massage parlours of Manila and Bangkok, the young women lining the roads in Eastern Europe that lead to the West. The majority of people working as prostitutes have been forced for economic reasons to choose between prostitution and starvation. Many courageously try to make the best of their lives, but, in having to choose between two cruelties, such a best is not much better.[34]

9 WANTING TO BE POWERFUL

When I was working in the National Health Service the local general practitioners frequently referred to me young married women with the diagnosis of 'frigidity', a condition which I was supposed to cure. Sometimes the problem was no more than tiredness, lack of privacy and boredom, arising as might be expected from having several small children in a tiny home and no spare cash for anything exciting and different. More often the problem was one of power.

A silent battle was being fought by the wife and husband over whose needs and wishes were to decide the pattern of family life. The battlefield was the bed. The problem was not a lack of sex but a lack of communication, for the partners never discussed what their real differences were. This battle over power had disastrous consequences for both partners, and for their children.

Some women try to use their considerable attractiveness in a bid to wield great power over men. They try to evoke the myth of the *femme fatale*, the woman who subjugates men by her sexual power, a myth which is reworked in different ways in every generation because many people, men and women, are still struggling, though they do not realize it, with their memory of a powerful mother who entranced and threatened them. Similar childhood experiences of cruelty are disguised and re-enacted in the sexual rituals of sado-masochism and fetishes.

Re-enacting childhood traumas in a mythical form does not enable us to master them unless we acknowledge the existence of the original experience. By master I mean finding a way of remembering the experience which is a true representation of what happened, and to which we have given a meaning which does not trap us in the past but allows us to get on with our lives. To do this we have to confront the past, not hide from it and not tell ourselves lies about it. The lies we tell ourselves through sex are just as destructive as all the other lies we tell ourselves.

Mastering the acts of cruelty and humiliation we suffer in childhood is not as easy as I have here made it sound. Anyone who feels in some way compelled to carry out certain acts which seem fascinating and repellent finds it very difficult on their own to get a grip on what is happening, in some way stand outside it, and, seeing it from another perspective, change its meaning. It is like on your own trying to climb out of a deep hole where you not only have to create the hooks and grappling irons but the wall itself which has to be climbed.

There are few people who can help. The profession of psychiatry has devoted its two hundred years of existence to denying the cruelty which children suffer, and, in insisting that it is our biology which is the cause of our distress, has created the profession's own forms of cruelty. Psychoanalysis is based on the notion that adults who recall being abused as children are simply reporting fantasies, while psychology all too often concentrates on the banal and the trivial. No wonder we don't understand what we try to do with sex.

Meanwhile, any woman who feels tempted to prove her power through sex should remember what happened to Carmen. Men, on the whole, are physically stronger than women, and a woman puts herself in potential danger when she is physically close to a man. Especially during sex.

10   WANTING REVENGE, WANTING TO HURT, HUMILIATE AND DESTROY

Sex offers endless opportunity for vengeance, but it hardly solves the perpetrators' problems.

Such revenge might be sought through repeated acts of apparently ordinary sex. Alan Moore wrote:

> Sex. For 25 years it ruled my life. I *had* to have it. Preferably three times a day between meals. And the more I had, the more I needed. I saw a woman – almost any woman

– and I wanted to have her. And my only regret was that I would never have time to get around to them all.

I tried. I had them in droves. Big ones. Small ones. Fat ones. Thin ones. Oh so pretty ones. White ones. Black ones. Brown ones. Yellow ones. Ones that I liked. Ones that I hated. I had them singly. I had them in pairs. I had them on buses. On trains. In cars. On planes. In the House of Commons. In a dog-kennel. In a German ambassador's bathroom. Up a tree. On my desk. Under my desk. In the Vietnamese ambassador's garden. Even in bed. So when, three years ago, I first met my mother, I suppose I should have known that the first thing I would want to do was to have her.

Adopted at birth, it took me 40 years to decide to search for my mother, and four months to find her . . .

She let me in through the kitchen, where we stood and simply looked at each other before moving towards an awkward embrace – and that's when it happened. One moment I was a forty-year-old child in her arms and then I was hit by a sudden and powerful urge to have her, right there and then, on the rather flimsy formica topped table on which we were plainly to have tea. And despite myself I felt myself harden.

I shifted position, then let go altogether. This was outrageous. Even for me. She was old enough to be my mother. She *was* my mother. This was sick. I was sick. I needed help. I sat down. If she'd noticed she gave no sign of it. She had something to show me, she said, and took from her handbag a small, plastic wallet which she handed me. Inside it were some credit cards and beside them were two polyphoto snapshots which I immediately recognized. They were of me on my first birthday: I had the rest of the set at home in an old photograph album. 'How?' I asked. 'Your mother sent them. I begged and begged and eventually, against all the rules, the adoption agency arranged it. Then I waited; for forty years I've waited for you to find and forgive me.'

And with the word 'forgive' it all began to fall into

place. It was not lust I'd felt a minute ago – well, it was, but that was only a symptom; at a much deeper level the cause was my desire to hurt and punish her for having given me away. And with this realisation came another: for 25 years that's what I'd been doing – revenging myself on as many women/as possible. Sex was my weapon; for me it had become an act not of love, but of anger – a compulsion to punish.[35]

Alan Moore's story had a happy ending for him and his mother, though perhaps the women on whom he revenged himself might not be so happy.

Some men try to solve their problems with their mothers by raping and killing other women. No such act of revenge relieves the man of his anger and hate, and so he goes on raping and killing until some other event – imprisonment or his own death – interrupts his activities.

Why do we try to use sex to solve all these problems?

Because we have so very few skills which we can use to solve them.

We are educated by our home, our school and our church in a way which actually prevents us from understanding ourselves.

To understand ourselves we need to be helped to discover that, even though the world might appear to be solid and real, what we perceive are the meanings which we have created. Instead, we are taught that the world is what those in power over us say it is, and if we don't see it like that we are mad and bad.

Because we don't understand our essential nature, we fail to understand why it is we misunderstand one another with such disastrous consequences. If we don't know that we exist as our own structure of meaning, we can never develop the skills necessary to understand another person and thus bridge the gap between us. Recently I went to see a National Theatre production of Shaw's *Pygmalion*. In the last scene of the play, where Henry Higgins and Eliza Doolittle rage at and taunt one another, while underneath loving and longing for one another, Shaw shows us two meaning structures in action, each displaying its values but without the slightest comprehension of the other. Henry, for all his study of how we talk, has no idea about how we create our own individual meanings. He cannot understand why Eliza does not see everything in the same way as he does. Eliza does not understand that the rigidity of Henry's meaning structure is a defence against his sense of inadequacy and helplessness. Instead she expects him to produce a response to her which lies right outside the range of his meaning structure. So they crash against one another, like two iron cartwheels grinding together, striking sparks in a futile display.

Deprived of the means of understanding one another, we are also deprived of the means to engage creatively with the world.

We are all born with talents for art, music, acting, writing, designing, building, discovering, but our education prevents us from realizing these talents. We grow up thinking that we have no talents, and even when we suspect that there is something we might like to do, our lack of confidence prevents us.

A few people manage to protect one talent from destruction, but at considerable cost to themselves, not least of which is their belief that if they inspect the processes of their talent the talent will be destroyed.

When I was gathering material for my book *The Successful Self* I asked two long-time, well-established, extremely successful actors, a man and a woman, if I could talk to them. Each refused, and gave as the reason that they feared that if they examined their talent they might lose it. Many writers, and not just Virginia Woolf and Sylvia Plath, believe that their creativity and their periods of being depressed have the same roots, and so they must not enquire into the cause of their depression. The result is that they waste most of their creative life by being depressed.[36] There are other writers and artists who, not realizing that they are trying to solve with sex the problems which sex cannot solve, persuade themselves that sex, especially sex with many partners, will improve their work. It is one way of collecting material to write about, but it does not improve personal relationships.

Whenever we designate one part of ourselves a no-go area

we prevent ourselves from becoming a whole person with access to all those parts of ourselves which our education has blocked off. Thus we, and the world, are deprived of what we might have become and what we might have created.

Our education deprives us of the vast range of channels into which we could pour that enormous stream of energy and enthusiasm which is the essence of being alive. Do you remember in your teens not knowing what to do with that energy? A few of us have the opportunity to pour some of that energy and enthusiasm into work or sport, but for most of us all we can do is try to pour our vast torrent of energy and enthusiasm down the narrow funnel of sex.

At certain times in our history attempts are made to do this by sexualizing every aspect of our lives while forbidding the public display of sex. It was said that the Victorians used to cover the legs of tables because table legs were considered to be sexual objects; true or not, it is an example of how, when all mention of sex is forbidden, every word and every object, however innocent, can take on a sexual meaning. At other times attempts are made to do this by treating every aspect of our lives as non-sexual except the public display of sex. My mother would have had the world believe that both her daughters were a result of Virgin Birth, while Madonna would have us believe that there is no sex act which she would not perform publicly, but for both women the degree to which sex is over-valued and obsessive is the same.

The apparatus we have for sex cannot take the load of significance we place on it. When John McVicar at the age of fifty-one had a prostate operation all he was worried about was whether he would still be able to achieve an erection. The *Weekend Guardian* gave him two pages, plus a picture, so that we could share his worries.[37] Women can worry about the relative merits of the clitoral and vaginal orgasms, or whether there is sex after the menopause. Rupert Haselden, writing about AIDS and the gay men like those who meet at the London Apprentice, a fashionable gay bar, said, 'We are retreating into our ghetto, resorting to each other for comfort when we should be asserting our presence in a world where sexuality should not matter. We are falling into each other's sweaty arms at the London Apprentice.'[38]

Perhaps the most bizarre aspect of our sexual behaviour is that we don't see how bizarre it is. The most immature, unreflective, and uncomprehending sexual behaviour is where 'You show me yours and I'll show you mine' is turned into frantic, repetitious, and ultimately unsatisfying attempts to be bigger, better, more different, more amazing, more shocking. This bizarre behaviour is called Adult, with Adult films, Adult videos[39] and Adult magazines. It is an insult to children to call such behaviour childish.

Not understanding ourselves it is no wonder we make such fools of ourselves over sex. No wonder we are so fascinated by stories of how other people make fools of themselves over sex. No wonder the media moguls make millions out of our foolishness.

No wonder our sexual behaviour breeds vultures in their millions. If we believe that all our worth and significance resides in our capacity to be sexual, no wonder we fear getting old.

However, even the media moguls have vultures that come home to roost. Thank goodness there's some justice in the world.

There is a certain satisfaction in seeing an avenging fate give the wicked their comeuppance. However, we are very foolish indeed if we tell ourselves the lie.

I'LL GET MY REVENGE AND THEN I'LL BE HAPPY

In May 1992, everyone in Britain was highly entertained by the revenge Lady Graham Moon took upon her faithless husband, Sir Peter Graham Moon. As well as his mistress, he cherished his car, his wine cellar and his Savile Row suits. Lady Sarah poured paint all over his car; she put a bottle of his wine along with the milk on the doorstep of every house in their village; and she cut a neat four inches off the right sleeve of each of his suits. Sir Peter responded by complaining to the press. His wife became the toast of Britain.

In the discussions about Lady Sarah's exploits the media involved me as an 'expert' on revenge. These discussions went on for weeks. I held forth about Lady Sarah's wisdom in making her husband a laughing stock rather than a corpse.

One of these discussions was on 'The AM Alternative' on BBC Radio 5 with Kate Saunders and the presenter Johnnie Walker. Lady Sarah spoke to us by phone from her home. She described her feelings of intense fury and frustration. Her frustration was not just the frustration we feel when we can find no way of expressing our anger. Her husband was acting as if there was no problem. He would not discuss with her what was happening. She needed to attract his attention.

In this she certainly succeeded. Johnnie Walker asked her whether Sir Peter was now talking to her. 'The lawyers are talking,' she said. 'I have, as they say, been cut off without a penny.'

As our discussion went on, Lady Sarah wondered if she should feel remorse. It sounded as though some of her relatives had been suggesting to her that a good woman must always be remorseful for her every action. I hastened to assure her that no remorse was necessary. She was a very wise woman for doing what she did.

And loved by everyone for bringing joy into our lives. However, her actions did cause some people, especially some men, anxiety. During those weeks there were reports of several women now being tried in court for acts of brutal revenge. A number of journalists contacted me to ask whether women had changed. Were women now taking revenge when in the past they did not, or were women always much more vengeful than men?

I pointed out that there was no way we could say that there were more vengeful women now than in the past because we did not have the necessary information to decide this. We can hardly say that women are more vengeful than men because it is men, not women, who indulge in endless wars of revenge. However, perhaps now that more women have been persuaded that it is acceptable for them to be assertive and be seen to protect their own rights, more women are prepared to carry out public acts of revenge.

A good woman has always been required to be long-suffering. She must not complain. She must endure insult and injury, and regard suffering as her cross. Women saints were always martyrs. Many good women, suffering at the hands of their husbands, bided their time and quietly took their revenge. I saw this happen with my grandparents, and subsequently with other couples whom I knew over many years.

When I was a child I spent much time in my grandparents' home, for my mother was very attached to her mother. Grandfather was always kind to me and told me stories of his youth in Scotland, but I knew that Grandmother and Mother were frightened of him from the way they reacted when he stomped, demanding and complaining, into the house. However, as grandmother got older (she died when I was twelve) her attitude to her husband changed. She showed him, and she showed all of us, that she thought he was a fool. She took all his power away from him, and she, growing frailer and frailer, took the centre stage of family life. He was left a lonely old man.

I have seen this pattern repeated, but earlier, in the lives of many couples.

In the first years of the marriage the man behaves with all the selfish arrogance to which most young men feel they are entitled. He thinks he can conquer the world with his cock. The young bride is entranced by this display, and accepts the insults about her incompetence and stupidity he heaps on her in the guise of jokes. She soon discovers that part of his most precious possession, his balls, are attached to him by the thinnest of thin string, and if this string breaks it would be the greatest disaster ever in the history of the entire universe, or at least that's how he sees it. Her duty is to protect his balls at all costs, but she must not let the world see that she is doing this. She must ensure that the world always sees him as a super-virile, impregnable man who never makes a mistake. If she has a car accident, it is always her fault, but if he has an accident, it is always someone else's fault. When I was married my husband would always summarize his position on this with, 'I mightn't always be right but I am never wrong.'

As time goes by the wife finds that the posture she has to adopt to support her husband while appearing to be supported by him increasingly tiring and painful. At first she adopts this posture without realizing that this is what she is doing. When she does recognize what she is doing, she feels sorry for him and wants to look after him, but, as the years go by and he never acknowledges his need of her, and indeed the greater his need the more he insults her, her love and pity diminish. One day she knows that what she feels for him is nothing but contempt.

If she is still economically dependent on him she keeps this knowledge to herself and bides her time. She plans revenge.

And her time comes. The children have grown up and left home. His sexual race is run. Young men scorn or patronize him. He might hold forth to his contemporaries about how he knows what's what, and he might take pride in what wealth and possessions he has accumulated, but he is totally dependent on her, and she knows it. Now it is time for her revenge. If she has been wise, over the years she has built up a life of her own with friends and outside interests. Now she lets him know that he will have to fit into her pattern of living, and if he doesn't, tough.

Whether she has been wise or not, she lets him see in no uncertain terms her contempt for him. Now she tells jokes to her friends about how silly he is. Now she refuses to listen to his oft-told stories, and walks out of the room while he is speak-

ing. Now she scolds him in public, and complains about him
to their children who side with her against him.

Only death can bring this vengeance to an end. No wonder
so many men fear growing old.

Not that this revenge brings the wife happiness, for every act
of revenge reminds her that she has wasted her life.

Men who suffer this revenge at the hands of their wives
cannot complain. They can grumble to their contemporaries
and tell the widowers among them how lucky they are, but they
cannot present themselves to the world as suffering victims.
There is no way they can attempt to win the world's sympathy
and be redeemed. They cannot confront the world's media on
the steps of a courthouse and present their side of the revenge
drama, as Kevin Maxwell did after becoming Britain's biggest
bankrupt. He said,

> I stand here today bankrupt with a deal of humility. Bank-
> ruptcy is a very public humbling. If there is a redeeming
> feature of the bankruptcy order, it is perhaps that the thou-
> sands of people who have suffered loss can take real satis-
> faction from seeing a former director – and, I suppose,
> above all, a Maxwell – suffer the consequences of their
> loss personally and in public. Perhaps those concerned
> believe this alone justifies the cost to the creditors of these
> proceedings, given the very small extent of my estate and
> my assets.[40]

Nice try, Kevin, but it's unlikely to be successful. Certainly
the people who have been harmed by your father will rejoice
in your humbling, but so will the people who, feeling that life
has not given them their just deserts, envy and hate the rich
and powerful. So too will all the believers in a Just World who
see your fate as evidence of its working. Even those people who
don't believe in a Just World are cheered by the slightest glimpse
of justice triumphant.

Revenge always takes one dramatic form – the vengeful victim and the aggressor, whose roles will alternate as the drama
goes on, with the world as audience. All three parties are essen-

tial to the drama. The drama starts with an injury, but an injury with special consequences. There are some injuries we can suffer, especially when we are feeling very self-confident, where we simply feel angry and express our anger immediately in some form or other. Our sense of being on the same level as the person who dealt the blow does not change.

Some injuries knock us off that level, or are inflicted by people whom we see as having some advantage over us. These are the injuries which create our need for revenge, for we feel not just pain but a threat to the integrity of our person. The injury threatens to annihilate our self, and that is the most dangerous threat of all. We must do something to defend ourselves and keep ourselves whole. Simply being angry is not enough. We must strike back at the person who dared to do this to us.

Discussions about the nature of revenge usually distinguish individuals seeking revenge for personal reasons and groups seeking revenge for social/political/religious/nationalist/business reasons, but in fact the individual and the group are not separate. The group is always made up of individuals with their own ways of seeing things, while as individuals we make membership of certain groups an essential part of our identity. Thus, whether we seek personal revenge or whether, as a member of a group, we take part in the group's drama of revenge, the processes are the same.

Seeking revenge is one of those activities where we like to tell ourselves that the consequences of our actions will be just what we want and no more. 'I'll have my revenge and that'll be the end of it,' we tell ourselves. We couldn't be more wrong.

Our act of revenge does to the other person what had been done to us – threatens the integrity of the self – and so the other person wants to retaliate. Other people can also be affected and want to retaliate.

Jesus advised turning the other cheek, but he didn't explain how to do this. He might have meant that you should have been feeling guilty about the injury you had inflicted on the person who is now injuring you, and so you can now interpret the injury you receive as the punishment you deserve. However, if you respond to the injury with 'I deserved that', you can

become very miserable if not depressed. Did he mean us not to retaliate destructively but imaginatively? Claiming the Moral High Ground can be effective, provided you have good PR. There is no point in claiming to be morally superior to the person who injured you if no one witnesses your claim. Martyrdom can be a very effective retaliation, provided you have a talent for pain, or at least the simulation of pain. Or did he mean the best revenge of all, which is to live well?

He might have meant that, but Christians have always preferred suffering, and martyrdom and revenge, like sentimentality and cruelty, always have a symbiotic relationship.

And so, in the name of all that is holy, the drama of revenge goes on.

More than three thousand people have died in Northern Ireland in the Catholic and Protestant drama of revenge. Most of those three thousand were not British soldiers or members of the militant groups of both sides, but ordinary people who just wanted a decent life.

As I am writing this in August 1992, we are learning of the appalling cruelties being inflicted on the Muslims and Croats by the Serbs. Their actions are a continuation of the centuries of wars of revenge between Christianity and Islam, and between groups of Christians.

When Germany and Italy conquered Yugoslavia in April 1941, they installed the Ustasha terrorist leader Ante Pavelic as head of the independent state of Croatia (NDH) in which was included Bosnia-Herzegovina. By the end of the year, even the German SS was appalled by the Ustasha massacre of the Orthodox Serbs, and Mussolini ordered his army back into Bosnia-Herzegovina to stop the persecution and keep the peace. Since the Germans and the Italians were the only foreigners in the NDH until a British mission arrived in 1943, this has remained the least known, as well as one of the most horrendous religious slaughters in Europe's history.

The Ustasha's policy to the 1,900,000 Orthodox Serbs in the NDH was first made public in June 1941: 'Convert a third, expel a third, and kill a third.' Already they had begun this gruesome work in Croatia proper, where the Serbs were about a fifth of the population. Later they turned their attention to Bosnia-Herzegovina, where the Orthodox then were 44 per cent of the population, while the rest were Muslims, whose ancestors had converted from the medieval Bogomil heresy.

The Franciscans, who had arrived in 1260 to try to win back these heretics with a series of Inquisitions, provided almost all the Catholic priests in Bosnia-Herzegovina. A high proportion of these had sworn the Ustasha oath on a gun, a knife and a bomb.

The Ustasha Minister of the Interior, Andrija Artukovic, set an example in May 1941 by carrying out the massacre of 4,000 Serbs in his native district of Herzegovina. In north-west Bosnia, the Ustasha started their purge of the Serbian Orthodox clergy when they seized the Bishop of Ganja Luka, shaved his beard with a blunt knife, gouged out his eyes, cut off his nose and ears, then lit a fire on his chest before despatching him . . .

The wholesale massacre of the Serbs began on June 28, 1941, in the region of Mostar and Capljina. The Catholic Bishop of Mostar, one of the two priests brave enough to denounce the Ustasha crimes from the pulpit, sent this account in a letter dated November 7 to the Archbishop of Zagreb: 'A reign of terror has come to pass. Men are captured like animals, they are slaughtered, living men are thrown off cliffs. At Ljubinje on a single day 700 schismatics (Orthodox) were thrown into their graves. From Mostar and from Capljina, a train took six carloads of mothers, young girls and children . . . to Surmanci . . . they were led up the mountain and the mothers, together with their children, were thrown alive off the precipice . . . In the town of Mostar itself, they have been bound by the hundreds, taken in wagons outside the town and then shot down like animals.'

The ravine where the women and children were killed is less than two miles from the Franciscan monastery at

Medjugorje, the site of the Marian apparitions which has drawn millions of pilgrims over the last decade.[41]

Who profits from these wars of revenge? Only the people who sell the participants the guns with which to fight one another.

In the language of revenge the metaphors used are often not so much of anger and injury but of dirt and cleanliness. Our education in virtue as children leaves us with a feeling that we are intrinsically sullied and dirty. Further injuries can leave us feeling even more intrinsically filthy. All religions have rituals of washing away this filth. Some use water, some use blood. Christianity uses both – water and the blood of Christ.

Since such rituals have a very temporary effect (as they must, since, if baptism made us clean and good once and for ever, the Church would have no reason to exist, other than to baptize babies), we have to find another way of disposing of the filth that we believe weighs on our soul.

We do this by declaring that we are spotlessly clean. It is our enemies who are dirty.

'Our soul,' the young Serb is saying, 'is cleaner than yours.'

Alexander is twenty, a first-year law student, who fought last year in the Yugoslav army in Croatia and is now an officer in the artillery reserves. He is a picture of national pride – tall, brown-eyed, well-spoken, steeped in the history of his people.

'In the West, you fight wars for reasons of self-interest. Our wars are fought for sentimental reasons.'[42]

Sentiment and cruelty – and 'ethnic cleansing'.

Wars of revenge rarely come to an end because both sides have learned good sense. I was going to put 'never' in that sentence because that's what I believe, but I don't have knowledge of every war that has ever occurred. I just don't know of any war which came to an end because both sides learned good sense. Sometimes two groups stop fighting one another in order to join together to fight a third group. That is just a continuation of the war.

Wars come to an end when both sides are greatly depleted economically, or one side is destroyed utterly. However, the side that wins does so at great cost. Destroying Carthage destroyed the Roman Empire, and winning the Second World War meant the end of the British Empire.

Sometimes two warring sides are taken over by a strong power. Such a power could undertake an educational programme which would get both sides to resolve their differences, but such a programme could hardly be successful if the strong power is still operating, as strong powers do, with its own array of enemies which further its purposes. After the Second World War the American government set up an educational programme to introduce the Japanese to the virtues of democracy, and very successful it was, too. However, the Americans did nothing to resolve the enmity between the Japanese and the Koreans because a Japanese and Korean alliance would not be in American interests.

Most strong powers who take over warring groups follow the practice used so successfully in the British Empire of divide and rule. When Tito came to power in Yugoslavia he did nothing to resolve the differences between the Serbs, Croats and Muslims. Indeed, he fostered these differences, so that when Communism came to an end there were no political parties in Yugoslavia, but only nationalist groups ready to start the wars of revenge over again.

Political parties of the kind which exist in the West could come into being only as the people gradually developed the meanings necessary for a democratic form of government to exist. These meanings include not only notions about ballot boxes and majorities but an understanding that we can enjoy freedom only to the degree that we can tolerate other people's enjoyment of their freedom.

Not that this is fully understood in the West. We might be able to tolerate the existence of people who hold different religious and political beliefs from our own, and some of us can even manage to tolerate people of different races, but there is still little tolerance for people who do not conform to the conventional way of life. Witness the persecution of those people who reject ordinary domesticity and instead travel around the country in cars and caravans. Witness, too, the contempt for those who cannot get work and so are unable to adopt the conventional way of life. Both these groups of people are a threat to those who sacrificed so much as children in order to become good. These people do not want any suggestion that this sacrifice might not have been necessary and that in this world virtue is not always rewarded.

Their envy and fear prevent them from realizing that freedom depends on tolerance, for if we do not tolerate other people's freedom we then have to try to confine them in some way. The prison walls we put around them confine us as well. We have to lock ourselves and our possessions away, and we have to limit and confine our meaning structure. Fear, prejudice and envy are the prison walls in our minds.

The Berlin Wall may have come down and the imprisoning Communist regime come to an end, but the prison walls of fear, prejudice and envy remain in Eastern Europe and the states of the old USSR. Democracy requires both tolerance and an acceptance of personal responsibility. Many people do not want to accept responsibility for themselves. In the West such people excuse their bad behaviour by saying, 'It's the fault of my genes' or 'It's my parents' fault.' In Eastern Europe and the old USSR such people long for the return of the totalitarian ruler, the Good Father who will take responsibility for everything that happens. They forget that, while we are not responsible for whom we get as a biological father, we are responsible for those who become our rulers. Totalitarian or democratic, rulers can rule only with the consent of the people. If no one becomes a member of the secret police, an informer, a torturer, a soldier prepared to kill his own people, how can a government rule through terror? Totalitarian or democratic, rulers rule because most of their people, by not recognizing their own responsibility, give tacit consent to the ruler's power. Thus we get, as Alistair Mant has pointed out, the leaders we deserve.[43]

Rulers maintain their position, first, by preventing their people from having the kind of education which allows them to understand the nature of personal responsibility. We may

not be responsible for or cause much of what happens to us, but we are always responsible for how we interpret everything that happens to us because we are free to choose from a vast array of possible interpretations. People who understand this are always a threat to those who would rule over them. (This is why totalitarian governments always persecute artists and why pseudo-democratic governments try to seduce artists by means of rewards and prestige.)

The second strategy used by rulers to maintain power is to create enemies of the State. Obedient subjects dutifully hate the enemies their ruler instructs them to hate. Thus there is now the re-emergence of anti-Semitism in the old Communist states. Elena Barikhovskaya, a member of the Russian lawyers' committee on human rights, wrote, 'Anti-Semitism is merely the political arena in which reactionary forces are battling to re-establish totalitarian rule.'[44]

The enemies and the righteous victims seeking revenge change over the years, but not the language used in the drama of revenge.

Michael Ignatieff wrote of how he read Maggie O'Kane's reports from Bosnia where friendly Serbian women and men tell her of how the Muslims 'kill new-born Serbian babies and drown them in the River Drina. They sexually assault Serbian children aged between nine and twelve, and they cut off Serbian men's penises.'[45] He realized that 'The language of blood libel has returned to Europe.'

A long and mournful entry in *The Encyclopedia Judaica* defines blood libel as the 'allegation that Jews murder non-Jews to obtain blood for use in Passover rituals'. The first recorded allegation in medieval Europe occurs in Norwich in 1144, where the city's Jewish community was accused of having bought a Christian child – the 'boy martyr William – and having crucified and tortured him'. In a later case in Lincoln in 1255, it was alleged that Jews had crucified another child. One of the monuments of our literature, Geoffrey Chaucer's *Prioress's Tale*, makes reference to the Lincoln case and holds the 'cursed Jews' responsible.

In vain did Jews plead, often under torture, that Leviticus and Deuteronomy explicitly forbade the consumption of animal or human blood. In vain did they cite their own dietary laws, which require the draining of all blood from meat to be eaten. Prejudice always has an ironic structure. The very nature of Jewish dietary law drew the neurotic Christian imagination to the subject of blood and built, upon the Jew's aversion to blood, the reverse fantasy: that Jewish ritual required it . . .

Jews, in vain, pointed out that Christians themselves had been the victims of the same structure of fantasy in the late Roman times. Jewish scholars were aware that Father Tertullian had complained in the second century after Christ: 'We are said to be the most criminal of men, on the score of our sacramental baby-killing and the baby-eating that goes with it.' If early Christians themselves were originally the victims of the fantasies they later turned on the Jews, we can only conclude that the basic structure of the fantasy – the murder of innocents, the consumption of human blood – is always independent of its target.[46]

In the language of revenge another meaning which has not changed down the centuries is the belief that a man cannot be a real man unless he is prepared to kill and be killed. Craig Newnes put this idea in its romantic form in his description of the good man: 'And sometimes, in our crazier moments, we still want to die for our country and be remembered as knights of the round table.'

Ken Lukowiak, never before having written anything longer than a letter, wrote an eloquent and moving account of his experiences as a paratrooper in the Falklands War. I met him at another exciting time in his life when he had just had his work accepted first by the *Guardian* and then by a book publisher.[47] What came across to me as we talked was that he thought his story was special, unique – as every soldier does. If he had told his story to my father who was an artilleryman in the First World War, or to an infantryman at Waterloo, a Roman centurion, an Assyrian warrior, they each would have said, 'Yes, that's what happened to me.' Terror, destruction, heroism, pain, futility – and the feeling that, 'Until now I have been playing at life. Now I know that life is real.'

Meanwhile, children rescued from Dubrovnik, Sarajevo and Mostar have been drawing pictures of their experiences.

Crouched in fetid underground shelters, they have endured night after night of shelling and weeks of hunger and thirst. Families have been split up and no one knows if their relatives are alive or dead. Some children have seen their mothers raped, their fathers' throats cut, and their homes burned down. One three-year-old drew a picture of his mother and painted blood pouring out of what appears to be an abdominal wound; another painted his grandmother, her body completely red.

The killers are often not strangers, but neighbours – men living in a previously close, intermarrying community who have turned into murderers. The four-year-old who says, 'Do not kill me, Uncle! I will be good!' speaks to the killer as a well-known and trusted adult he is used to calling 'uncle'. It is as though the child thinks that, if only he were good enough, the violence would stop. Some of these children have lost both parents and, like many children, understand the death of those they love as happening because they have been naughty. It is a terrible burden of guilt for any child to bear . . .

Most of these pictures have been done by pre-school children, but we also have ones from older children. In these, there are obvious gender differences. The girls draw flowers, women in frilly dresses and people busy collecting water for cleaning and cooking – somehow conveying a reassuring sense of normality. The older boys, however, focus on the fighting. They draw strutting warriors, men firing guns, bayonets and tanks with intricate detail and precision, often cramming in every weapon of destruction they can. The greatest danger is that children who live with the reality of violence grow up to become violent in their turn. Perhaps we ought to ask what we are doing to our children's minds. While boys cherish an image of manhood like this, can the killing stop?[48]

Language connects the individual to society, and society to the individual. We are born into the language our society speaks, but the language our society speaks changes because individuals change the language. We live in language like a fish lives in water. Language penetrates our being, envelops and supports us. When individuals and groups change the language, we change.

The language of revenge and war changes us.

We might live in language like a fish lives in water, but, as the ancient Chinese said, 'The fish is the last to discover the water.' In an effort to help us discover how the water was changing, the *Guardian* printed the following.

All the expressions below have been used by the British press in the past week.

We have	They have
Army, Navy, Air Force	A war machine
Reporting guidelines	Censorship
Press briefings	Propaganda

We	They
Take out	Destroy
Suppress	Destroy
Eliminate	Kill
Neutralise	Kill
Decapitate	Kill
Dig in	Cower in their foxholes

We launch	They launch
First strikes	Sneak missile attacks
Pre-emptively	Without provocation

Our men are ...	Their men are ...
Boys	Troops
Lads	Hordes

Our boys are . . .	Their men are . . .
Professional	Brainwashed
Lion-hearts	Paper tigers
Cautious	Cowardly
Confident	Desperate
Heroes	Cornered
Dare-devils	Cannon fodder
Young knights of the skies	Bastards of Baghdad
Loyal	Blindly obedient
Desert rats	Mad dogs
Resolute	Ruthless
Brave	Fanatical

Our missiles cause . . .	Their missiles cause . . .
Collateral damage	Civilian casualties

George Bush is . . .	Saddam Hussein is . . .
At peace with himself	Demented
Resolute	Defiant
Statesmanlike	An evil tyrant
Assured	A crackpot monster.[49]

We should try to be aware of the language we use because it becomes the assumptions on which our decisions are based. If the British soldiers are lads and the Iraqi soldiers merely hordes, then our meaning structure can protect us from pain and pity when the hordes are burnt alive in their tanks.

We should try to be aware of what our meaning structure will allow us to do. The more absolutes our meaning structure contains, the more imprisoned we are, thus dooming ourselves to repeat our errors until death.

In 1990 the Polish writer Ryszard Kapuscinski was flown secretly to Nagorno Karabakh, which is an enclave within Azerbaijan. Three-quarters of the population are Christian Armenians and the rest Muslim Azerbaijanis. Fighting began in 1988 over plans to unite with Armenia and to date casualties include some 2,000 killed and 270,000 homeless. He wrote:

For the Armenians an ally is anyone who thinks that Nagorno Karabakh is a problem. The rest are enemies. For the Azerbaijanis an ally is someone who thinks that Nagorno Karabakh isn't a problem. The rest are enemies.

The extremism of these views is notable. There is simply no question, being among Armenians, of saying, 'I think that the Azerbaijanis are right'; or, being among Azerbaijanis, of saying, 'I think the Armenians are right.' Nothing of the sort – they hate and they kill. It is sufficient in the wrong place or among the wrong people to say, 'It's a problem' (or 'It's not a problem') to expose oneself to strangulation, hanging, stoning, or burning. Nor is it conceivable to make this statement in Baku (Azerbaijan) or Yerevan (Armenia): 'Listen, decades ago (and who among us still remembers this), some savage Turkish pasha and the equally savage Stalin threw an awful cuckoo's egg into our Caucasian nest and since then we have spent the whole century wearing ourselves out and killing each other, while they lie in their musty graves chuckling to themselves that the joke has gone so far. And yet we live in such poverty, with so much backwardness and dirt around us. Let's make peace and get down to work!'

This person would never be able to finish what he was saying because, as soon as both sides realized what he wanted to say, the unhappy moralist and conciliator would be deprived of his life.

There are three plagues which threaten the world:

The first – the plague of nationalism.

The second – the plague of racism.

The third – the plague of religious fundamentalism.

These three plagues have the same characteristic, a common denominator – their aggressive, all-powerful, total irrationality.

In a defeated mind one of these plagues will find a home. In such a mind burns a holy stake, which is just waiting for a sacrifice. Any attempt at quiet discussion will miss its aim. It is not talk which interests him, it is a declaration of beliefs, so that you agree with him and admit that he is right, so that you sign the accession. Otherwise in his eyes you have no meaning, you don't exist, because you are counted only as a tool, as an instrument, as a weapon. There are no people – there is only the cause. The mind touched by such a plague is a closed mind, limited, monothematic, revolving exclusively around one motif – the enemy.

Thinking about the enemy gives us life, allows us to exist. That is why the enemy is always present, is always with us. When near Yerevan the local guide shows me one of their basilicas, he asks me, 'How could they build such a basilica?' When, later, in Baku, the local guide shows me a row of decorative, secession apartments, he finishes his explanation with the contemptuous question, 'Could the Armenians have built such a building?'

On the other hand, there is something to be jealous about. They don't trouble their minds about how the world is mapped out, or about the fact that man's fate is uncertain and fragile. They know nothing of the anxiety caused by some of those normal questions which we all ask, like What is truth? What is good? What is justice? They know nothing of the anxiety which oppresses those who ask themselves the question: Am I right?

Their world is small – it consists of a few valleys and mountains. Their world is simple – on one side of us, the good people, on the other them, the enemy. Their world is governed by exclusivity – it's either them or us.

And if there is some other world, what could they want from it? To leave them in peace. They need the peace so that the one can count the bones of the other in all exactitude.[50]

We hold on to our absolute beliefs in the attempt to make time stand still and the world stay the same. 'Revenge,' said Sheldon Kopp, 'is a form of nostalgia.'[51] Longing for the security of timelessness, we fear growing old for that shows that time is passing.

When we hold our beliefs tentatively, aware that we can never be absolutely right, and even if we are right it isn't possible for us to know that, we hesitate to impose our beliefs on other people. When we hold our beliefs absolutely, we believe them to be absolutely true, and so we do not hesitate to impose them on other people. Indeed, we are impelled to impose them on others because we need all the time to be reassuring ourselves that our beliefs are absolutely true.

Imposing our meaning structure on other people is the exercise of power. Rulers impose their meaning structure on their subjects, and parents impose their meaning structure on their children. Children sensibly resist this, but when the parent describes the world in terms of absolute truths, young children accept what they are told, because a world of absolute truths seems to be comfortably secure.

Remember the insecurity of wondering who you were and what your place in the scheme of things was? How secure you would have felt if your parents had told you that you had been named after a great hero whom everyone revered. That answered your question, 'Who am I?' You are a person with all the qualities of a hero. And you know what your place in the world is. You are going to be a great hero, just like your namesake.

Suppose you had been told that your name was Kevin Barry O'Donnell and that you were named after a Republican hero executed early this century. Would you not feel that a certain expectation had been laid on you? Especially when your father was a man of very strong views.

At the church door there was a further delay. Much of the conflict in Northern Ireland centres on symbols and the priest, Monsignor Liam McEntegart, refused to allow the two coffins inside unless the Irish tricolour was removed.

Over years of Republican funerals the practice has emerged that the flag is taken off outside the church along with the IRA black beret and gloves. James O'Donnell, Kevin's father, would have none of it.

Emanating a calm fatalism, he argued with the priest for 25 minutes – with the crowd shivering in the carpark

– before he got his way. The coffins were allowed inside draped in the tricolour.[52]

Kevin Barry O'Donnell was twenty-one when he was shot by the SAS as he and his IRA companion Sean O'Farrell made their getaway from an attack on Coalisland RUC station.

Parents put their dreams of revenge on to their children, and children put their dreams of revenge on to their parents.

When we are children and suffer cruelty and humiliation at the hands of the adults who have power over us, the integrity of our self is greatly threatened. We have to do something to defend ourselves, and more often than not all we can do is in terms of fantasy, not action. We dream of revenge. One day we will show them.

Such dreams can prove fruitful. They spur us on to achieve, and we· do achieve. However, we can be satisfied with our achievements only if our original dreams of revenge were no more than the booster rockets on a spacecraft. They start us off, and then they fall away, forgotten. If we hang on to our dream of revenge, no achievement is good enough. By the time we do achieve outstandingly, most, if not all, of those we wished to vanquish are no longer there to be amazed at our magnificence and to humbly beg our pardon. Even if they are still there to witness what we have done, they remain incorrigible in their attitude to us. We can cause ourselves a great deal of misery by refusing to accept this. I came across this kind of pain often when I was working in the National Health Service.

Charlie had spent his life trying to outwit and defeat his father. Every game he had ever played with his father since his earliest childhood his father had won. I knew Charlie's father – he had a garage I used occasionally – and I met Charlie when, deeply depressed, he was admitted to hospital. He told me that his business had failed, but it gradually emerged that although he and his father had been in partnership, his father had arranged matters so that when the business failed Charlie lost everything and his father nothing. This was an action replay of every game Charlie had ever played with his father. Why didn't he refuse to play any more games with him? Wasn't it obvious that the way he constantly denigrated his son undermined Charlie's self-confidence, thus leading him to become depressed? All Charlie would say was, 'I've got to beat him. Just once. I've got to beat him and prove myself.'

This dream of revenge served two functions. If fulfilled it would boost his self-confidence enormously, and it would prove that his father really was an honest, generous man, the kind of father every boy wants to have. Charlie could not bring himself to face the reality that his father was a liar who denigrated his son in order to maintain his own precarious self-confidence. Charlie is now, I understand, out of hospital and living with his father.

Psychiatric hospitals provide the setting for dramas of revenge that have been running for decades. Some children conceive their dreams of revenge, not in terms of achievement but in terms of exposing the wickedness of the parents. The basic plot is, 'You've hurt me. I'm going to show people what you've done. Then you'll be sorry.' However, there is a problem about this plot.

Suppose you as a child get beaten by your parents. You might be able to go to the police or the social services and show them your bruises, but there is always the danger that they'll say, 'You're a wicked child and you deserve what you got.' (Many children suffer great cruelty at the hands of their teachers, but they don't tell their parents because they know that they will side with the teachers. Children know that adults stick together.) If the police and the social services take you seriously you could end up losing your comfortable bedroom and your mother's good cooking. So you need another way of displaying your injuries.

You become ill. Some people develop physical complaints which are completely impervious to medical cure, even diagnosis. Others develop some nervous complaint – a fear of open spaces, obsessional washing, a refusal to eat, depression or highly eccentric ways of talking and behaving. (Just what the person chooses depends on whether the person is an extravert or an introvert and how great is the peril the person is in.[53])

Family therapists like to home in on these dramas very early and confront all the players with what they are doing. Traditional psychiatrists focus on only one of the players, turn that player into a patient, and, by taking the side of the parents against the child, ensure that the drama of revenge continues until the death of the child. The death of the parents does not end the drama, because the parents live on in the child's imagination, and the drama continues.

Many other dramas of revenge are fought out in families decade after decade. Many children create their fantasy of revenge when they discover that the justice of the Just World has failed them. Their fantasies of revenge and recompense concern not so much their parents as their siblings. The parents are fought over as possessions. 'Mummy belongs to me, not you.' They see their siblings getting more than their just desserts. They become envious and vow revenge, and family life, especially in 'a close family', as the media so heartwarmingly describes families where opportunities for in-fighting are limitless, allows revenge and retaliation to be acted out for decades, generation after generation. In such families the participants, like the Armenians and the Azerbaijanis, want to be left in peace so that 'the one can count the bones of the other in all exactitude.'

Parents often give their children the means whereby the children can wreak their revenge on them. After a lecture I gave on depression a middle-aged woman sought me out to ask a private question. She was a big, bony woman with a hard face, one of those faces that we develop when we are hard on ourselves and hard on other people. She said, 'What can you do for a woman who becomes depressed when she remembers what she did to her children?' I talked to her about talking to her children, acknowledging that certain things happened, and saying that she was sorry. Not a satisfactory answer, for her children would not listen. She had been hard on them, and now they were hard on her.

Children, as the recipients of the parents' cruelty, learn the means whereby they can try to get revenge. They can also learn what will hurt and humiliate their parents the most. Marie, an ex-nun, told me how, when she was a child, her mother had forced her to attend church because she thought the nuns would make Marie be obedient. Her mother never attended church and had little time for anything religious.

Marie decided on a form of revenge which some children do as a joke to tease their parents. They obey their parents' order to the letter. The father of one lad I know scolded him for playing in the hot sun and unwisely said, 'I never want to see you without a hat.' His son obeyed him fully. He wore his hat at dinner, in bed, under the shower, everywhere. Marie decided on the same form of revenge, but more seriously. She became very obedient, and who is more obedient than a nun? It took her years to realize that hers was not a vocation but a revenge.

One of the ironies which we need to recognize and accept is that something which is essential to our survival can also destroy us if we are not careful. Fantasies of revenge can save us when we are being attacked and humiliated, but putting such fantasies into action is always risky. The drama of revenge played as a comedy can resolve bad feelings and bring about a reconciliation. Play it seriously, and it becomes a tragedy where everyone suffers. There is no 'happy ever after'.

All our acts have consequences. These are not part of the working out of some Grand Design of rewards and consequences, nor are they signs of the intervention of some Divine Overseer or the wild vagaries of Blind Fate. The consequences of our acts arise from a network of interlocking events in which we have played a major part.

When we are born a vast array of possibilities lies before us. Our educators narrow the range of possibilities. They say, 'You can't do this', 'You must do that.' In our teens and twenties we make choices which narrow the range of possibilities even more. Most of us build a cage for ourselves from which escape seems impossible. Whatever we do, our choices have long-term consequences, but because we do not understand this, we act blindly, unthinkingly.

We act without thinking beyond tomorrow. We tell ourselves fairy stories. Sometimes we have a vague sense of unease about what we are doing, but we ignore it. Sometimes we know that what we are doing will lead to disaster, but we feel compelled to act as we do.

In our teens and twenties we lay our vultures' eggs. In our thirties we begin to see what we have done, and we are horrified. Some of us try to change what we are doing, but we cannot undo the past. Others of us feel bound and helpless.

We see our future coming towards us, and we do not like what we see.

We fear growing old.

What can we do?

Live in terror and despair, or accept that what has happened has happened. Time is irreversible and always moving. We have to live with our injuries and our failures whether we want to or not.

The only compensation is that, terrible though our vultures may be, we can always learn from them.

CHAPTER 5

From absolute truths to uncertain wisdom

NOT EVERYONE is afraid of time passing, growing old and dying. Some people, I found, said, 'Every age has its benefits. The trick is to make the most of them at the time. I don't want to die a painful death, but death itself doesn't bother me.'

Such people did not hang on to the past, trying to make it into an unchanging absolute.

These people looked to the future with hope, not fear, but it was not the hope that in a Just World their rewards would come. It was the hope engendered by the understanding that in this 'random universe to which we bring meaning'[1] a multitude of outcomes is possible. As Ludovic Kennedy wrote, 'The only certainty is that life and its origins are a marvellous mystery and happily will always remain so.'[2]

Some of these people spoke of the pleasure of being the age they were and not striving to appear older, as they had when they were young, or striving to be younger, as many of their contemporaries did. Others spoke of how age is a matter of attitude. Ron Janoff described meeting his contemporaries at high school reunions:

> ... there are people who are now middle-aged, which could be anywhere above forty, and who you realize haven't changed because they were old when you knew them when they were young. They were always like little old people. Now that they're in their late forties they simply became more like the old people they already were. This isn't unusual. You know I work at the university. I work with a lot of people who are very young – fifteen and up. To me there's a category of being old which means fixed in your ways and not too flexible – lack of flexibility, and sort of, not narrow or selfish necessarily, but keeping the range of experience around you very limited. That's what old means to me, I guess, and young means the opposite – flexibility, willingness to explore, discover and so on, and they don't necessarily correspond to ages. There are many people beyond middle-age that I would think of as very young, and there are people definitely when they were young they were already old.

As these people described how their earlier fear of old age and death had fallen away they showed that this change came about not in isolation but as part of a major change in how they saw themselves and their world. Some had gone searching for a better understanding, while some, overtaken by events which challenged their beliefs, were forced to question and so change.

What they all reported was the discovery that the world was not fixed and absolute, as they had been led to believe. What they had taken as absolute reality was naught but a dream. They could stay on in this dream only so long as they did not test the absolute truths they held so dear, but once they did question, the absolute truths crumbled. What they were left with was uncertain wisdom. Such uncertain wisdom changed how they lived their lives and how they saw the passing of time and growing old.

Such uncertain wisdom relates to every aspect of life and can be expressed in a multitude of ways. Here I have chosen five aspects which recurred in the discussions which I had about the getting of wisdom. The expressions of these uncertain wisdoms I have taken from Sheldon Kopp's Eschatological Laundry List, now in his book *No Hidden Meanings*[3] and its companion volume *What Took You So Long?*[4] If you find Sheldon Kopp's brief statements confusing, you are still holding on to absolute truths. If you are in possession of uncertain wisdom his statements are crystal clear.

1   SEEING THE EMPTINESS OF AUTHORITY

No one is stronger or weaker than anyone else.
  Everyone is, in his own way, vulnerable.
  There are no great men.
  If you have a hero, look again; you have diminished yourself.

Believing that God is watching over you, that the Government is guarding your interests, that the Keepers of Morals and Standards are always wise, and that Heroes are Good Incarnate might create a sense of comfort and security, but what do you do when you discover that God might watch over the faithful but He does not protect them, that the Government guards only its own interests and that of its friends, that the Keepers of Morals and Standards ignore reality, and that Heroes have feet of clay?

The first authority whose emptiness we might see is that of

our parents. This always comes as a shock because as children we want to feel that our parents are strong and wise and hold up the sky over our heads. Wise parents know that if their children are to become adults, and not merely children in adult bodies, they must outgrow the authority of their parents. Alan Brien wrote, 'I think it is the duty of all parents to demystify, to profane and humanise their role in their children's eyes. It is hard work, not always pleasant but essential if we are ever to accept each other as we ought to be, as soon as possible, as equals.'5

Not all parents can accept this. The biographer of Freud, Ernest Jones, was one such parent. His son Mervyn Jones, the novelist, wrote:

> My own father, Ernest Jones, was a psychoanalyst. On the face of it he was excellently equipped to be a father . . . Human insights and human relationships were his particular line of country . . . I admired my father enormously. He was better at everything than I could ever aspire to be . . . I knew, as soon as I could understand anything of the kind, that in his work he was a man of great distinction . . . It was the distinction and achievement of Ernest Jones that prompted a goading, frustrating question: if he was so damn good at everything else, why couldn't he be equally good at being a father?
>
> Then, being the son of a dedicated Freudian was bound to confront me with a particular difficulty. I learned (not from my father who was averse to talking about professional matters and certainly never sought to indoctrinate me, but from my general reading) of the existence of the Oedipus complex. I don't recall my exact age at the time, but I know I was seized by panic. Did I really want to kill my father? Did I want to make love to my mother? (The idea held no attraction for me whatever.) I asked my father, attempting to put on an air of detached intellectual curiosity, whether this complex was indeed universal in mankind or whether it admitted of exceptions. He assured me it was an integral part of the human condition, whether

in the primeval forest or in the most sophisticated and cultivated environment. To have discovered its universality, he explained, was the mark of Freud's genius. I felt – as the son of a Calvinist preacher might have felt on making acquaintance with the doctrine of original sin – the weight of inescapable doom. I did not want to hate my father, yet, by failing to hate him, I was repudiating his creed.

There was a further difficulty: once I knew about the Oedipus complex I was debarred from the kind of disagreement, or straightforward conflict, with my father that was available to other sons. If I was rude to him, if I rejected his advice on any matter, if I forgot (quotation marks here – 'forgot') to buy something he had commissioned me to buy when I passed the shops, I was not simply annoying him – I was exemplifying the Oedipus complex in classic form. In my teens I argued with him a great deal, particularly about politics. I naturally felt on the merits of the question I was right, and sometimes I was. But I was in a no-win position (a phrase that, in my youth, hadn't yet been coined) because my argument, being an expression of Oedipal rebellion, could not be judged on its merits. I became more intense and heated and overstated my case. My father then gave a quiet smile, looked at his watch, and departed for his consulting room or his study.

In this relationship my father was above all a figure of authority . . . In his world, however, he was not the supreme authority, that position being reserved for Sigmund Freud. It was painful for me to realize that there was someone who could correct or rebuke my father, just as the headmaster of my school could correct or rebuke me. Many years later, I read my father's letters home to my mother from San Cristoforo – the place where, in 1932, the mandarins of psychoanalysis, led by the egregious Otto Rank, convinced Freud that Jones was an unworthy disciple and imposed a humiliating censure on him. When I read these letters, my father was long dead (so was Rank) and I was almost sixty years old. But I felt the same mingling of grief and outraged anger − 'how dare they do this to my father?' − that I might have felt had I still been a boy . . .

I am inclined to think that the most devastating moment in a child's life comes with the recognition − which all must experience, except perhaps the children of the Dalai Lama − that a father's supremacy is not absolute, nor universally admitted . . .

Looking at myself as best I can, I should say that my best quality as a father is a negative one: I take no pleasure in the exercise of power . . . I found power over my children unpleasant and embarrassing. I was impatient for them to grow up and make their own decisions without authority from me.[6]

No doubt Ernest Jones, were he to observe his son's refusal to don the mantle of paternal authority, would have dismissed this decision as being no more than the defence of reaction formation! Ernest Jones, like many other psychoanalysts, accepted the ideas which Freud had put forward as Absolute Truths, and so had to make everything that happened fit his master's theory. He did not see the emptiness of authority because he felt that he could not live without some supreme authority to protect him.

However, some people do manage to outgrow the need for a supreme authority.

When Geraldine Bedell went to interview the actress Sheila Hancock she found that Sheila had just heard that a demonstration at Sellafield Nuclear Power Station had been banned. Sheila's mother and first husband died of cancer, and four years ago she herself developed breast cancer. Now she said to Geraldine,

'My first inclination nowadays is to go, though I was brought up to believe that They were always right, that They wouldn't have built it if it was dangerous, and then I would have thought, "Quite Right, all those people are being naughty and making a mess". I grew up with the idea that there are rules you didn't question, which has made for a lifetime of belated questioning. Now I have no respect for authority whatsoever, but it's been a long journey' . . .

When her mother and husband died of cancer within a year of each other, Sheila Hancock not only became a campaigner for hospices and a bereavement counsellor, she also lost her religion. She had prayed nightly and sought out a church wherever she had been on tour; now she simply wasn't interested. 'I just got fed up of asking, "Why suffering?" I looked at Alec at the end and thought, "I'm not going to bother with this anymore. I've got other things to do with my life, practical things."' She also discovered feminism. 'Then everything started to irritate me. Every time someone said Our Father, I felt excluded.'

Her own cancer made her reconsider. 'I began to feel the lack of any kind of inner life, spiritual support. It's quite bleak for me not to have a religion.' So she recently, tentatively, began to get involved with the Quakers. 'I'm not committed to anything yet, but I do go and there's just this hour of silence, no hierarchy, prayers, vicars. It's very feminist, open to everything, just a gathering of people who think something might be there.'[7]

Sheila 'remains self-deprecating; she retains a sense of herself as ordinary'. When we come to see that those who claim authority over us are not part of some absolute authority but simply ordinary, vulnerable people engaged in a play whose aim is to entrap and use us, we realize too our own ordinariness. This is not the humility which takes pride in itself, but the recognition that everyone is ordinary, and that no one has to earn the right to exist, nor is anyone born with the right to be superior to others.

In contrast to Sheila Hancock is the former World Champion racing driver Niki Lauda. Having survived a major crash, Niki Lauda went on to put into his airline business the same single-minded determination to achieve perfection that he had put into driving.

After one of the LaudaAir planes crashed in May 1991, Niki Lauda's friend and biographer Heinz Pruller wrote,

> The boss and owner of LaudaAir – 70 pilots, 200 hostesses, total staff 575 people – is just through the worst phase of his life. Only slowly the shadows of the tragedy are disappearing. 'It was an accident that happens once in a million years,' Niki says. 'But why did it happen to *me*?'
>
> And sensationally, he asks himself: 'Why didn't I fly the plane myself? I keep asking myself. Because, in this case, I would have known exactly what happened. Maybe not for long – but I would have known the reason for this terrible crash.'
>
> One thing, though, is absolutely certain. It was not the fault of Niki's pilots, nor the fault of LaudaAir. 'And for sure it was not a service or a maintenance mistake,' says Niki firmly . . . 'I was absolutely sure that, in flying, accidents can only happen through human error. Whatever happened has been analysed clearly: a cargo door in a Jumbo that had not been properly locked, for instance. Then come I, my LaudaAir line, looking for perfection in every detail, from cleanliness to the food to the last bolt. And then my technical wonderthing, my masterpiece, crashes in the jungle in Thailand. I will never understand, until I know why.'
>
> Being Niki Lauda, he will find out. But why did it all happen to him? 'Destiny? – I don't know. Ask God. Maybe He wanted me to go through all that.'[8]

Interpreting every disaster that befalls you as a lesson which God is teaching you for your betterment is a form of the belief in a Just World. But what vanity it involves! God arranged for 223 people to die in order to advance Niki Lauda's education!

God is essential for the maintenance of vanity, both personal and national. One way of trying to persuade yourself and other people that you are powerful is to claim monopoly of God's power. This keeps God very busy, for so many people call on Him. Within the space of one week during the Gulf War in

1991 these were some of the calls He received:

We are being faithful to the values which God almighty has inspired in us, for we have no fear from the forces of Satan, the devil that rides on your shoulders.

Saddam Hussein, letter to George Bush

The Saddam Hussein regime is now clearly heading for destruction. We can thank God for that.

Paul Johnson, *Daily Mail*

Iraq and Palestine will be together side by side and after the great battle, God willing, we will pray together in Jerusalem.

Yasser Arafat

Whatever Saddam Hussein says about a holy war, we are the ones who have been given a special mission by God.

Major Mohammed Abu Amnah, commander of one of Saudi Arabia's forward combat squadrons

We pray to God for victory for his soldiers.

King Fahd, Saudi Arabia

Every time the sirens sound, we rush to this mountain to shout Allah Akbar (God is great) and pray the missiles find their target in Tel Aviv.

Young Palestinian, West Bank

The Jewish God will not allow this murderer Hussein to succeed. God will defend the state of Israel.

Phone-in caller, London

We know that this is a just war, and we know that, God willing, this is a war we will win.

George Bush

There come times when we must fight for peace, I pray we will be on God's side.

Billy Graham

We pray that God brings us peace very soon, that he shows those responsible that they should abandon immediately this war which is so unworthy of humanity.

Pope John Paul[9]

God is not only very busy, he has to be all things to all men (and women). To some he is the avenging God, and to others the kindly, forgiving God. But whatever form God is required to take, belief in any absolute truths always produce the same results, as Jill Tweedie described.

They stopped me in the street and told me that Jesus loved me. There were four of them, two lads, two lasses, nice smiles, nice clean hair, nice clean eyes bright with concern for the state of my soul, and the sight of them, the look of them, filled me with such unexpected dismay that it was all I could do not to hit them.

When they trailed off, singing reproachfully, I went on feeling dismal. True, religion was never my favourite thing but it's part and parcel of life, as an outsider you soon learn to steer around it, switch off the God-spots on radio and telly and otherwise stay clear. So why should four perfectly harmless young people suddenly pitch me into such gloom. What's new?

What's new, at least in my lifetime, is the way religion has grown thin in the middle and disastrously over-crowded at each end. There are the doves, a mawkishly lovey-dovey lot, and there are the hawks, never more dangerously hawkish, while in between, where once could be found a decent intelligence, some aesthetic delights, some dignity, some ancient wisdom, a certain stoic disci-pline, there is a vacuum. In other words, from my point of view, very little left to admire but a lot more to fear and, as the millennium approaches, the imbalance seems all set to get worse.

The 1990s have been designated The Decade of Evan-gelism . . . [The effects of the Evangelical Movement] however well-meant are dire. It can take hold of perfectly normal, idiosyncratic individuals with their normal share of distinguishing features, warts and all, and melt them down in the twang of an evangelical minister's guitar into one great featureless blob that smiles all the time, sings soppy songs, and keeps up a constant bleat about loving,

caring, sharing and the wonder of Jesus's (and I quote)
'flipping marvellous brilliant good news'. To attend a
church service run by such folk is to know what it's like
to be dunked fully clothed in a vat of lukewarm treacle.
Indiscriminate 'love' of the kind they practise makes your
ordinary promiscuous physical bonking seem positively
uplifting by comparison – at least it's real, at least it's
natural and no one expects you to smile all the time.

The hawks, on the other hand, will have no truck with
love at all, spiritual or physical. They are fierce, predatory,
and interested only in laying down their own version of
spiritual laws which they force as many people as they can
to obey out of shame but, most satisfactorily, out of fear.
Anyone who does not believe as they do is seen as part of
an evil conspiracy against their God, deserving only of
contempt, the utmost intolerance and every sort of punishment up to and including death.

Hawks and doves, however, have two things in
common. In the name of religion both offer status, power
and respectability to men who in other walks of life might
well be dismissed as mildly doo-lally, or, in the hawks'
case, raving mad, very bad and dangerous to know. And
both share entirely closed minds . . .

Doubt is anathema to (the closed mind), yet doubt is
the only truly human condition, our burden but also our
glory, and to reject doubt's saving grace turns us into so
many robots with floppy disks where our brains should
be.

Doubt is the light in the tunnel, a kind of spiritual
Rentokil guaranteed to keep at bay the worst depredations
wrought by religion which, left untreated, will in one way
or the other bring the house down. Watch the hawks now
on the rampage from Northern Ireland via the Gulf to the
furthest reaches of the Himalayas – any other group under
any other banner but religion who could wreak such
havoc, stir up such tragic and violent hostility between
man, woman and child would long ago have been seen
for what it is, a plague upon humankind whose festering

roots lie deep in the holy books. And what are the doves doing in this wreckage? Roaming the streets with silly grins on their faces telling people that Jesus loves them.

But yesterday I heard one of them declare they'd have the whole country saved for Jesus by the year 2000 and, just for a moment, I glimpsed the cold gleam of a hawk in that dove's eye.[10]

'Faith,' wrote John Lahr, 'is nice but doubt will get you an education.'[11] It is hard to get such an education. In totalitarian countries, doubt the absolute truths of the state and you will be imprisoned, tortured, killed. In those countries which like to call themselves democratic we may doubt what politicians tell us, but religious doubt is much harder to express. In the USA God and America are absolute truths which must not be questioned. In Britain the BBC gives airtime to religious believers but not to agnostics, humanists and people who simply think that religion is irrelevant. If such doubters do make their views known, the religious police move in to stop them, as the columnist Mat Coward found.

More people die in this country from listening to *Thought for the Day* than from smoking – this is a scientific fact. (For the scientists among you, allow me to explain my method: I smoke a cigarette, then take my blood pressure. It is unchanged. I listen to platitude for the day, and take my blood pressure again. It has gone crazy.)

Agnosticism is the traditional religion of the British, yet nowhere is it recognized. Serious newspapers run endless messages from Anglican bishops about love, and profitable papers run endless front-page stories about Anglican bishops and other people's bottoms. When was the last time the *Mirror*'s headline read: 'Agnostic Nabbed In Nooky Nest: Frilly Knickers Were Gift For Wife Says Unbeliever'? . . .

Every time I write about religious tyranny – which, to be honest, is more often than is good for my blood pressure – I get dozens of sweet letters from devout Christians, full of charity and forgiveness for which such people are noted. 'Soon you will die,' they say, 'and burn in hell forever, and I'll be glad.'

One old darling wrote to me every Saturday for six months, predicting: 'Next Tuesday your children will perish. Vengeance is mine sayeth the Lord!' One day, in his excitement, he forgot to decapitate his headed notepaper. I replied thus: 'Eldest son died Tues, precisely as predicted. One down, three to go. Amazing prophecy! What do you fancy for the Derby?' As it happens, I've never owned a child, but Mr Goodwill-to-All-Men wasn't to know that, and his correspondence ceased.[12]

Mat Coward's correspondents demonstrate their belief in a Just World where anyone who criticizes them and their beliefs is punished by a vengeful God. The reality is that the world – everything that exists – is neither just nor unjust but simply is. 'Just' and 'unjust' are ideas which we impose on the world.

However, it is easy to argue that we live in a distinctly unjust world where the wicked are rewarded and the good never get what they deserve. Indeed, believing in a Just World is a way of hiding from the real terrors, cruelties and injustices of this world.

Jill Tweedie, Alan Brien and I were discussing this one day. Jill said:

'One of the things that I have learned is almost useless to try and pass on. It is almost impossible to put chapter and verse to it because it consists of endless examples and statistics to back it up and so on, which one can do painfully and you could put it all down. What it amounts to is that the corrupt, the liars and the wicked in the simplest, childhood sense, run the world. There is no question in my mind that that is so, and it is certainly not what I was led to believe or did believe when I was a child.'

Alan agreed. He said, 'It is because most people are good that the wicked thrive. If you made an image like a computer print-out of the world, like they do with the economy, and then you showed it to a man from Mars, he would say, "Of course, the wicked have to win." This is because they have got everything on their side, particularly the fact that they are not seen as the wicked, they are seen as the upper classes, the best people, the beautiful people. They are seen as all these things, and on top of that they are exciting.'

Seeing the rich and powerful as being larger than life and more significant than those who are not rich and powerful is one of the lies we tell ourselves in the hope that we, somehow, some day, will share in this excitement. We create heroes in the same hope. Instead of asking ourselves, 'How can I develop myself and give my life more significance?' (something not easy to do considering the education we have had), we create fantasies about those people we see as being exciting and significant, and in doing so, we diminish ourselves. Moreover, since very few of those people regarded as exciting and significant are old, and those that are old present themselves as for ever young, we fear time passing, for with it go our hopes that one day our dreams will come true.

Our dreams that one day our lives will be changed by our being taken into the magic circle of the exciting and significant people are built upon a much older and deeper belief.

It takes great honesty to admit to this belief. Alec Jenner, Emeritus Professor of Psychiatry at Sheffield University, told me, 'Right from the beginning I wanted to be God and have everyone obey me and love me. Everybody wants to be God. All these Gods! It's not surprising there's so much trouble in the world.'

He went on, 'When I was twelve I decided that I was going to be the world's greatest scientist. But I thought I wouldn't start just then. I'd enjoy myself first.'

Although Alec didn't become God, he became many other things, including a bee-keeper. He said, 'I enjoy status and power, but they're not important. It's important to me that I don't invest myself in things. It's important to me that I enjoy myself. I enjoy my bees more than I enjoy status and power.'

Alec is right about us all wanting to be God. When we discover that we can't be God most of us settle for justice. (Though the hankering after being God never entirely disappears.)

A notion of justice seems to be one of our basic forms of

thought, though the content of this form varies among individuals and societies. Such a form of thought is necessary to us because we have to live in groups, and because our life story, to be bearable, must promise a balance and a closure. However, it is foolish in the extreme to believe that there is a system of justice existing in some absolute reality outside our concepts of justice, for then we help perpetuate the injustices of this world, and we increase our sense of being helpless and insignificant. Belief in the absolute justice of God or 'the market' has enabled many people to refrain from helping the poor because the poor are deemed to be wicked, or lazy, or necessary so that the non-poor can practise the virtue of charity. Absolute Justice leaves little room for luck or mercy.

Once we see that justice and authority are not absolutes imposed on us from on high, but are simply meanings which other people create and want to impose on us, we realize that we are free to question everything that people who claim to be in authority say.

Now we can see that we don't have to accept all those pronouncements about age. There is no absolute law which says that you have to have made it by thirty, or are finished at forty, or are worthless and useless from sixty until death.

You are free to be yourself and to express yourself and the age you are in whatever way you want. You are free to make yourself miserable because you are getting older. You are also free to enjoy whatever age you are. You don't have to be anything except yourself.

2 LIVING IN FAMILIES

The answers keep changing. The questions remain the same.

These questions concern how we can organize our family life so that our two continual but contradictory needs are met. Always each of us wants to be an individual, and, simultaneously, we want to be a member of our family group. We cannot solve this problem by concentrating on one need to the exclusion of the other.

If we decide to abandon all claims to be an independent

individual and instead cleave totally to our family, we lose that sense of being a person and become nothing but an appendage to another person. I have seen such people, adult children who have never separated themselves from their mother whose desire for such a symbiosis is as great as the child's. The adult children are such sad, empty people, always fearfully awaiting their mother's death.

If we decide to separate ourselves totally from our family group to be an individual with no group ties, we condemn ourselves to a life of loneliness. We also become very peculiar, if not crazy, people. The important function of other people in our lives is that they are always ready to tell us when they think that we are not sufficiently accurate in our constructions of reality. They are not always correct in this, and often their criticisms have motives other than the desire to help us, but their constant presence helps us to work at our most important task, a construction of meaning which approximates reality as closely as possible.

Thus the question for each family is how to organize family life so that each member can create the optimum balance between being an individual and being a member of the family group.

The answers to this question change because economic circumstances change. Families which work together as well as live together, as in peasant cultures, create answers very different from those whose economy is based on the father going out to work.

The answers change with changing social circumstances. Families with little opportunity for education and social advancement find answers which are very different from those of families who have access to a vast array of educational and social advantages.

Of course a great many families are not in the business of asking this question. These families are organized in a hierarchy where only those at the top have the power and right to be an individual. Those lower down the hierarchy, usually the women and always the children, have to adapt their individuality to the demands of those further up the hierarchy, and so they suffer.

All members of the family suffer when the family's strategy for living is determined, not by themselves, but by some religious or political power. Such powers present their strategies as absolute truths. They are not concerned with creating the optimum balance between the individual and the group because such a balance helps to create independent, questioning individuals. These powers want to create people who believe that to be good they must always subsume their needs to the needs of the group. In such families the parental figures are powerful and the children suffer, but are forbidden to complain about their suffering. Consider the Betsimisaraka tribe.

It's no joke annoying the ancestors in Ambodirafia, a village of 124 houses on the east coast of the Indian Ocean island of Madagascar. The Betsimisaraka tribe who populate that region still adhere to animist traditions, most of which centre on the omnipotence of the dead.

Every 12 years Tangalamena, who acts as the official go-between for the living and the dead, presides over a ceremony in which bulls are sacrificed to pacify the ancestors. The bones of the dead are removed from their tomb, reclothed in fresh shrouds, and offered sweets and other luxuries. People come from miles around to pay their respects.

If the ceremony goes wrong, they can make your life seriously unpleasant. They might strike you down with illness or refuse to protect you from witches. The worst thing they can do is blight your staple crop, rice.

Ambodirafia is dependent on rice. People often eat nothing else. They are largely self-sufficient in food; they have to be, as they are virtually cut off from the rest of the world. To reach the village one walks for more than an hour along a muddy tunnel of palm and banana trees.

The ancestors have a lot to answer for. In the process of trying to please them by adhering to traditional rice-growing methods, the villagers are destroying their lifeblood and threatening one of the world's most precious natural treasures.

Ambodirafia lies on the edge of Betampona, a lowland rainforest with more than 200 tree species and teeming with wildlife including the unique Malagasy primate, the lemur. In eco-jargon, its biodiversity is among the richest on the globe.

One tenth of the surface of Madagascar used to be covered by tropical rainforest but today Betampona is among the last reserves left. The island, which hosts hundreds of unique species of plants and animals, is being stripped of its forest at the rate of 200,000 hectares (750 square miles) a year, largely to make way for rice. Much of the island is already barren and the United Nations estimates that at current rates it may lose all its rainforest within 30 years.

But the inhabitants of Ambodirafia need more land to feed their malnourished children. And they need to carry on practising their traditional farming, called *tavy*, which involves slashing down trees and burning the land. Or the ancestors will be annoyed.

Every year during December and January a thick cloud of smoke hangs over the hillside as local farmers burn their fields in preparation for the sowing of rice, a ritual bound up closely with their worship of the dead.

The results are plain to see. Betampona stands on top of the surrounding hills, neatly defined like a flat-top haircut. Below it the fields are sparsely vegetated with traveller's palms and coffee bushes, resembling a stubbly face. The further down towards the sea the more bald and barren the land becomes.

Erosion of the island's deforested, terracotta-coloured soil is thought to be occurring at a faster rate in Madagascar than anywhere else in Africa. Around Ambodirafia there are red gashes in the hillsides like ugly shaving wounds where chunks of the land have simply slid down into the river.[13]

In ancestor worship, as in all religions, no one is allowed to grow up. Believers remain for ever children dependent on their parent figures, some imaginary, some as superior people who represent the imaginary parent figures. No optimum balance between being an individual and being a member of the family group can ever be reached.

The Christian Church condemns ancestor worship as heathen and wicked, but then instructs the faithful to honour and obey their parents. Many families in Western societies live as the Betsimisaraka do, always in fear that they will upset their ancestors. In some families the worrisome ancestors are well and truly dead, and in others the ancestors always come to Sunday lunch, but the children feel that they must always defer to and obey their ancestors. Many of these children, even when they are approaching old age, still work hard at keeping their house and garden immaculately tidy, not because they enjoy doing it, but because they fear their parents' wrath. They work, not like adults attending to a job, but like children scurrying around, wanting praise for their industry and feeling aggrieved when it does not come. If their parents have taught them that the only people who are allowed to call the doctor are the deserving good who are very, very ill, they go through life thinking, 'I'd rather die than call the doctor,' and, sooner or later, they do just that.

In some families the parents claim that it is their right as parents never to allow their children to be independent adults. One of the readers of *Chat* magazine wrote to me about this.

In one issue of *Chat* I had answered a letter from a reader who had asked my advice about how to make her two-and-a-half-year-old son be obedient. I replied by saying that it is easy to make children be obedient. All you have to do is to terrify them into submission. However, fear drives out love. Your child will cease to love you, and what the child as an adult feels towards such parents is not love but guilt.

Signing herself Mrs M. B., my reader wrote,

> I just couldn't help but write when I read your reply to the Lady whose 2½-year-old was rebelling against her.
>
> I've been looking for an answer like you gave to the Mother all my life (I'm 50 years old).
>
> I had a strict upbringing and had to obey my parents

all the time, never having my own opinions, even to this day. If I don't agree with them I'm always wrong. They didn't often take the time to listen, it was always little girls should be seen and not heard, and I've never fought back in any way, in fact I feel it has spoiled my marriage with the way I've always been with Mum and Dad, in always considering them first before anybody else in my life. I would have felt guilty not doing this. I've always tried to be the good, obedient girl they wanted me to be.

I hope I have tried to be a Mum like you spoke of and that my Son can talk openly with me, but I know my upbringing is bound to have rubbed off on him in some way, and I have tried to have a more modern approach and thinking about what he should and should not do – and of course, as far as Mum and Dad are concerned I'm wrong there.

I have been wondering all my life what the problem was and now you have told me in your reply to this Lady, that I have a fear of my parents instead of loving them.

I'm glad I read your reply, because now I feel that I'm not always wrong with what I do or say, and it has helped me greatly. Thank you.[14]

Many adults feel guilty because they don't love their parents. Once they realize that no one can love to order – love is always spontaneous – and that they are frightened of their parents, they can give up telling themselves that they feel guilty. If, in your childhood, you became an expert in being good, you also became an expert in feeling guilty. Most of your decisions are formed in the context of 'If I do/don't do that I'll feel guilty', and 'Because I have not done enough/well enough I feel guilty', so thinking and talking about guilt becomes a habit. You often say you feel guilty when what you are feeling is discomfort or unacknowledged irritation.

Once you realize that you are frightened of your parents you can see that you are reacting to them as if you were still a small child. But you're grown-up now. What is there to be frightened of? Or don't you want to give up your belief that your parents are larger than life, heroic figures who will always be there to give you their protection in return for your obedience? In that case you will fear their growing old and dying even more than your own.

Some parents, not wishing to lose the power which their children have given them (people are powerful only if their subjects see them as being powerful), get very disgruntled when their children no longer obey them and hang upon their every word. Other parents, having gained wisdom themselves, are glad when the barrier of the child's fear disappears. Now reconciliation and friendship are possible.

If we do not free ourselves from our parents, if we do not come to see our parents as human-sized people instead of giants who tower over us, we not only damage ourselves, we can also damage our own children because we see in our children characteristics which belong to our parents, and we respond to these characteristics in ways which we dare not use in response to our parents. Children of demanding parents can interpret their children's legitimate demands as being unreasonable, and then punish their children in ways which they dare not use against their parents. Freeing yourself from your parents can make you realize that just because your daughter looks like your mother doesn't mean that she is your mother with all of your mother's irritating habits and beliefs.

While we are still tied to our parents we cannot make an optimum balance between being an individual and being a member of a family group because we for ever oscillate between feeling resentful because we see our family as smothering us and fearing being expelled from the family group because we fear that we cannot manage on our own.

Mrs M. B. was fifty when she was at last able to make an optimum balance between being an individual and being a member of the family group. Some people start this process much earlier, in their teens and twenties, but progress can be slow because in years of teenage rebellion we might know what we are struggling against but not what we are struggling towards. We know that we want to be an individual, but we don't see how we can reconcile this with our need to be part of a group. Often we align ourselves with a group which we do not realize is not markedly different from our family.

Lou Miele, a devoted family man, surprised me when he said that he had entered a monastery when he was twenty. I knew that his grandparents had been Italian immigrants to America, but now at forty-seven he showed no interest in religion. He explained:

> I already knew a world of books when I was in my teens. It promised what only the imagination can know. I wanted a venue which would allow me into the world of imagination. My happiest times were in a library.
>
> No one was religious in my family except my grandmother who had no influence. I was expected to become a professional, but to stay within the world my family defined. I wanted to escape it, but I saw no avenues. You could be educated, but that meant strictly the professions. There were no intellectuals. Intellectuals were always the enemy and always to be feared. My family didn't know what to make of them. I began to develop tastes along those lines and I saw nothing in my world that supported that. I didn't know what I could become without being trapped. In the high school I went to we were taught by Benedictine monks. They were the only people I knew who were free of the world I wanted to escape. It looked like a magic place. It was an escape which my family could not reject. I could beat them at their own game. It was a rebellion centred thing. I had to escape the family, and then I had to escape the monastery.

At twenty-three he left the monastery because it did not offer the balance of being an individual and being a member of a family group, something which he later found with his wife and son. When I asked him how he now saw death he said, 'There's no after. Life ends. I don't particularly relish the idea but I don't think it bothers me. It did bother me years ago, when I was in my twenties and I had lost that one compensation that religion offers.'

Freeing ourselves from our parents and creating the optimum balance between being an individual and being a family member requires us to come to an understanding of how the family has functioned, and how the meanings which the family has created become embedded in our own meaning structure.

It is not just that we acquire in childhood many of the attitudes, prejudices and beliefs held by older members, but we acquire, through our interpretations of what our family members say and do, our own interpretation of who we are, especially of just how we are good and how we fail to be good. Our interpretation of who we are can itself be interpreted in two ways, 'I am good' and 'I am bad'. For instance, you might think of yourself as being a sensitive person. Your 'good' interpretation of this could be 'I am very aware of other people, and of art and beauty.' Your 'bad' interpretation could be 'I am easily hurt.'

Such alternative interpretations emerged in a long discussion I had with my friend and agent Imogen Parker who, when she was coming up to thirty, had urged me to write this book.

In all the years I had known Imogen I had always seen her as immensely talented, confident and competent. I knew she had had some difficult times – the tragic death of her father, the uncertainties of the publishing industry, a couple of excessively difficult men – but I had not seen that at times she went through what she called 'periods of huge self-doubt'.

When, as children, we become convinced that we are bad and unacceptable, we have to devise ways of defending ourselves from other people, for if they see how bad and unacceptable we are, they will hurt and reject us. Imogen's defence had been to form friendships with people belonging to different groups, and to each friend she would reveal a different aspect of herself.

She said, 'I just wanted little bits of myself to be known rather than the whole of myself whatever that might be. It's easier to show little bits of yourself and never actually deal with people getting close to you who might then threaten you or make you feel vulnerable.'

What she did not want people to see were her 'periods of huge self-doubt'. Then, 'I feel that I'm just nothing, absolutely nothing, that I only exist as a kind of conduit.'

'A conduit for other people's work?' I asked.

'For other people's everything. I think that I became an agent has something to do with the fact that I'm quite used to negotiating within my family. I'm very used to calming people down and translating what they want to say to somebody else. I can be good at that. When I get depressed I think I don't exist at all. I'm just there in order to make things better for the people around me. Everyone around me, even my family, thinks that I'm terribly strong. If I tell them I'm not really strong they say, "Don't be silly. Of course you are."'

Imogen went on, 'It also makes me feel that I'm completely fraudulent somehow. I appear to be something that I'm not. If I'm in a low period I can feel that my whole life's a fraud.'

I replied, 'Once you've learned how to be depressed it's easy to do it again. It's seductive. You can slip into depression like into old clothes.'

'Yes. You can also turn anything round, even things that you're good at you can make into things that you're bad at.'

I asked her what for her was the opposite of being a conduit.

'I suppose being a separate person that people look after, being somebody that has a separate identity.'

'What do you see as creating your separate identity?'

'I do feel I have a separate identity. I suppose I've always been acknowledged as such, but I don't think I've been tended to or made allowances for. That obviously goes back to family. When I'm feeling low I feel as though I don't really matter unless I'm doing something for someone, and that almost counts me out. I am somebody who is essentially a very independent person but who, in a bad state, thinks of herself as being a conduit because that means that I actually depend on others for my own sustenance.'

'You're just a useful tool.'

'Yes. I find it hard to be coherent about that because that's something that has very much changed in my life since my father died. When he died I was extremely unhappy. That did shock my family and quite a lot of my friends. That made me feel even worse. However, allowing people to show that they wanted to support me made me more balanced about myself. It also made my life simpler because I was no longer a go-between for my father and other family members.'

'That was where you learned how to be a conduit.'

'Absolutely.'

Thus Imogen saw herself as a negotiator. Her 'bad' interpretion of this was that she was so totally absorbed into the family group as to become nothing but a conduit which put one family member in touch with another. Her 'good' interpretation of herself as a negotiator was that she had a special talent which she could use professionally to great effect. (This was a realistic interpretation, for Imogen was regarded in the publishing world as one of the best literary agents in Britain.)

However, her family had pushed her to the extreme of being a completely independent, self-sufficient individual. She knew that she needed a better balance than that between being an individual and a member of the family group. She needed to be an individual to whom the family showed concern and care. However, she could not reach this balance until she was able to trust people enough to show her need. Her father's death enabled her to do this.

I asked Imogen how she felt about rushing up to forty.

She said, 'I don't really think about being forty. I've never really thought I've got a biological clock, although I would like children. I suppose I don't want children so much that I'm desperate about it. I'm thirty-four. I don't think about forty as "Oh my God, that's the end of everything." I see my life more as a continuum than I used to. Certainly when I was coming up to thirty I was scared about it. It was such a relief to actually become thirty and discover that life was actually the same. I don't think I'll have that problem when I'm thirty-nine.'

I asked, 'Do you feel more of an individual now than you did before you were thirty?'

'Yes. Absolutely. Far more confident. The major thing I've learnt is something that I completely despised when I was in my twenties. This was the value of experience that people talk about. Unless you have experience, you can't see the value of it. It might be a middle-aged thing to say, but in every kind of thing – driving, job, relationships – experience counts for so much. It gives you confidence, and if you feel more confident you do feel more independent.'

Early in our conversation Imogen spoke of how, as a student at Oxford, she had been very good at scoring points in arguments.

Now she said, 'I think that's a waste of time. What is important to me is to know what my limits are. That knowledge is very liberating. I don't mean limits in terms of mortality, I mean what I can put up with and what I can't. I feel I know where I stand on lots of things, and what's worthwhile making a fuss about and what's not.'

Learning what is worth making a fuss about and what is not is a task with which children get very little help from adults. Generally children are told that whatever fuss they make it is a fuss over nothing. Being allowed to make a fuss, especially when it is a something which matters to you, is an important part of being an individual in a group. Yet so often children have been prevented from speaking out on their own behalf.

I have a small flat in Coram Street, London, a few blocks from the delightful Coram Gardens where adults can go only if accompanied by a child. Of these surroundings Lloyd de Mause wrote, 'Even though Thomas Coram opened his Found-ling Hospital in 1741 because he couldn't bear to see the dying babies lying in the gutters and rotting on the dung-heaps of London, by the 1890s dead babies were still a common sight in London streets.'[15]

Between Coram Gardens and Coram Street is Brunswick Square, a monstrosity of 1960s cement, where I shop in the supermarket. Most evenings three or four teenagers are hanging around the square. They should be hanging around school yards and discos, and complaining that their parents expect them to tidy their rooms. Instead they are trying to cadge money from the shoppers as they leave the supermarket. The teenagers are homeless, hungry and ill. They have little more economic and political power than the babies in the eighteenth-century dung-heaps.

The teenagers in Brunswick Square have little understanding

of the functioning of political power, although they are its victims. Yet they see very clearly what is happening to them and their fellows. What makes childhood a nightmare is that children, especially small children, see directly, clearly and immediately what happens around them, but they lack a framework of meaning by which they can explain to themselves what they see.

Jill Tweedie described this to me. She said:

'I believe that children always know what is going on emotionally. Every pain, every pleasure in everyone in their own environment they understand and know. The only thing they don't know is the reason. They do not know why this is happening. As a child I used to see this as colours around a person. I used to see my mother and sometimes the colours around her were grey shot with red, and sometimes they were pink and sometimes pale blue. She seemed to carry these things round. It used to change, and I used to see it change. I used to see two people collide and the two capsules around go crash, but I didn't know why. Children don't know why and therefore they cannot give any value to it. They don't know whether it means everything or nothing. It's a real horror to be a child, especially to be around unhappy people. Especially if you ask why and you are told that there is nothing happening. To me childhood life means deciding that either you trusted adults or you trusted yourself. I decided not to trust adults. This is why I didn't want to grow up. Some children decide to trust adults, but I didn't.'

Those children who decide that the safest way to live is to identify with the adults, to be good in the way that the adults want them to be good, become old while young in the way that Ron Janoff described. This is the kind of trust which is along the lines of 'if you can't beat them, join them'.

There is another kind of trust which children can develop, and that is the trust that grows when, as a baby, you know that your parents see you as the person that you are, they take your point of view seriously, they try to meet your needs as well as the situation will allow, and, when they cannot meet your needs, they try to explain to you why, and help you deal with your disappointment.

Over the years I have observed parents who regard their

children's needs as demands which should be ignored or punished, and parents who regard their children's needs as legitimate requests which should be acknowledged and, where possible, met. The actual time taken in suppressing a child's needs or in meeting them barely differs. However, in the long run, the child whose needs are met makes fewer demands than the child whose needs are suppressed or punished.

Parents, even well-meaning, loving parents, often ignore or brush aside their child's needs because the parents are busy. Yet, actually, such parents save little time.

I have seen this in the way my friend Jo Pearce handles her son Miles. I met Miles, now twenty-one months, the day after he was born when Jo and her husband Jeremy Halstead brought him home from hospital. I have watched Miles and his mother as she fed, changed and bathed him. At first Jo seemed to me to proceed at an extraordinarily slow pace. She and Miles would stop what they were doing to talk to one another, or she would wait while he looked around, or burped. An efficient mother in a hurry could have fed, changed or bathed Miles in a third of the time. Then I realized that an efficient mother in a hurry might have the task completed, but a hurried baby will not settle. By the time an efficient mother has got her baby quiet and settled, Miles and Jo have arrived peacefully at the end of their journey and had a nice time along the way.

Jo's patience with Miles will enable him as he gets older to be patient with other people. I have seen this with Ed Janoff, the thirteen-year-old son of Ron Janoff and Diana Leidel. I first met Ed when he was four, and then and subsequently I saw how patient his parents were with him. When Ed was twelve his sister Elizabeth was born. I have never seen a boy Ed's age be so patient with a baby. Instead of living totally within his own selfish world, as so many young teenagers do, he is aware of her perceptions and needs, and he responds lovingly to them. The only impatience he feels is towards adults who keep asking him what it is like to have a baby sister.

However, bringing up children in this way requires parents to have more strengths of character than simply patience. Children whose parents take the children's point of view seriously become used to presenting their point of view with all the unquestioned certainty of the sun rising, and they develop excellent skills in argument. Since their parents have not presented themselves as omnipotent, omniscient gods, their children see them as fallible human beings, and are greatly amused and critical.

I have seen all this happen in the Ives family. I have known Marc, now twenty-three, since he was five, and Naomi, now fifteen, since she was born. Their parents, Helen and Galen, have always treated Marc and Naomi with a patience, understanding and love which is rare among parents. As a result they have children who continuously discuss and, where necessary, argue, who make very funny jokes (I think they're funny) at their parents' expense, and who are the best of friends with one another and their parents.

Whenever I am with Marc and Naomi I am struck with how much they are at ease with people older than and different from themselves. They have never had to develop that defensiveness which children need when they live in a world of adults who notice them only to criticize them. Because Naomi and Marc have never had to develop that defensiveness they treat other people as real persons, not objects. They always talk to me as the person I am, not as an object labelled 'one of my parents' old friends'.

My friends Jo and Jeremy, Ron and Diana, Helen and Galen, all had the opportunity to ponder the questions of family life and to find some satisfactory answers before they had their children. Most of us don't, and later in life, when we wish we had done things differently, we wonder if it is possible to put things right. We can't go back and change the past, but we can offer our adult children the opportunity to renegotiate the balance between being an individual and a member of the family group.

When I asked Alan Brien what he would say to his children he said, 'I would say, and to some extent I have said, forget about me. I am sorry that because of the accident of biology and psychology, parents seem to have this terrible effect on their children. It bears no relation to any reality, I am not this tremendously powerful, noble, interesting, famous, achieving, whatever you think of this person. I am not. I am just like anybody else. I have achieved some things, and I have done some things, but you should be able to know what they are and to see how they compare to the fathers of your friends and you will find it more or less the same thing.

'So forget about that and don't think are you going to please me. Am I going to be impressed by what you do? You are not going to be like me and, although I may appear to be saying that, take no notice because I should know better and you should know better. You must live your own way of life and when you are interested in your husband or wife or lover or family or job, that comes first. It will distress me greatly if I think that you are saying, "Well, I would like to fly around the world with you, I would like to do this but it is Dad's birthday and I have to be with him." I have got my own friends, I have got my beautiful wife, I have got a job and the things I am interested in. To know that you are happy and doing what you want to do is enough for me, and you don't have to come to see me ever. You can go off and spend the rest of your life doing it, and I shall be pleased because I am not going to be deceived by being twisted into this thing. I release you from the spell, you can go and be like everyone else. I think I have done that now. My daughters now see that it doesn't matter what I think about them, they haven't had to do something in life to please me.'

Only when we release ourselves from our parents' spell can we establish our optimum balance between being an individual and being a member of our family group, and with that abandon the hate that we, as the young, have for the old. Only when we, as parents, let our children be themselves can we establish an optimum balance which is based on friendship, and with that abandon the hate which we, as the old, have for the young.

Then we no longer fear growing old.

3 BEING A PERSON

All of you is worth something if you will only own it.

Whenever I give a talk about how we experience our sense of existence and see the threat of the annihilation of our sense of existence, several people in the audience will say, 'I don't know whether I'm an extravert or an introvert. Can you be a bit of both?'

I try to explain that I am not talking about *types* of people, but about the *reasons* why we do what we do. The people for whom I use the shorthand term 'extravert' always have reasons to do with maintaining their relationships with other people and warding off rejection and isolation. The people for whom I use the shorthand term 'introvert' always have reasons to do with giving them some sort of achievement and warding off losing control and falling into chaos.

Every time I have this discussion I think, 'How can you not know why you do what you do?' But of course I know the answer to that.

When, as children, we have been lied to, and told that our own truth is no truth at all, we get very confused about just what our truth is.

Consequently, some extraverts very readily stop trying to pay attention to their internal reality of thoughts and feelings, and instead pay attention only to what they do in their external reality. They will say to me, 'I enjoy being with people and I enjoy being on my own. Doesn't that mean I'm an extravert and an introvert?', and not be aware that, just as they spend time with people in order to foster their relationships, they have time on their own in order to foster their relationships with their books, or their rose trees, or their cuddly toys, or all of the objects which they have turned into human friends.

Some introverts pay close attention to their internal reality, but only in terms of what they *ought* to be thinking and feeling, not what they *are* thinking and feeling. If they believe that they ought to be a happy wife and mother thinking only of others, or a good team man concerned only with the success of the team, they can be unaware that the reason they want to be a good wife and mother or a good team man is because then they will have that sense of achievement which confirms their sense of existence.

Knowing your reasons for doing what you do helps to give you a sense of being grounded in reality, being part of everything that is, belonging in the world and in yourself which allows you to abandon absolute truths, discover uncertain wisdom, and, far from being frightened of such uncertainty, see it as opportunity and hope.

For such people the reasons they do what they do have a self-evident quality. When Lou Miele was telling me about his years in a monastery, he said, 'When I went into it I wasn't thinking I was escaping, but I know now that that was what I was doing. I saw it as a chance for self-fulfilment and self discovery.'

'Why,' I asked, 'is self-fulfilment important?'

'That seems like one of those self-evident building blocks that you can never explain in any other terms. It's one of those givens. It's like saying, "Why did you feel hungry?"'

Lou found my way of describing introverts as people whose every decision and action was based on wanting a sense of achievement, organization and control as interesting but obvious. Equally obvious was my observation that what introverts fear most is the loss of control and falling into chaos.

Many people, unaware of the reasons which underlie their every action, are greatly shocked when they encounter those conditions which pose, but which they do not recognize as posing, the greatest threat to their sense of existence. One of my readers told me how comforted she was to discover that what she felt when she was under great stress was the fear of herself crumbling. She wrote:

'The fear is, as you say, of finding that what I hold on to disintegrates in my hands, and what I stand on is not solid ground. I fear losing hold, losing my footing, and nothing will stop my fall. I fear I will fall to pieces, and nothing can keep me together.'[16]

Only a poet can convey the quality of the fear experienced. Andrew Motion, feeling secure in himself and his world, was walking, in daylight, down a familiar street when

> a man with no face lurched out from behind a tree
> and tried to kill me.

He fought back and the man with the knife ran away. I have met Andrew Motion only once, but from what I know of him and his work I would guess he is an introvert. Introverts are usually very calm in a crisis. Later, when everything has quietened down, the emotions which they had so carefully isolated in the crisis burst forth. When night came,

> the knife became
> an adder's tongue

and what he held on to disintegrated in his hands.

> But you were asleep and made no sound
> when I left your side without a word
>
> and slipped downstairs to my room underground
> a grown man like a frightened child:
>
> *The fire is out at the heart of the world;*
> *all tame creatures have grown up wild.*
>
> *The lives I trusted, even my own,*
> *collapse, break off, or don't belong.*
>
> I leant my head on the window pane
> and the sharp-edged garden, lit with rain,
>
> shimmered a million knives; the wind
> caressed them with its painful hand.
>
> *The fire is out at the heart of the world,*
> *all tame creatures have grown up wild –*
>
> *All except you, your life like a cloud*
> *I am lost in now and will never be found.*[17]

When we fail to understand what such an experience is we can be all but destroyed by it. When we do understand it our lives can be transformed.

When I first met Heather some ten years ago the solidity of her ice-cold depression seemed to be her only defence against the disintegration of herself. All that she had strived for, all that she believed in, had been thrown into doubt. She planned her suicide – off the cliff at Beachy Head – but she was a devoted Christian, and God's love held her back.

We talked over many months, and she began to glimpse two pieces of uncertain wisdom, namely that what she called God's love was actually the unacknowledged love she had for herself, and that the Christian vision of a Just World was an illusion. (Heather might have given up her belief in a Just World, but she will never give up her belief in an unjust society!) However, such wisdom could not come into its own until she had dealt with her philandering husband.

Not long after she found herself a deserted wife and a single parent – not much of an identity on which to build a new life. With a need to achieve and with much perseverance and risk-taking (trying to escape from the poverty trap in Britain requires more courage than that of a Stalag escapee), Heather got work as an untrained social worker and immediately had to assume the duties of a trained social worker. This work allowed her to adopt a new identity. She now had a role in society which enabled her to act effectively.

However, she was not out of danger. Her job was temporary, and government money for social workers was scarce.

Heather rang me one evening to say that in six weeks' time she would be facing the dole again. She said, 'When I got the dismissal notice I felt that when the job disappeared I would disappear. I felt that I was no more than my job.' Only her job gave her value. No job, no value. No right to exist. She felt terrified, the terror of the imminent annihilation of herself.

She had set out for Beachy Head. She told me, 'I was very frightened. I was facing my annihilation. I didn't know what would happen. I would disappear or I would come out whole. As I drove there I wanted someone to stop me. But when I got there I walked and thought. Then I stood on Beachy Head and felt my past connect with my present. It gave me a sense of wholeness. It was a religious experience of the very broadest sort. Now I know that, no matter what happens, I go on existing. I have value in myself. The job isn't important.'

In her bad old days Heather was totally convinced that there was a Law of the Universe which said that she would never get a job. Now she thought perhaps something would turn up. And it did. Another job.

One evening when my television was on but I was out of the room I heard someone say, 'If I am in the minds of others then I exist.' I thought, 'There speaks an extravert.' And then, 'What a terrible way to live, always in fear of being forgotten. Old age would have special terrors, as those who knew you die before you do.'

Introverts, under stress and losing confidence in themselves, find their external reality becoming increasingly unreal. For extraverts it is their internal reality which becomes unreal. My friend Stephanie – zoologist, newspaper columnist and critic, yoga teacher, musician – in September 1991 described this sense of unreality in a letter to me.

That sense of unreality I often have, sometimes very badly indeed; the feeling that I am utterly insubstantial, invisible or perhaps created of some fine, gossamer-like stuff that scarcely picks up the light in bright sunshine. When one feels that insubstantial one feels, also, very tired indeed and quite unable to do the things a substantial person would do in order to grasp hold of the oyster that is the world, let alone open it. Also, when one is that nebulous and that tenuous, everything one does or can do seems just as nebulous and tenuous. Obviously, nothing one does can have the least significance, and there is very little that is worth the monstrous effort it takes. Which is why my thesis never materialised and why the book I keep thinking about doesn't start. The ephemeral leaders and reviews etc that I do write seem appropriate to my nebulosity: like me they vanish in the sun, and if someone mentions some-

thing I've written I'm astonished. This same sense of insub-
stantiality was there when I undertook a big piece of
scientific editing during the late eighties. When I look at
that work now, vigorous and erudite, it seems as though
I must have been taken over by someone else, someone
positive, strong, assured and probably fun to know. It is
a peculiar feeling. And I ask myself if one day a bell will
ring or a light will flash and suddenly, at long last, I'll
begin to feel myself solid beneath my fingers. Will I suddenly know that 'This is happening to *me*, now, here?'
Will I feel secure that this knowledge won't slip away
again? The answer seems to be No. The nothingness, the
invisibility, the sense of inward dissolution, will always be
there, if not gobbling me up, then waiting in the wings
for a vulnerable moment. The only way is to Act As If:
Act As If I exist, Act As If I'm totally aware and living
fully in my skin, Act As If what I do is important, despite
the evidence there seems to be to the contrary. And that
is to Act As If I'm my own best friend – doubly difficult
to be doubly insubstantial.

By then Stephanie had come a long way on her journey of
self-discovery. In October 1987 she had just dared to begin that
journey. She wrote:

The joy is in saying, I too can lay out my terrors; I too
can understand that I have them and even why I have
some of them. To me they are real terrors and terrible
terrors, and knowing that other people have them doesn't
help much. What does help is being given permission (or
giving myself permission) to look at them and describe
them and say hello to them and put out a hand and stroke
them – and so the great shapeless monsters rearing out
of the dark become manageable creatures. With love perhaps they can become purring cuddlies – a grotesque hope
at the moment, but why not indulge in something way
out for once.

I've wondered why these panics and terrors should be

emerging now, after years of seeming to be OK. I think it's because my writing has turned me into something of a local celebrity, discussed and gossiped about, respected by some and loathed by others. And I'm terrified. Suppose they find out what I'm really like: weakminded and feeble, mentally and physically a perfect slug of laziness? I'd shrivel up to nothing – as shapeless, formless and empty as a pricked snail. (What a good word 'shrivel' is, applied to the ego: very vivid image of the healthy ego as plump, silvery grey, floating jauntily like a barrage balloon with endearing ears: most of the time, though, shrivelled, dark, no silver lustre; just a poor, withered thing like a pinched and toothless mouth.)

When we embark on a journey of self discovery we are not always aware of the progress we are making. By 1991, Stephanie had found a compatible therapist who could accompany her on part of her journey. In September 1992 she wrote to me:

The therapy sessions continue, and I'm content now not to hurry-hurry-hurry but let things move at their own inherent pace. Change creeps up on me quietly, sometimes taking me unawares. Things which were impossible even a few months ago are gradually becoming possible. Instead of saying, 'I can't, I'll disintegrate, I'll crumble to dust, I'll fall through every available crack!' I've said yes with only minor misgivings to a high level invitation arising out of my writing. I also offered to speak at a meeting of a political organization, and managed it with such aplomb that I won their applause – even though they disagreed with most of what I said: not bad for a lifelong fearful speaker. I even agreed a few days ago to take part in a fashion show and strutted my stuff beaming and feeling marvellous. In short, there's an increasing sense of self – a solid, likeable centre that is me. I don't, except as a memory, still have the dreadful feeling that I have no centre, and that in a crunch, such as travelling or at a strange social gathering, or during a public speech, I'll dissolve from the inside out.

Perhaps it is only when one moves beyond those feelings that they become clear enough to describe. A year ago, 'dissolving from the inside out', leaving a ghostly or pained shell that looked like me, would not have occurred to me. If it had, it would have seemed too threatening to put into words.

Stephanie went on to tell me of the adventurous enterprises she had undertaken in music and yoga, and then said:

I've started to take some interest in the Chinese martial arts, and attended an introductory talk and demonstration recently. At question time the young teacher listened politely to various irrelevant questions and, several times and before he could respond, I heard my own voice snapping out the answers – and collected a lot of those 'What a know-all' and 'Who does she think she is?' looks. That solid centre of mine is beginning to feel its oats and trying to make up for decades of silence and false humility. It's going to get me into trouble.

However, the kind of trouble which Stephanie and other self-confident people get into when they speak out and present their own point of view is much more interesting, enlivening and real than the alternative of hiding away in lonely, frightened misery.

Our reasons for seeking relationships or a sense of achievement press upon us as needs which demand to be met. When we recognize the reasons why we do what we do we realize that we should organize our lives so that our needs can be met.

If you're an extravert and you want a chance to be happy, you must recognize your need for relationships, and so organize your life so that you have many good relationships. You must recognize your fear of being alone and see it, not as something despicable or so alien and frightening that it must be fled from, but as nothing more than the contrast to your need for people, a contrast which does not exist in reality because, even though you feel as if you will disappear if left completely alone, you won't. You're stuck with you for the rest of your life.

If you're an introvert and you want a chance to be happy, you must recognize your need for a sense of achievement, and so organize your life so that you are able to set about tasks which fulfil this need. You must recognize your fear of losing control and falling into chaos, and see it, not as something despicable and frightening, or as something you deny by taking self-righteous pride in the way you and you alone are always right, but as nothing more than the contrast to your need for order, clarity and control, a contrast which does not exist in reality because, even though you feel you will shatter if you lose control and fall into chaos, you won't. You're all of a piece for the rest of your life. You're also stuck with external reality, no matter how unreal it might appear to you. Moreover reality – everything that exists – is moving and changing all the time, so your idea that you can get the universe, or any part of it, under control is an illusion.

Those people who don't recognize their reasons for why they do what they do fail to organize their lives appropriately, and live with a painful, unnamed longing which, as time passes, seems less and less likely to be met. And so they fear time passing and getting old.

Some people recognize their reasons but then organize their lives so that the need is not met. However, they promise themselves that one day they will get what they want. Many extravert men accept their family's and society's demand that they be achievers, do well, and enter positions of lonely authority. They promise themselves that, come retirement, they'll play lots of friendly games of golf, or surround themselves with friendly books, or look up chums from schooldays. Many introvert women accept their family's and society's demand that they become wives and mothers, and so devote themselves to their families, an occupation which allows little sense of achievement. They promise themselves that once the children are grown up they'll go back to studying, get a degree, paint pictures, travel the world.

And what happens? They discover that they should not have waited until middle age to put their plans into operation.

Friendships should be fostered life-long, and not seen as objects to be picked up when convenient. A sense of achievement needs to be based on the self-confidence of being able to operate as an individual in your own right. Being nothing but a wife and mother does not foster such self-confidence.

Many of the people who successfully change their career in mid- or later life have actually been laying the ground for this by maintaining the necessities for it. Others, finally recognizing what they need, summon up the courage to create new relationships or to confront the world as an individual.

Those people who have, in effect, spent their lives living a lie and who feel that they are not brave enough to change their lives do not lose their longing to live their own truth. And so they fear time passing and growing old.

4 THE JOURNEY OF SELF-DISCOVERY

Childhood is a nightmare.

But it is hard to be an on-your-own, take-care-of-yourself-'cause-there-is-no-one-else-to-do-it-for-you grown-up.

We must live within the ambiguity of partial freedom, partial power, and partial knowledge.

The journey of self-discovery is the process whereby we discover that what we see as the world and ourselves are not the fixed entities we always thought them to be but are simply our interpretations which we are free to change, and whereby we apply this new understanding to our lives.

Some people do this by going into therapy. Most people do it by observing, thinking, reading and discussing. It is a never-ending process, for there is always something more to be understood, but always, somewhere in the process, there is a moment of enlightenment when we see the world afresh.

We might have lived without contemplating and questioning what we do, or we might have devoted ourselves to finding The Answer to the Question of the Meaning of Life, hoping to discover the Ultimate Absolute Truth, but, whatever, enlightenment is the discovery that to live without thinking is to be merely an automaton, and to expect to find The Answer is to be always disappointed and misled. Enlightenment is the discovery of mindfulness and our own truths.

Over the years I have encountered many people who set out on a journey of self-discovery and, in the course of this, became independent, aware adults. Sadly, I have encountered many more people who refused to set out on that journey and who, consequently, remain children, even though they carry out many adult tasks.

I used to meet many of these children when I was working in the National Health Service. Such children were the doctors and nurses who held firmly to the belief that their patients suffered from mental illnesses which had a physical cause. Children too were the relatives of the patients who insisted that the patient was insane and that they were perfectly normal. None of these people dared to look at their lives and question.

Nowadays I meet such children masquerading as adults in my lectures, on my travels, and in politics and the media.

There are those people who have heard me talk, or have read one of my magazine articles, and who ask me in tones of great puzzlement, 'But surely you don't think that what happens in childhood has any relationship to our adult lives? Children don't take things in and remember, do they?' As often as not the person asking the question is a devoted parent who has expended much time, effort and expense in teaching his or her children all manner of things intended for a lifetime's use.

I met many politically active people when my book *Living with the Bomb: Can We Live Without Enemies?* was published in 1986.[18] Then the nuclear threat was at its height, and there was much public debate. It seemed to me that wars would never come to an end until we addressed the question of why groups of people always see certain other groups as their enemy. In my book I set out the reasons why enemies are necessary – they unite the people in a group against the enemy and provide a repository for the excessive anger and hate which results from the way we bring up our children. To end wars we have to change the way we form our groups and how we bring up our children.

Many of the people who had devoted themselves to the cause

of peace found my message quite unacceptable. I would say that we are all aggressive, and necessarily so, otherwise we would be annihilated by other people, if not physically, then as persons, for other people want to impose their structures of meaning on us. These Peace People would advance upon me threateningly, declaring, 'How dare you say I am aggressive!' They were certainly not going to embark on any journey of discovery of their own aggression.

Then there were all the Important People, the politicians and scientists. At conferences where they spoke I was not given an opportunity to speak, except, perhaps, to ask a question. I always asked, 'Do you think it would be possible for the human race to live without enemies?'

My question was usually treated with contempt. A sentimental question from a stupid woman. Of course there would always be enemies and wars. How else would men fill in the time between birth and death if they couldn't make and use weapons?

At one large conference on nuclear proliferation held in Geneva in 1985 I put this question to the famous Carl Sagan. Other men on the platform to whom I had put the question just muttered, 'Of course there'll always be enemies,' but Carl refused to answer. After the meeting I accosted him and asked him why he had refused to answer. He said, 'The others had answered your question.' I pressed for his answer to my question, and he angrily replied that of course there would always be enemies.

Afterwards I wondered whether it had just been his vanity which stopped him from merely echoing the answers which the other men had given, or did he realize that this string of answers, all affirming that enemies and wars would go on and on, showed how futile such an expensive and pretentious conference was, and how futile the efforts of the participants. Then all the talk was of the dangers of nuclear war now that so many countries had the capacity to make nuclear weapons. Eight years later this danger has not gone away, but what has arrived meanwhile is Saddam Hussein in Iraq and the new round of the Balkan Wars.

Of more recent years I have encountered directly or second-hand those media people (chiefly men) who decide what should appear on our television screens. All the people I know who have made the journey of self-discovery are keen advocates of such a journey, so I can only assume that the media moguls have not made this journey and have no wish to do so. They certainly will not sponsor any programme which asks the question, 'Why do we behave as we do?' They relegate the very occasional programme on subjects like depression to daytime, 'women's' television, but all they allow to prime time television in the study of human behaviour are shock-horror programmes on sexual abuse or the crimes committed in the name of therapy, or else pretentious presentations of medical propaganda. As a result television viewers are much better informed about the mating habits of the Bolivian loop worm or the defensive tactics of the Transylvanian pork bat than they are about their own behaviour.

Of course there are many splendid programmes made by investigative journalists and many fearless, intelligent interviewers. They are the glory of the British media. However, they do not look beneath what is being studied and ask, 'Why do these people behave like this?'

They might explain that two warring groups are traditional enemies, or that an ageing dictator wants to hang on to power, but this is as far as their explanations go. In the story as they tell it each person has a fixed character and personality, and all the person's actions follow from that. There is no sense that the person has reasons, and behind that reasons for reasons, and that these reasons are not fixed entities but structures which the person can choose to change. Tito was not compelled by his character to act out the role of a dictator who maintains his power by fostering racial hatred on the principle of 'Divide and Rule'. He had a choice between doing this or fostering racial harmony. To explain Tito's actions in terms of 'a lust for power', or to explain widespread murder, torture, destruction and theft in terms of 'all people are cruel if given the opportunity' explains nothing, and certainly does not provide a platform from which we might explore how to change.

I sometimes wonder how much investigative journalists investigate their own reasons for what they do. A crusade for social justice might spring from personal injustice in childhood, and a crusade for truth might spring from personal betrayal in childhood, but if such crusaders are not aware of the connections they might not want their cause to be completely successful, and justice and truth to triumph, for then they would have lost the stage on which they parade their sensitivity and virtue.

So I cherish those people who have found the courage to set out on the journey of self-discovery.

A journey of self-discovery sounds like a very selfish, self-absorbed enterprise, yet it is actually a journey from selfish self-absorption to the freedom of just being yourself.

When we live without awareness of what we do and how we arrived at the set of reasons, attitudes, opinions, beliefs which direct our lives, we live with little direct awareness of other people and the world. All our observations of other people and our world are made in relationship to ourselves. We are concerned with how another person compares with us or thinks of us. Other people do not exist in their own right with aspects of their lives where we play no part, but are merely bit players in the drama of our life. We think of ourselves as being at the centre of the world. Where we live is to us the centre of the universe. Anything which we cannot relate to ourselves in any way, however false or tenuous, is boring, incomprehensible, silly.

My friend Peter Barkworth told me how, early in his career, he was in a play with Clive Brook who, he said, was a nervous, odd man. One evening when the two of them were waiting in the wings Clive said to Peter, 'Now I'm going to tell you something very important. Don't forget it. The older you get, the worse it gets.'

'It' was anticipatory anxiety. However, over the years Peter has found that for him 'it' got better, not worse. Dressing-room nerves, he believes, are a waste of time and effort. What is needed is concentration.

Peter told me that he had been in his first long run when he was twenty-three. He said, 'What I couldn't cope with was the frequent repetition, more than I had ever experienced, eight times a week, week after week. I knew the play too well, like a tourist guide. I didn't need my whole mind to do the words. The proverbial thing for actors is to do the part while thinking about what's for dinner or doing a shopping list. What I did was to let part of my mind join the audience where it watched me. I became self-conscious. My lips became dry, and I couldn't smile naturally. My movements became jerky and mechanical.'

Worried about this he confided in the very famous and delightful actress Athene Seyler. She said, 'Oh, I hadn't noticed,' and went on to tell him that he must not think about himself but concentrate on what the other actors were doing. 'Think about how pretty your leading lady is, or wonder what Clive has done to his hair.' After the next performance she said, 'I was watching you tonight. You are very good in it. And what you said about yourself doesn't show.'

Peter told me, 'I did appreciate the wisdom of that advice. It was a constant help, though it was not until I taught at RADA that I was fully able to put her advice to complete use.' Years later, when he became depressed, an image came very powerfully to him of a camera turned on him and observing him. The trick he discovered was to say to himself, 'Turn your camera round the other way.' Now the camera observed other people, and he ceased to be depressed.

Before this time, when he lived alone, he would stand at his window, watching people go by and feeling very lonely. Once he understood how the camera worked he realized that the man at the window had been seeing the passers-by only in relationship to himself. Now he knew that to be happy he needed to observe people as themselves.

The less we understand ourselves, the more self-absorbed we are. The actress Anna Massey spoke of this self-absorption when she described her process of self-discovery through therapy.

My parents split up when I was one and my nanny brought me up. These depressions started after she died when I had to face up to retrospection. She had been the bolts and braces of my life and after her death I had to learn how to live. I had done nine years' meditation but that did not solve my problems.

Analysis was very painful at times, but joyful as well. It rejoined me with my instinctive optimism. It was wonderful to accept and enjoy life after periods of not getting out of bed. It enables you to understand yourself.

Previously I was manifestly selfish because my own problems blocked off any understanding of other people's. It's like a brass band playing in your head so you can't begin to hear a delicate distressed violin playing in another person's mind. That protects you in some ways, but also makes you an impossible person. I think I am much more sensitive to other people now . . .

During the process you go through an immense amount of self-absorption and become even more of a pain but you come to understand yourself. Not everybody needs it but I think a lot of people could benefit immeasurably. Analysis opens you up to life. In retrospect I wish I could have started much earlier. But you have to be ready.[19]

In the state of selfish self-absorption we cannot help but make some serious errors in our relationships and in our choice of career. Lou Miele began his journey of self-discovery while he was in the monastery, and this showed him that he had to leave.

Lou told me how he had developed a form of self-inspection that was very intellectual. In the monastery, 'Psychological issues are transmuted into other metaphors and you inhabit moral and theological landscapes of one kind or another.'

Then he left the monastery.

I left all these structures. I had a very clear sense that the universe was value free, and that I was another set of loose atoms in it. The meaning was to be invented. I was both thrilled and horrified. All things were possible. You could be anything you liked. I came to therapy with a real vengeance. I felt I had developed some patterns for making good choices and not just scatter energy.

Therapy played a huge role in reaching contentment. It taught me the habit of facing myself square on. Therapy has to become the centre of your life for a time. It's a tremendously narcissistic enterprise. I chose to become someone that I am fairly content with. The surprises with self are fewer. Reality now is much more predictable, much less a roller coaster ride. Much less thrilling, much more contentment than it was twenty years ago. I find many compensations for what I do in the present, but there is a bit of nostalgia for when the world was being created by me and my friends, and we could work magic wherever we were.

Some people fear to set out on the journey of self-discovery because they fear growing older. They fear they will lose the magic of being young of which Lou spoke, when we feel that we have discovered delights which no one else has discovered. (Every generation of young adults believe that they invented sex.) But that magic will disappear, journey or no journey.

Some people fear to set out on the journey because they feel it will show them that nothing can be put right. The actor Daniel Massey found that this was not the case.

I feel, so to speak, a stranger in the family in which I was born. This has caused me much pain. The source of it I hid for much of my life, and when you hide from that kind of truth it catches up with you. Psychotherapy has helped me to come to terms with this. Indeed, it has changed my life. No, I don't talk about it much. On the whole, apart from those who have been damaged them-selves, people don't understand. If I have any envy it is for those who've had a wonderfully sustaining early life of love and understanding, because that is what a child needs to help it on its way to self worth, value and a sense of being loved, and of how to relate to other people. You can, however, repair damage, integrate, find that value in yourself, learn to love and be loved. It's regeneration, I suppose.

I've carried damage through my life – this isn't self-pity, it's a fact . . . Children who are unhappy when they were young and live through difficulties and bad relationships, tend to gravitate towards difficulties when they grow up, because that's what they've been conditioned to. There's no question that you develop patterns, sometimes very destructive ones. That's without any shadow of doubt why my two marriages broke up. But the wonderful thing is that whatever time you come to account and face it, it's enormously rewarding. And you can make it right – it's never too late.[20]

Therapists can be useful companions on the journey, but they must be outgrown and left behind. Some therapists resist this. They want to keep their patients in their thrall so as to maintain their power, prestige and wealth. Some do this by insisting that they have secret knowledge which makes them wiser and stronger than their patients who vainly try to get the therapist to use his supposed knowledge to make them better. Other therapists hold on to their patients by demanding gratitude and inspiring the patient's guilt.

The system of health care often makes it very difficult for people to recognize what is being done to them, much less to break away. But some people manage to do this. Some people strike out on their own, and others get together to help one another.

In June 1992 a sixteen-year-old girl was ordered by a judge to accept a therapeutic regime intended to compel her to eat. After my letter about this case was published in the *Guardian*[21] Pat McNeill wrote to me enclosing one of her cartoons. She said:

I enclose a rough for a pic strip based on the experiences of a self-help group for recovering agoraphobics. Your letter in today's *Guardian* re anorexia will make a lot of sense to our group which have, like the anorexic girl, all been offered NHS 'treatment' which was no more than attempts to remove (by skimpy, rather bullying de-sensitization courses) or chemically palliate the phobic symptoms.

In the virtual absence of really solid NHS psycho-

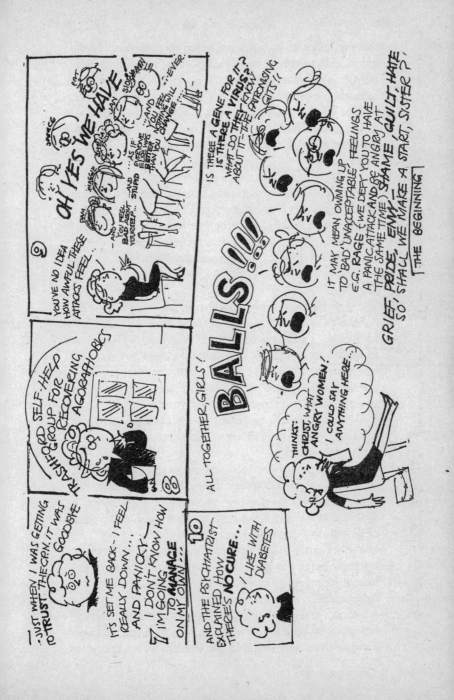

therapy, and with myself, a recovered agoraphobic, as facil-
itator, our members have pulled each other up by the
bootstraps, discovering themselves to be real people with
individual attributes and talents who learned early in life,
and for good reasons at the time, to suppress feelings. Real
achievements have resulted (though husbands, significantly, are not all that delighted at losing their wee wifies'
dependency).[22]

It is not enough just to recognize what society has done to
us which leads us to feel shame, guilt, hate, grief, pride, envy
and fear. We need also to recognize how we adapted to the
world's onslaught in order to preserve our pride.

Laura, at twenty-four, recognized this. In a letter to me she
said:

> The individual probably knows as much as anybody else,
> but the adult world begins by telling you that it 'KNOWS
> BETTER'. Until you feel you 'KNOW BETTER', you
> feel you are not capable of making decisions for yourself,
> when, in fact, you have always been capable of making
> decisions for yourself – it's just the rules that change as
> you get older and more aware, not your*self*.
>
> What no one tells you is it is *your* world out there, just
> as much as it is theirs. They covet it just as much as you
> covet your world.
>
> I grew up in a world of everyone else 'KNOWING
> BETTER' – I think everyone does – but my defence to this
> dependency was to create my own internal world where I,
> for once, knew better. And this is the world I am terrified
> of giving up – my own inner security . . .
>
> We're born into a world where everything – conditions,
> rules, language – is all pre-set. People don't feel that they
> have the power to change any of that, they just learn the
> rules and live their lives, and that's that. We consider it
> mankind's greatest ability to adapt our environment to suit
> ourselves, to change our surroundings to make life easier
> for ourselves. But, I think, we use this as an excuse to

protect ourselves from change; we don't change ourselves because changing our environment is easier.

If living with others proves difficult, we create a world that lets each of us live on our own. If reality gets too tough, we make up other places to live. People created fire because they were scared of the dark. People invented the wheel because their feet got tired. I create barriers because caring costs me more than I'm prepared to give.

Not going into a supermarket was easier than making myself talk to somebody. Writing this is easier than going around to somebody's house and telling them. Explaining myself to them. Letting them know I'm a human being too.[23]

However, letting other people know that you are a human being too means letting people know that you have needs. Like many people, Kay, after a childhood where she suffered much cruelty, struggled on in a hugely unhappy marriage for many years rather than ask for help. She explained to me:

I always thought I had no rights (having no earnings or status helped with that one), who was I to burden other people with my problems, they had enough of their own (I was always much aware that other people had problems), I thought they might break down completely if I added mine to them. Pride played a large part in my not being able to ask for help. I remember thinking, 'I don't know what would happen to me if I didn't have my pride.' My guilt, for not being good enough, and my pride in not admitting it, were the two things which held me together, but they prevented me from moving on faster to a solution.[24]

So she began her journey not in the company of another person but with books. She told me:

I have this great sense of freedom now (I used to read your books in secret for fear of criticism!). Without your books I really do not know how far I would have ever got on my own – it seems that your books have put into words and images shadows that were already in my mind. They made a complete form of something within me which was whispy and translucent – very profound and difficult to handle in concrete terms. My mind had all the answers, of that I was sure. I knew within myself I had the capacity to heal my own wounds but I needed guidance and clarity. These are what you have given me, and this enlightenment is the greatest treasure I could ever hope to have received.

The important thing for me is that now I can be myself. I no longer feel at odds with the world – in fact I know I can fit into the world *and* hold on to my own perceptions and conclusions. I appear to have always monitored my own thoughts and reactions to other people and events. Sometimes I am not sure whether this is a natural instinct which most people seem to lose or whether I developed it because I had to rearrange and modify my behaviour in order to survive. I wonder sometimes if I could have survived either physically or psychologically had I not been fairly adept at responding in a way that rectified reality for the other person.

I have never been able to talk to my mother about her treatment of me as a child, but my father told me a few years ago how sorry he was for not protecting me when I was small. I can't even picture him when I was a child. He was a shadow in the background. He knew I was being ill-treated but he couldn't do anything about it. He knows how much I appreciate his being able to acknowledge my childhood pain, and he knows I understand how it happened, and that it isn't necessary for me to confront my mother. I have no wish for either him or my mother to suffer any guilt. My father is still afraid to stand up for himself. It is so sad but not everyone gains wisdom as they grow older. My mother maintains you cannot change (despite the evidence of my changing); she believes that she is always right; she is positive she is a good wife and mother; she cannot 'see' anyone's pain except her own, which is basically that life has not been fair to her.[25]

What damage do those people do who refuse to set out on the journey of self-discovery? If your mother won't care for and comfort you, you soon learn not to care for and comfort yourself. Part of this journey of self-discovery is learning how to care for yourself, not in the silly self-absorption of those purveyors of Recovery and the Inner Child, but in the awareness that caring for yourself is part and parcel of caring for others, and living comfortably with yourself is part and parcel of living comfortably with others. Caring for and living comfortably with yourself allows you to recognize how your creativity has its sources in your earliest childhood.

Jean Medcalf told me how her counsellor had told her that, because she had not been comforted as a child, she found it hard to comfort 'my own child'. She wrote, 'My mother used to be alarmed when she saw me cuddling my children and say, "Don't pet them!" She was born in 1897. Can you tell me why in those days she would have thought it so wrong to have made so much of a child? I was born in 1931.'

Jean's problems were 'panic attacks and a general fearfulness about things in general and not valuing myself very much.' She sent me some of her poems. Her search for and misunderstanding with the child she had once been she called 'Counselling'.

Right then, Child, I said this morning firmly.
Now what's all this about – tell me all that's in your mind.

Well, said Child, you've been ignoring me when I cry,
You shut the door on me and say hard luck –
You must get over it.

I'm often busy, I replied,
With cooking, and cleaning and washing up –
Someone's got to do it.

I know, said Child, but I could help you there.
How? said I. You're no good for anything.

Child shrank. Sorry, said I,
Let's start again.
But you are a liability, you know –
You're far too sensitive.
What good are you? You tell me.

Child looked up –
I've written all those poems,
All those stories,
I've made creative clothes
And knitted, and made a beautiful garden.

Did you do all those things? I asked amazed.
Yes, said Child, and I'll do more if you'll let me.

What is it that you need? I asked, subdued.
Well, said Child,
You've never asked me that before and it is about time,
I've been asking for sixty years and you haven't listened to
    me.
Sorry, I murmured – do go on.

I need time to myself, to dream and think and read
I need to be looked after.
I've hardly ever had toys
I love the country, trees and grass
And I'm good at sewing and colours.
Child seemed to grow in stature.
And then she stamped her foot.

But most of all I want you to listen to me more –
You're often busy, like your Mother used to be.
I remembered her busily scrubbing the floor while I called,
    'Look what I've made!'
And was silent.

So I gave Child a little kiss
Not too big or she might get above herself
Or above me;
And when I told my Mother about Child
She cried in fear don't pet her
And who wants to look at her anyway.
It's a wise mother who knows her own Child.[26]

Jean wrote that poem in October 1990, when she was still hoping that someone – God, or her counsellor – would give her The Answer to it all. In March 1991 came her moment of enlightenment.

I said to God last night
'Help me.
Please send me
St Michael and all angels
One flaming sword and a golden chariot
To carry me off from my misery.'
He didn't answer.

I asked again
'Help me
Please send me
A burning bow
A Jacob's ladder and, if you like,
Half a dozen cherubs.'
Still He said nothing.

'What about seek and you shall find?' I said crossly.
'What about knock and it shall be opened to you and all
    that?
Where are You when I need You!' I shouted.

I heard a rumble of thunder.
'Oh dear,' I thought, 'now I've annoyed Him.'

'I did say please first time,' I said
'So how about a teeny weeny harp
Or a fluffy pink cloud to cheer me up.
Any sign will do – I'm not fussy.'

I thought I heard Him smile
But I saw it was only a rainbow.

So in the silence I waited patiently
And what do you think He sent me?

All His loving kindness –
And it was there all the time
Inside me
And I hadn't even noticed.[27]

Jeremy Henzell-Thomas, emerging from severe depression, wrote of his enlightenment,

Through this catastrophe I have learnt at last to understand why I was never at peace.

I sought certainty to hide my fear, but seeking certainty only increases fear because nothing is ever certain. There is always the possibility of loss and change. There is no perfect security in which everything is ordered and arranged. Nothing can be perfectly right all the time. Nothing can be totally controlled, and ambiguity can never be eradicated.

There is freedom and hope in the realization that nothing is certain, nothing secure. Suddenly, the shackles are loosened from one's perception of the world, and one sees a shifting scene in which the images are light and airy, no longer fixed and immutable. This is the door of perception into the mist, the letting go through the illusion of forms.

When certainty is destroyed and one has faced and survived the annihilation of the old self, even though the old self fought desperately for its survival, and failed, there is a palpable sense of rebirth, at first tentative, and then more confident. One looks around, and the world is no longer a wall to surmount, a grim edifice to scale. What one does is no longer a joyless, exhausting task to be carried out with stern efficiency and matchless competence. Neither is it done anxiously, in anticipation, already suffused with the spectre of the next daunting task to be accomplished.

But there emerges from this painful rebirth a sense of lightness, as if an old skin has been shed. There emerges the sense that one no longer possesses the world, and one is no longer possessed by one's need to possess it, but that all the forms one sees are merely shifting shapes which have no immutable reality of their own. And one sees that everything will pass away, but that beyond the illusory forms everything merges into the One.

Enlightenment is not a sudden transcendent experience. It requires a painful death in which every anchor is pitilessly wrenched away until one is left utterly alone in the cavernous emptiness of oneself. One searches desperately for old footholds, for some sense of continuity, but there is nothing to catch hold of. There is only a bottomless chasm of black negation.

In this place one gives up one's need to make the world conform to one's will. One understands that all things must be as they are, and it is nothing but absurd pride to imagine that one can push anything into a place where it does not belong.[28]

The picture of the passage from absolute truths to uncertain wisdom as a journey has been with us for a long time. The *Dhammapada*, the Sayings of the Buddha, written two thousand years ago, gives some ageless advice about the journey of self-discovery.

If the traveller can find
A virtuous and wise companion,
Let him go with him joyfully,
And overcome the dangers on the way.

But if you cannot find
Friend or master to go with you,
Travel on alone –
Like a king who has given away his kingdom,
Like an elephant in the forest.

Travel on alone
Rather than with a fool for company.
Do not carry with you your mistakes.
Do not carry your cares.
Travel on alone
Like an elephant in the forest.[29]

5 COMING TO TERMS

You are free to do whatever you like. You need only face the consequences.

Let me explain what I mean by 'coming to terms'.

Coming to terms is not the sorrowful resignation of those who have tried to make the world what they want it to be, and failed.

Coming to terms is not the cynical resentment of those who believe they have been cheated of their just rewards.

Coming to terms is the awareness that everything changes, and that this is all right. We might have been successful in imposing our will on part of the universe, we might have had the good fortune to be rewarded for our efforts and avoided being punished for our failures, but all this will pass, and that is all right. We are part of the continual process of birth, life, and death, and that is all right.

Coming to terms is the understanding that everything that happens has good implications and bad implications, and that is all right. We rejoice in the good implications, and endure as best we can the bad implications.

Coming to terms is the understanding that the reality of what exists is far more marvellous than we can imagine, and that is all right. We no longer need to dwell meagrely in the pallid, magical fantasies which purport to explain life, but instead live richly in the enjoyment of what is.

We can look at the world only through the frame of the theories we have created about the world. Our frame determines what we see, and what we see has good and bad implications for us. In the fourteenth century the frame through which people saw the world was almost entirely magical. Accordingly,

> People lived close to the inexplicable. The flickering lights of the marsh gas could only be fairies or goblins; fireflies were the souls of unbaptised dead infants. In the terrible trembling and fissures of an earthquake or the setting fire of a tree by lightning, the supernatural was close at hand. Storms were omens, death by heart attack or other seizures the work of demons. Magic was present in the world: demons, fairies, sorcerers, ghosts, ghouls touched and manipulated human lives.[30]

Such a vision made the world seem a much more exciting place to live than it actually was, but it also made it a much more dangerous place. How could people protect themselves other than by prayers to God and by trying to be good?

There are many people today who see their world through the frame of magic. Their world is peopled by angels and devils, or succoured by beneficent powers of Mother Nature, or fought over by the forces of good and evil, or dominated by the powers of distant planets. They do not want to give up their belief in magic for they believe that the world seen through the plain spectacles of the inquisitive, doubting, questioning scientific mind is a very dull and boring place.

Such a belief is actually the scar of a severe childhood wound. As children, when they were inquisitive, doubting, questioning and creative as all young children are, they were severely punished for wanting to know what the world was really like. Their little hands were slapped for touching, their little bodies were roughly wrenched away from interesting sights, they were scrubbed and shouted at for being dirty, doors were closed in their faces. The source of their curiosity turned dangerous. And so, as Laura said, 'If reality gets too tough, we make up other places to live.' These people made up their other places, and they fear to leave them.

However, in such magical worlds they are helpless. We have no control over magic, other than to know that it is not real. Once we think it is real, we are helpless in the power of the magic and of those people who, in claiming that they can control the magic, lie to us.

On a plane flying to New York I sat next to Ken, a twenty-two-year-old student returning from his first trip abroad. He told me, 'I can't imagine getting old – grey hair and all that. I expect to die young. I've got a short life-line.' He showed me his palms. His life-line was indeed very short. It was shorter than my life-line, and palmists have been telling me since my teens that I would die young.

He told me that he intended to pack everything into his very short life. He would do everything, and he would write music which would be remembered for ever.

I asked him about his grandparents. All were still alive and at a good age. Had he ever inspected their life-lines? No.

Ken had a wonderful excuse for never doing anything he doesn't want to do. He can't afford to waste his precious time.

A belief in magic can always be used to avoid personal responsibility. 'I can't help being like this. I'm a Gemini.'

Believers in magic include many of those extraverts who are sure that if the world was a calm, secure place, and if they lost their anxieties and confusions they would become so bland they would disappear. They make sure that once a crisis in their life is resolved another appears. Telling their troubles to an audience assures them that they exist, but they hang on to their troubles as they would hold on to a lifebelt in a raging ocean. They are a source of endless income and annoyance to therapists.

To come to terms, the magical belief which most of us have to give up is the belief in a Just World. Some people say that they have given up their belief in the Just World, but the way they say this reveals some sadness and bitterness. They are, in effect, mourning its loss. Mourning is the process whereby we try to keep in existence that which we have lost, so in effect they have not given up their belief. Like the people who believe in magic, these people suffered a wound and made a sacrifice which, it seems, only the promise of a Just World could compensate.

Coming to terms involves accepting that we have suffered wounds and losses for which there is no recompense. There was no special reason why we suffered. We were simply unlucky to have been in that particular place at that particular time. However, being unlucky in the past does not mean that we won't be lucky in the future.

One version of the belief in the Just World is that there is an Answer to Life. Nowadays there are many people who purport to have set out on the journey of self-discovery when in fact what they are looking for is The Answer to Life. They believe that once this Answer is found, everything will fall into place, all confusions resolved, all suffering ameliorated and compensated for, and they will live happily ever after.

In the seventies such searchers for The Answer were called group groupies. They went from one therapy group to another and became experts on every kind of therapy, however exotic. Such an enterprise then appealed more to women than to men. Now a great many men, each claiming to be a New Man, have joined their ranks. Such New Men have taken to the Wild Man philosophy of Robert Bly. Andrew Anthony attended a Wild Man weekend in Dorset run by James Hillman and Michael Meade.

After a number of discussions and much beating of drums have passed it becomes apparent that for the majority on the course it is not their first crack at self-discovery. An impressive level of therapy literacy is displayed by nearly all. Hillman has only to mention an exercise and the men embark on it with the unhesitating assurance of old-timers.

For example, when Hillman suggests letting our bodies do what they tell us to do, not only do scores of men suddenly throw their limbs in every conceivable direction with the uninhibited fervour of a primary school drama class, but they are also able to describe exactly what they were feeling while doing it immediately after, and with stunning candour. 'It made me feel incredibly feminine,' says one. 'I wanted to get down and eat the grass,' says another.

Between them they've tried it all: Buddhism, Marxism, psychotherapy, astrology, Christianity, transcendental meditation, rebirthing, EST, Jungian analysis, acupuncture, LSD, management training. And now they're having a go at being a man.[31]

The searchers for The Answer have yet to understand that there is no Answer, but a vast array of ironic contrasts in a world where every event and every meaning we create has good implications and bad implications.

Some of these ironic contrasts are peculiar to our own individual lives. For instance, because I, like everyone else, want to have everything, I often think how nice it would be if I became immensely successful in my work. My books would sell in their millions and the media moguls would be falling over themselves to get me to present my views. However, the basic thesis of my work is that we are very poor at understanding ourselves, that the majority of people do not want to understand themselves, and that the powers of the State and the Church do not want us to understand ourselves. If my work became popular it would mean that its basic thesis was not true.

So what's to do except be amused, be pleased when some people thank me for my work, be reassured that there are people who want to understand themselves, and hope that their numbers are growing larger.

Some of these ironic contrasts exist in all our lives. Death, for instance. If no one ever died, if we all lived for ever, we would not know that we were alive. We have the concept of life only because there is death.

Part of coming to terms is accepting the presence of death in our lives, and recognizing its importance. This means recognizing that everyone will die and that there are no exceptions, recognizing that the process cannot be prettified or glossed over no matter how we might try, and recognizing how death can show us what is actually important in our lives.

The death of people close to us forces us to realize that we will die. My friend Ann said:

'When I was growing up two of my sisters died, and then my brother committed suicide. That hurt me greatly. It made me realize you've got to cope whatever happens. I was twenty-six and he was thirty-one. After I was married our little girl Lisa died at three-and-a-half. I think I've grown up with death. It's been part of my life, which I think has made me accept it better. I feel it doesn't worry me. I've been nursing. You don't forget things but you've got to get through them and over them. They're part of life. You can't let them pull you down. I'm lucky. I've got lots of pluses. A happy marriage, nice children, lots of friends.'

Ann did not run away from the knowledge that she would die, but built it into her life by choosing a career of which death was part, and by seeing that it was always part of family life. The cartoonist Charles Addams came to terms with his own death by laughing at it. The doom and gloom of the Addams family, and Charon rowing his boat across the River Styx were presented in the context of everyday practicalities. In this cartoon Charon's craft is organized like the airliners we know so well (see next page).

Charles Addams's friend Wilfred Sheed wrote of him:

Insofar as Charlie had any message at all (and he resisted the idea firmly), it would have to be that there is *nothing* in this world or the next too horrible to laugh at. And in case you're worrying, it might be worth adding that no one ever faced the prospect of his own death and whatever else more serenely, or died more peacefully, than Charlie himself.[32]

Trying to prettify the process of death can lead us seriously astray because at some stage in our lives the reality will burst in upon us. Madame Bovary thought that to kill herself all she had to do was to take some arsenic, lie down, and quietly slip

away. Many of the people who take overdoses of drugs make the same mistake. Death is usually messy, often painful, and always real. Making up pretty stories about it does not make it less real.

One of my Catholic friends told me that the nuns had taught her that no matter how she died she would always have time to repent of her sins before expiring. Now she is a doctor she knows that this is not true.

Another friend, Merle, and I met when we were teaching together in the sixties. She was a science teacher, and she always read widely in her field. However, as the years passed she found science, particularly the biological sciences, less and less satisfactory. She began to explore alternative studies – homoeopathy, herbal medicines, ayurvedic medicine, aromatherapy – and she began to find some better answers to her questions. These studies took her into yoga and the Eastern philosophies, and these, along with her quest for self-understanding, brought her a sense of self-acceptance and peace.

Merle had had in her life several close brushes with death, the first being rheumatic heart disease and high blood pressure. She needed to live to a grand old age to do all the things she wanted to do, but she had to make some kind of reconciliation with death. She had to find a meaning for death with which she could live.

Death, she decided, was just part of Nature's plan. Nature was kindly, so as we grow old, gradually coming to the end of our natural span, Nature helps us withdraw from life slowly, gently, closing down the faculties which allow us to interact with our environment. Our hearing becomes less acute, our eyesight dims. We withdraw slowly, gracefully, acceptingly into the end of our cycle, still within Nature's care.

Then her friend John died. John was a vibrant, active, supremely intelligent seventy-nine-year-old. His presence lit up the room. He challenged and informed his companions. He read, his garden was an experimental and visual delight. Then suddenly he was dead, his body invaded by a massive cancer. Merle was distraught. She had lost a friend, and her framework for death fell apart.

Merle wrote,

'Even for the elderly, Death may not be part of a slow with-drawal. Death can strike rapidly and overwhelmingly enough to annihilate all of the vital Life Force of the individual. John's death was very rapid – a matter of great fatigue that swamped his strength in a matter of three days, for only two of which he was conscious, so that he ceased to be. The sudden "snuffing out" made coping with his death very difficult.'[33]

Through its history the Christian Church has had many prac-tices aimed at reminding people of the imminence of their death. Such a warning was aimed at reminding people of the necessity of being in a state of grace which would allow them to enter heaven. Perhaps what we all need are daily reminders of our death, not to fix our minds on the hereafter, but to warn us not to squander our precious time. We need to be constantly aware of how important it is to live as much as possible in the present and to know what really matters in our lives. Some of us learn this only after a brush with death.

I had been invited to give an evening lecture for a weekend course organized by a Catholic women's group in Ireland. There I met Ursula.

Ursula was to me a typical Irish matron – short, stout, with a kindly face that had rarely been cherished with creams and powders, sensibly cropped grey hair, competent, experienced hands, her conversation about children and grandchildren. Her home, I was sure, was immaculate and her cooking nurturing and satisfying. She had raised her children with love and firm-ness, and with respect for the Catholic faith.

Yet she was not other-worldly. When, after my lecture, she settled into her seat in the college bar I expected that she would enjoy a drink as the other women there were doing. But she did not. As she explained, she had had an operation for gall-stones which had been disastrous. Now she could not drink any alcohol, and she had to limit what food she ate and what exercise she took. 'I don't mind,' she said, 'It's not a problem.'

The next morning after breakfast she greeted me. Most of the women went from breakfast straight to Mass, but Ursula suggested that she and I share a sofa and talk.

She questioned me about some aspects of the talk I had given on depression, and in my reply I made some comments about how, to be free of depression, we need to learn the value of living without the security of a belief in the Just World.

Ursula said, 'You know I was sick, dangerously ill. That changed me. I used always to be busy, thinking about what had to be done. Now I take one day at a time, and I enjoy it. I used to be houseproud. Now, if I feel like it, I leave the dishes in the sink, close the door and go for a walk along the beach. I always had things put away to use only when special visitors came. Nice things I never used. When I came home from hospital I got them all out and I use them. I get the pleasure of them. I've learned to say no. I don't do anything I don't want to do. I take the time to do the things I want to do. All my life I've been afraid of dying. Now I'm not afraid to die. I used to dread lying in my coffin and feeling the clay coming down on my head, but now I know I won't be there to know about the clay. I won't be anywhere,' and she smiled in satisfaction as the women returning from Mass filled the room.

Many people will argue that dying means going somewhere else. Such a belief can be comforting, but it can prevent the believer from being able to live fully in this life because the urgency of enjoying and making the most of life is missing. Moreover, if the imagined hereafter is seen as part of the workings of the Just World, then the believer has to live this life in terms of the next life and not in terms of this life.

If death means not being anywhere, it shows us that we should make the most of being somewhere. This is all very well when we enjoy bountiful good fortune, but what can we do when we are not fortunate, when we encounter major disasters? How do we come to terms with that?

Some people, reluctant to give up their version of the Just World, try to find an explanation which can be derived from their thesis about the Just World. Niki Lauda saw the disaster of his plane crashing as God teaching him a lesson. Other people interpret the disaster as God pointing out a pathway down which they must go. Such a pathway never leads to taking things easily. It always points to further achievement, either in terms of greater obedience to God or to carrying out some good works. Whichever, the ultimate goal is unattainable, for the person can never feel that he is good enough or has achieved enough. To believe that you have earned top marks in being good is to commit the sin of pride, and the ills of the world are without limit.

Some of the people who decide that the meaning of their disaster is God pointing the way to good works do achieve marvels from which many people benefit.

When his eight-year-old son developed cancer of the nervous system in 1974, Bob Woodward established the Cancer and Leukemia Childhood Trust (Clic). It was, so he told journalist Helen Kendall, 'his unswerving Christian faith which enabled him to bear that sorrow. He was "shown a way" to come to terms with his grief.'

Clic has given enormous help to stricken families and helped further research. The father of a child helped by Clic said of Bob Woodward, 'He is Clic.' However, 'Recently Mr Woodward collapsed. It was feared he had suffered a heart attack, but doctors who carried out extensive tests said he was suffering from stress. Now he has been told he must slow down and learn to let others take a more active role in the organization . . . [He] finds it difficult to rest.'[34]

Other people come to terms with their disaster. They see it as bad luck. They do not expect the world to recompense them fully for their loss. They try to make the best of their resultant circumstances. They allow themselves to be angry and sad.

At nineteen Ian Waterman had a bout of an undiagnosed illness, perhaps glandular fever or gastric flu. He took a few days off work, but got progressively worse. One day he got out of bed and collapsed in a heap, not paralysed but unable to negotiate the movement of his body. By the time doctors had managed to diagnose what was wrong they had decided that he was a hopeless wheelchair case.

What had happened was that a rare immune reaction to a common infection had wiped out a specific part of his peripheral nervous system, that which controls proprioception, or the sense whereby we know the position, state and movement of our body in space. We each have a mental map of our body. Ian Waterman lost his map. He is the only person in Britain who is known to suffer from this condition.

He has no sensation of touch from the neck down, although he is aware of pain and temperature. He has no idea where his body is unless he can see it, and so he avoids the dark. Sent home from hospital for his mother to look after, he was a six foot three inches rubber doll. Eventually he was offered rehabilitation, and slowly he developed strategies for moving by making the most of what abilities he had left.

Telling his story, the journalist Liz Hunt wrote:

Learning to move again, he developed a successful career in the civil service, and for six years enjoyed a 'deliriously happy' marriage. But life dealt him a second serious blow when his wife died from cancer. He couldn't cry at her funeral because tears would have blurred his vision, and then he would have been unable to walk.

He is now retired (at thirty-nine) and lives with his second wife, Linda, near Kendal in the Lake District, in a farmhouse that they are renovating. He left work because he wanted to enjoy life while he could. 'I'd proved a point: that I could work and live independently. But I suspect that as I get older, I'll be less able. I want to enjoy life while I can.' His aim is to one day open a hotel in the Lake District for the disabled, and he is working on a guide to the area for people with mobility difficulties.

Mr Waterman insists that he is no 'tragihero' who has triumphed against all the odds. 'Life isn't like that. You are presented with a particular set of circumstances and you deal with them as best you can. Of course it is tough and you do ask "why me?"' But when you realize that there isn't an answer, you just get on with it.[35]

On 18 November 1987, Kwasi Afari-Minta was at King's Cross underground station when an escalator exploded into flames. Thirty-one people died and dozens were injured. Kwasi was one of the most badly burned.

He is a musician and before the fire was a record producer. Now his face is very badly scarred and his hands, locked clawlike at the knuckles, cannot play a guitar. Recovery from his injuries was a very slow process. Finding a new way of life took much longer. He learnt a new way of making music by using a computer. To support himself he drove a cab. But how to deal with other people? How to come to terms with what had happened? He said:

I don't think I'm being over-sensitive, I mean, what makes an adult say – so that I can hear – 'Wow, man, God, he's really ugly'? What makes a person need to say that? If schoolchildren pass along the road and start laughing at me, I don't mind. They're not grown-up enough to know what hurt is. But if somebody on the bus or train stares at me for a long time, or I overhear them say something, it does disturb me.

One day I was sent down to pick up a girl – she had an unusual amount of freckles on her face, masses of them. And when I got there the girl looked at me oddly. She didn't talk much but just kept looking, and when we arrived at our destination she was still looking at me intently. I asked her why she was doing that, and she said, 'Why are you looking at me?' I said I wasn't looking at her, and she replied, 'But you were.'

Finally I said, 'Look, if you think you've got a problem with your freckles that's up to you, but really you're all right, you know, you shouldn't worry. You still look nice. But if you let it get on top of you, maybe think that you can't get a boyfriend, the next thing you know you'll be thinking of suicide, and that's no good.'

Before the fire, Kwasi said, 'Failure wasn't part of my vocabulary.' Now 'I challenge myself.' He set himself challenges like being able to control a car gear stick. 'If I am able to do these things I feel satisfied. But when I can't I feel very low. In big things, as in small things, I wrestle with the possibility of success and failure.'

'Once,' he said, 'I was a very, very confident person. But now

I am sad, my new personality has made me sad. You can say that sadness is part of everyone's life, that some of the best black music has been sad music. But I say to you this African music is happy music. South Africans may use ballads and voices to propagate feelings about apartheid. Americans may use blues to sing about slavery. But in West Africa we're not used to being sad. If somebody passes away even the funeral is a celebration. So you see what this fire has done? It's taken something of my Africanness away. How would you compensate for that?'

There is no compensation for such sadness, for there is nothing that can remake the past and take the sadness away. Many people, bitterly regretting that events in their lives have left them feeling sad, go into therapy in the hope that therapy will cure them of their sadness. Imperceptive and/or dishonest therapists will encourage them in this aim by telling them that they cannot be considered to be well or whole while the sadness persists, a ploy which ensures the therapists' continued income.

Part of coming to terms is accepting that this sadness is not something alien thrust upon you but an essential part of you. You are sad, but you need not be sad all the time. Kwasi found that he was sad when, in Peter Barkworth's phrase, he 'turned the camera on himself'. When he turned the camera on other people he was not. He said,

'Sometimes, when my friends come around – friends that I had before the fire – I forget the scars on my hands and I don't see my face. Then I can dwell in my old self for a while. I can see myself really flourish. But no sooner am I aware of that blessed release than it is disrupted by someone who sees me for the first time and creates a tension.'[36]

When we turn our camera on other people in order to see them as no more than a curious object we injure them and injure ourselves for we make ourselves less than what we might be. When we turn our camera on other people and see them as people, when we let our sadness create the frame whereby we see other people we are able to make that most human, creative leap of the imagination – empathy. We are able by this means to leave the lonely prison of our individual worlds and be close to other people.

It is yet another of those ironic contrasts of life that it is sadness which brings people close together, not joy and happiness. You might have enjoyed the best of times with a group of friends, but it is not until disaster strikes one or all of the group that true friends are revealed and bonds formed which are way beyond ordinary friendships.

Our sadness, too, can strengthen our understanding of how we are always part of everything that exists.

Bernadette Connole told me how, at twenty-two when she had just started her career in journalism, she was sent to cover a horrific car accident where several people died.

I had no way of coping with it, so I spent that weekend looking at books and art, things which were beautiful, because I had seen things which were horrific. After that I developed this as a principle. I've had to report on a lot of murders, and I've seen wars, and I've seen a lot of distress that most people wouldn't be subjected to, particularly a woman. The way I developed originally to get around it was to look and see very concrete beautiful things. But I also realized it was important not to talk to people about it because if you said to some of your male colleagues that you couldn't face it, then it was an excuse not to allow you to do those police rounds again. So often I find, particularly today, that well-meaning friends can interfere with your spiritual journey. They can say, 'Just pull yourself together', or 'I could cope with that', and they're putting their judgements on you. So rather than talk to people about it, except to those people I think are capable of understanding, I just look at things that are beautiful.

Another technique I developed in New York when I was covering an assignment for the United Nations. I was at a function at the UN where Mrs Thatcher and Ronald Reagan had been talking about poverty. I walked out, and two streets down on the Lower East Side there were mice going across a newspaper, and there was this guy, and I took the newspaper off him and he was dead. He'd been

dead for two days. Being from Australia I hadn't experienced people dead in the street. That weekend I spent at
Ithaca planting trees and canoeing because it was my way
of getting in touch with the earth. I felt very much
betrayed by the people I had seen at the UN, by the
Reagans and the Thatchers who said they were concerned,
but it was obvious they had no concept of the common
man. Again if I had expressed that I would have sounded
like a middle-class idealist who couldn't cope. So I found
the answer in the earth, because there was no way of justi-
fying that insanity. I use the same principles today. When
I have something to work out I know I will eventually
work it out. I think, if we expect things from people,
people will always let you down. But the earth won't let
you down. It's always there. I do a lot of swimming at
Bronte. You don't have to make an appointment to catch
a wave. The wave is always there.

It is sad that we usually acquire our uncertain wisdoms late
in life after much hard experience. It is sad, too, that we so
rarely acquire these uncertain wisdoms from our elders. In the
ordinary modes of teaching the young will not learn from the
old. Of course, while with very good reason the young hate
and distrust the old, they will not learn from them. However,
what the young do learn is not from what the old say but from
what they do.

When I asked Diana Leidel what uncertain wisdoms she
would want to teach her son Ed she said, 'To be fair. I don't
know whether I've communicated that to Ed or he's communicated that to me. I also think to work with intensity. To be
involved in whatever you're doing. I would hope to communicate to him to choose something that is challenging and pleasing
to him and devote himself to it. To make choices. I think that's
something I didn't do for a long time. Time and chance make
choices for you, and you don't get the satisfaction that you
might otherwise have. And to love, to show that you love, to
make space for it.'

Here Diana was describing how she actually lives her life.

Her uncertain wisdoms are there every day for Ed to see.

'Time and chance make choices for you.' There is that word 'time' again.

What uncertain wisdoms are there about time?

CHAPTER 6

From absolute time to created time

MIROSLAV HOLUB'S poem 'Brief Thoughts on Time' concerns a cannon 'which is perched on the walls of a castle overlooking a city. A stranger comes to the city and is immensely impressed with its orderliness and efficiency. He is told that the good order of the community has much to do with the firing of a cannon from the castle walls at precisely one o'clock every day.

'He goes to see the cannon and asks the soldier how he can be sure it is always precisely one o'clock when he fires. "Ah," says the soldier, "each day as I come up here to fire the cannon I pass the jeweller's shop. In the window is a chronometer and beside the chronometer is a sign which says, 'This is the most accurate chronometer in the world.' I set my watch by it and then proceed up the walls."

'The stranger is impressed and as he walks back down towards the city he passes the jeweller's shop. Sure enough, there is the chronometer and the sign. "How," he asks the jeweller, "can you be sure that your chronometer is the most accurate in the world?" "Well," says the jeweller, "every day a cannon is fired from the walls of the castle at precisely one o'clock. I check my chronometer against it and it is always right."'[1]

Time is our creation.

All our ways of measuring time, keeping time, being on time, picturing time, enjoying time, fearing time, are our creations.

We think of time and space as being essential attributes of the universe, but they are simply concepts which we have created in order to make sense of our experience. If we, and any other self-conscious species, didn't exist presumably the universe would still be there, doing what it does, getting bigger, getting smaller, staying the same or whatever, but there would be no 'bigger' or 'smaller', no 'before' or 'after', just as there would be no colour, merely different kinds of light bereft of any eye which might call them 'red' or 'green' or 'white'.

In his study *The Natural Philosophy of Time*, G. J. Whitrow wrote:

> From all the evidence we conclude that our conscious sense of time depends on the mechanism of attention and the coding and storage of information in the brain rather than on any specific internal organ of time experience. It is affected not only by our general mental and physical state, including our age, but also by the nature of our surroundings and by the culture in which we live. *Our sense of time is neither a necessary condition of our experience, as Kant thought, nor a simple sensation, as Mach believed, but an intellectual construction*. It depends on processes of mental organization uniting thought and action. It is a late product of human evolution, in all probability closely related to the development of language. Moreover, we have no reason to assume that any living creature other than man has the capacity for temporal awareness.[2]

What amazing creatures we are! And how tragic that we don't appreciate how amazing we are. We denigrate ourselves, and create imaginary superior beings to admire and obey, instead of understanding what extraordinary feats all of us achieve every moment of our lives.

Here we are, part of a wondrous universe, yet we have no way of apprehending that universe directly. Our problem is 'that human beings cannot obtain an objective view of the universe. Everything we experience is mediated by our brains. Even our vivid impression that the world is "out there" is a wonderful trick. The nerve cells in our brains create a simplified copy of reality inside our head, and then persuade us that we are inside it, rather than the other way round.'[3]

We look around and see what we think is the world out there around us, and we confidently act upon that world. 'The way in which the world looks sensible and final at any moment,' said the poet Les Murray, 'masks the vertiginous process of its continuous creation and destruction.'[4]

It is tragic that we don't understand this vertiginous process, for on those occasions when the process fails, as it does when we are greatly frightened, or very tired, or ill, or dying, we see our creations just as creations, and, like a tightrope walker suddenly discovering the perilousness of his position, become very afraid. The people around us become afraid too, and call us mad, or demented, and treat us at worst harshly or, at best, with uncomprehending compassion. Or else they insist that we are undergoing some magical, mystical experience. They say that we are in touch with spirits, or God, or are having an out-of-body or near death experience.[5] This explanation might please us for it gives a special significance to our lives, or it might frighten us for it makes us feel alien. In either case we are mistaken because for human beings our experience is commonplace.

Because we don't understand that we create our world we find it exceedingly strange that time does not always behave in the orderly fashion that our measurements of it imply that it should. We are puzzled because sometimes time goes fast and sometimes slowly, or that past time can seem more real than present time.

Because we don't understand that we create our own individual time we are not aware that the regularities we observe in the measurement of time are simply agreements we have made with one another. Because we think that time is an absolute attribute of the universe, going on whether we are there to see it or not, we think that we all mean the same thing when we speak of time. But we do not.

Within our social group we share certain constructions of time. You and I read a clock face or a digital clock in very much the same way. However, you might regard punctuality as an essential virtue and I might not. Accordingly, when we arrange to meet at 18.00 you would interpret this 18.00 precisely, while

I would see it as 18.00 give or take twenty minutes. If I asked you why punctuality was important to you, you might say, 'Time is precious', thus applying to time an image which I did not share.

The constructions of time which we share with other people and our constructions of time which are totally idiosyncratic are never separate entities but operate within the wholeness of our meaning structure. However, here, for the sake of a clear argument, I shall set them out separately.

SOCIAL CONSTRUCTIONS OF TIME

We see time as we do because, as a species, we live on earth. If we lived in another part of the universe we would see it differently. In his gem of a book *Time in History*, which anyone interested in time should read, G. J. Whitrow explained, 'The time kept by us in civil life is based on the rotation of the earth, which gives us our day. Similarly, the earth's motion around the sun gives us our year. If, however, we lived on the moon, we should find that, since the moon spins on its axis so much more slowly than does the earth, each day as determined by the moon's rotation would in fact be equal to a month.'

However, 'The way in which the terrestrial day is divided up into hours, minutes, and seconds is purely conventional. Similarly the decision whether a given day begins at dawn, sunrise, midday, sunset or midnight is also a matter of arbitrary choice or social convenience.'[6] The ancient Egyptians chose dawn as the beginning of the day, while sunset was chosen by the Babylonians, Jews and Muslims. Western Europe used dawn until the advent of the striking clock whereupon midnight was chosen as the start of the next day.

Perhaps the only concepts about time which all societies throughout history have in common is that of day and night. I say 'perhaps' because there could conceivably be a society which found no reason to distinguish night from day. G. J. Whitrow said:

There is no intuition of time that is common to all mankind. Not only primitive people but relatively advanced civilizations too have assigned different degrees of significance to the temporal mode of existence and to the importance or otherwise of the temporal perspective. In short, time in all its aspects has been regarded in many conceptually distinct ways.[7]

You and I live in a society where the past, present and future are seen to be separate and distinct. This is not common to all cultures. The anthropologist Evans-Pritchard studied the Azande of southern Sudan and concluded that 'for them present and future overlap, so that a man's future health and happiness depend on future conditions that are regarded as already existing. Consequently it is believed that the mystical forces which produce these conditions can be tackled here and now.'[8] The Azande see their world in terms of magic. They make decisions and resolve disputes through ceremonies which are deemed to be able to contact the future which is present. The ability of chickens to survive doses of poison feature in such ceremonies. It is an interesting way to live, but tough for chickens.

The Nuer, whom we now see on our television screens as victims of war and famine, was another tribe studied by Evans-Pritchard. He found that they had no word for time and needed none, for they did not conceive of time as something which could pass, or could be saved or wasted. Instead they thought in terms of the order of their social activities and important events, like floods and pestilence. Years for the Nuer were cattle years. Drought and famine must now be changing their chronology.

LANGUAGE CREATES REALITY

Different languages create different kinds of time. 'It is only in Indo-European languages that distinctions between past, present and future have been fully developed.'[9] In English 'the future is predominantly to lie before us, while in Hebrew future events are expressed as coming after us.'[10]

However, English did not develop distinct ways of identifying future time until after the Norman conquest. Old English
merely adapted the present tense to indicate the future. According to historians of time, the reason for this change was Christianity which required the faithful to look to the future and
consider their salvation. Moreover,

> Time for Christians began with the Creation and would
> end with Christ's Second Coming. World history was
> bounded by these two events. The spread of this belief
> marks the divide between the mental outlook of Classical
> antiquity and that of the Middle Ages. Moreover, our
> modern concept of history, however rationalized and secu-
> larized it may be, still rests on the concept of historical
> time which was inaugurated by Christianity.[11]

In Christian Europe time was seen as a straight line. Other
societies, like the Balinese, saw time as a circle. A new-born
baby was his grandfather returning. In a circle there can be no
progress, just a return to the beginning. Linear time allows
linear progress, and so the idea of progress entered Christian
societies. (On a visit to Bali in 1986 I got the impression that
the Balinese had developed the notion of progress, at least in
the form of, 'The more tourists, the more money'.)

However, in Christian Europe the notion of progress was
first confined to that of personal salvation. In the fourteenth
century:

> Fortune's wheel, plunging down the mighty and (more
> rarely) raising the lowly, was the prevailing image of the
> instability of life in an uncertain world. Progress, moral
> or material, in man or society, was not expected during
> this life on earth, of which the conditions were fixed. The
> individual might through his own efforts increase in virtue,
> but betterment of the whole age would have to await the
> Second Coming and the beginning of a new age.[12]

The notion of progress came into being in the eighteenth

century, partly because of the invention of the marine chronometer 'which revolutionised navigation and thereby saved
countless lives',[13] and partly because 'the intellectual optimism
that characterized the age of enlightenment was based on a
forward looking attitude to time.'[14] The eighteenth century also
saw the beginning of the Industrial Revolution which changed
how people experienced time.

In previous centuries time was amorphous. It stretched or
contracted, or just hung around in gossamer vagueness. Events
were not precisely recorded, but left to be remembered by some
aspect which gave them significance. Only the nobility had their
day of birth recorded. Few people could worry about turning
thirty because few would know exactly when they would turn
thirty.

The Industrial Revolution changed all that. Time became real
and precise.

When Benjamin Franklin was drawing up his list of virtues
for self-perfection he did not include punctuality. In his day
punctuality was a virtue that few people could aspire to, for
only the wealthy had watches which they could carry with
them.[15] The poor factory, mill and mine workers had no alarm
clocks. The owner of the local industry appointed official knock-
ers-up who ran along the streets and banged on the shutters of
each house. The industrial owners controlled the functioning
of the clocks in the factories, mills and mines. Unscrupulous
owners would alter the clocks so as to lengthen the working
day.[16]

The Christian calendar contained a great many holy days and
feast days, and people were not used to working a six- or seven-
day week for fifty-two weeks every year.

With time now a precious commodity, factory owners
were beside themselves over how to get around ecclesiasti-
cal time and secure worker acceptance of the more
demanding work schedule . . . For the most part, the new
class of owners was unsuccessful in converting farmers and
tradesmen into disciplined factory workers. They were too
settled into the temporal orthodoxy of an earlier epoch.

But it soon became apparent that their children, still temporally unformed, provided a much more convenient labour pool for the new industrial technology. Child labour was cheap and could be easily moulded to the temporal demands of the clock and the work schedule. By spiriting children away at the tender age of five to seven to work up to sixteen hours a day inside dimly lit and poorly ventilated factories, the owners insured themselves a captive and manipulable work force that could be thoroughly indoctrinated into the new time frame.[17]

Before the Industrial Revolution most people living a rural life worked when there was work to be done and otherwise were idle. With the spread of factories came the work ethic. '"Lost time," said Poor Richard's Almanac, "is never found again." The work ethic was based on the notion that each working moment was unique and irrecoverable.'[18]

Time became money – not much money for the workers, a great deal for the owners. And the owners owned time because they controlled the clocks.

The Boer War changed all that.

The expression 'wristwatch' did not enter English until nearly 1900. Widespread use of the wristwatch, and the universal awareness of horological time, did not come until after such watches had been worn by servicemen in the Boer War (1899–1902) to synchronize the movements of their army units. Only when Americans could afford to buy watches and clocks and had found ways to make them in unprecedented numbers did they begin to wear wristwatches and measure their lives in minutes.[19]

The Puritan founding fathers in America had believed in a Divine Providence. 'To everything there is a season, and a time to every purpose under the heaven.'[20] Now time and progress appeared to offer an alternative to God's plan. If you worked hard and did not waste time you would make progress. Your efforts would be rewarded. But time was a hard task-master.

'Efficiency', an American gospel in the twentieth century,

meant packaging work into units of time . . . Time entered into every calculation. An effective America was a speedy America. Time became a series of homogeneous – precisely measured and precisely repeatable – units. The workday was no longer measured by daylight, and electric lights kept factories going around the clock.[21]

By the 1930s in America time had a powerful meaning, more powerful than God. People did not have to believe in God but they did have to believe in time. Their life in society depended on it.

America beamed its message across the world. In the late 1930s and early 1940s I was at an Australian school where the day was divided into eight forty-minute periods, and woe betide you if you were late. On Saturdays I went to the cinema where the newsreels were usually more memorable than the films. Each week there was a newsreel from America called *The March of Time*. The presenter, a man, had that sort of deep voice which gives every word a resonance of great significance. When the music and drums boomed he would intone, 'The March of Time', as the title was superimposed over pictures of tanks rolling, guns firing, and uniformed figures – Hitler, Mussolini, Stalin, various generals – paraded themselves. Then followed two or three news stories, and, as the credits rolled, again the voice intoned, 'The March of Time'. All this weighty significance given to 'The March of Time' seemed to bestow a supremely important meaning to the news. Yet the message of the whole series seemed to be that, though events of importance do occur, they, like everything else, can never delay or deter the relentless march of time.

I saw this newsreel every week. It is a wonder I didn't just lie down and let time roll over me like a steamroller.

Instead, I set out to control time. I acquired clocks.

When summer time last came to an end it took me an hour to reset my clocks. There are two clocks in my bedroom, one in the spare bedroom, one in my study, one in the living-room, two in the kitchen, one in my car, and there's my wristwatch. Then there are timers for the fax, the telephone, the central heating, and three light switches. I've really got time under control.

But it always slips away from me. Just when I think I've got hold of it, it gives a canny wriggle and it's gone.

My array of clocks represents both my social understanding of time and my own personal meaning for time.

PERSONAL CONSTRUCTIONS
OF TIME

Social constructions of time and personal constructions of time are interwoven. We present ourselves as dealing with time in the socially accepted way, but our personal constructions intervene.

Scott Budge, in his study of family businesses, found that one factor which could bedevil such businesses was the intervention of personal constructions of time when social constructions should be paramount. He wrote:

> Time is different in the discourses of family and business. Business time draws its referents from its technico-rational basis in capitalism. That is to say, time is clock and calendar time, with deadlines and the apparent possibilities for time management. One is on time, just in time, or late – any way, it is time measured by the clock. In business time is linked with another apparently rational system: money. 'Time is money' said Benjamin Franklin . . .
>
> Family time, on the other hand, cares little for the clock or calendar. Daddy and daughter can both act as if she were sixteen again when she is in her early forties. Second-generation Chief Executive Officers can still be defining themselves in agreement or disagreement with their fathers twenty years after the father has died.[22]

Our personal constructions of time take the form of images, and these images appear in our conversation. An American surgeon whom I heard talking on the radio said, 'These anti-cholesterol drugs could have effects down the road.' His listeners knew that he was talking about time and not literally about a road. A friend telling me how busy her husband was said, 'He's working like there's no tomorrow.'

When Jill Morrell heard that, at last, John McCarthy had been released by his kidnappers, she said, 'Time can now start again.'[23] How aptly this image captures the sense of being trapped and immobile which we feel throughout that space of time when we know that someone dear to us is suffering or missing and we do not know what the outcome will be. Once we do know the outcome, whether joyful recovery or discovery, or sorrowful death, we are released. Time indeed starts again.

In adult life we are so familiar with our images of time we take it for granted and do not think about them. We forget how we learned about time. U. A. Fanthorpe recaptured our childhood experience of time in her poem 'Half-past two'.

Once upon a school time
He did Something Very Wrong
(I forget what it was).

And She said he'd done
Something Very Wrong, and must
Stay in the school-room till half-past two.

(Being cross, she'd forgotten
She hadn't taught him Time.
He was too scared at being wicked to remind her.)

He knew a lot of time: he knew
Gettinguptime, timeyouwereofftime,
Timetogohomenowtime, TVtime,
Timeformykisstime (that was Grantime).
All the important times he knew,
But not half-past two.

He knew the clockface, the little eyes
And two long legs for walking,
But he couldn't click its language,

So he waited, beyond onceupona,
Out of reach of all the timefors,
And knew he'd escaped for ever

Into the smell of old chrysanthemums on Her desk
Into the silent noise his hangnail made,
Into the air outside the window, into ever.

And then, *My goodness*, she said,
Scuttling in, *I forgot all about you.*
Run along or you'll be late.

So she slotted him back into schooltime,
And he got home in time for teatime,
Nexttime, notimeforthatnowtime,

But he never forgot how once by not knowing time,
He escaped into the lockless land of ever,
Where time hides tick-less waiting to be born.[24]

When my friend John Purnell was a small boy, like the boy in the poem, he learned about hurryuptime, don'twastetimetime and makethemostofyourtimetime, and these kinds of time became central to the way he saw himself and his world. When I first met him in 1953 he was very much in love with my friend Nan. He had been a teacher but had left and set up a small garage business with his brothers. Within the space of a few short years and much hard work on his part Purnell Brothers became one of the biggest car businesses in Australia. John still operates in makethemostofyourtimetime but his hurryuptime has mellowed into workplayandresttime.

One evening John and Nan and three of their grandchildren, Stephanie, Jaime and Josh, gathered around their large dining-table where I gave them several sheets of paper and a pile of coloured pens.

'Would you,' I asked, 'draw a picture of you and time.'

They set to work. This is what they produced.

John's picture with its endless stream of clocks reflects what G. J. Whitrow said: 'Most of us feel intuitively that time goes on forever of its own accord, completely unaffected by anything else, so that if all activity were suddenly to cease time would still continue without any interruption.'[25]

Along with the regular flow of time goes life's endless vista of mountains, but John has drawn himself as bigger than the mountains so there is no doubt that he will be able to climb them.

Nan has pictured time as a road which she journeys along. The journey starts with herself in her family group – John and their daughters Jane and Kate. On another occasion Nan had told me that the best time in her life was when her daughters were little, so perhaps that is why she started her time road with depicting that point in her life rather than any earlier point. From the family group she and John go on, their daughters having left them, but then the grandchildren arrive. They too leave Nan and John who then travel together. Now they seem to be moving faster, and at the furthest reaches of the road they seem to be separating. This sense of speed and change is balanced by the drawing of a solid house with smoke coming out of the chimney and flowers round the door. This, so Nan told us, was their family home.

I know this house well. It had been a pretty little white cottage when they first moved into it with Jane as a toddler and Kate a baby. Over the years it has been extended and given an additional floor, so now it is a substantial and handsome mansion. Although Nan and John have other homes and spend much of their time travelling around Australia this house is the pivot of Nan's existence, her point of fixity in the universe of change.

Stephanie was five. She drew a very colourful picture with herself in a blue dress smiling at the world, a flower beside her and four birds above. That, her mother Kate told me, was the way she always drew herself. She linked herself very clearly with time. Her time was day and night. The first circle represented day with green grass at the bottom and blue sky above. The second circle was night with a black sky and a yellow star above the green grass.

Jaime was eight. In this colourful picture she depicts her life and time as being in stages, herself as a baby with her mother, at eight, sixteen and forty. Her four images of herself are looking out at the world, and looking into a mirror, for at eight she was increasingly conscious of herself. She had a strong image of herself as a baby. Those of us who were born before the advent of the video camera know ourselves as babies and small children only from the inside-looking-out view of our memories and from family snapshots. Jaime, so she told me, had often watched the family video of her first birthday party. She was very conscious of seeing herself and of how other people see her.

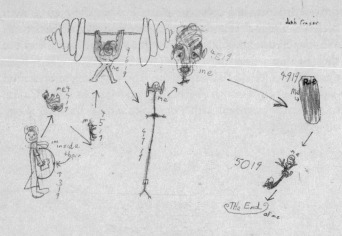

Josh pictured his life and time with the macabre humour of a ten-year-old boy. He presented himself in the form of the events in his whole life, and time as the numbers or imaginary dates beside each stage in his life. The sequence begins in the bottom left-hand corner with himself inside his mother's womb. Then out he pops, and rapidly grows into a very strong young man. From there to adulthood – the long line and a face on wheels – and then to the skull-like face of old age. A large arrow takes him to his coffin, decomposition and 'the end of me'. Josh, so I found in a conversation with him elsewhere, had no belief in an afterlife.

These were five people I knew very well. I was not surprised to see a consistency between their images of themselves and time and who they were as people. Our personal construction of time is central to the meaning structure which is our self.

The next group of friends I involved in such drawings were people I had not known as long as I had known Nan and John and the children, so this time I recorded their descriptions of their pictures.

Lou Miele, his wife Midge and son David, Ron Janoff, Diana Leidel and their son Ed and I were on holiday together on Block Island off the Atlantic coast of the USA. One evening after dinner we gathered around the dining-table where I had provided paper and coloured pens. I asked them to draw a picture of themselves and time, and they worked away diligently. When everyone had finished I asked each of them to talk about their picture.

David was fourteen. He placed time as an hourglass as the centre of his picture on a green circular background. From bottom left to top right time was traversed by yellow suns and yellow cloud representing summer vacations. To the top left and bottom right were two heavy, black, august buildings representing school. Beyond each of these were the promises of the future, a mortar board and a diploma, each emitting rays of golden light.

David said, 'It's the cycle I'm stuck in of the vacation and school cycle. The whole focus of my life right now in school is sort of exciting, I like to learn, but I really get tired of it. The vacation is over too soon. School and vacation is a sort of a cycle and I'm caught up in it. This vacation is too short and I'm not looking forward to another year of high school. Right now I can't even think about what my life's going to be in the future. I'm stuck in this higher education warp. I go to school and I do pretty good, I know it's important to learn, so, I know it's something I have to do, so it's sort of like a cycle I just have to go to school.'

I asked, 'Do you see any point where you'll break out of that cycle?'

'When I go to college it'll be a different sort of cycle. I can't look into the future so much. I'm deep into my school career. That's what I think about now, but I guess, I think college'll be different, possibly more fun, and then I guess, I'll have to think about life after college. I'm not sure what I'm going to do, I guess that cycle'll end when I get out of high school and out of college and into the adult world.'

'Might be another cycle or something straightforward?'

'I'm not sure. It depends on what I do. I mean, I sort of like school. You have to go to school to become what you want, and when you become what you want you pick and choose. Depending on what kind of career I choose it might not be a cycle. It might be different. I may make a lot of money and I can choose what I like. I can go off and vacation whenever I want and choose what to do rather than be stuck in a job which I just keep doing. It could be a cycle because I could get a regular job, big business man, and work nine to five every day and then take vacation every summer just like school. I'd like to do something more than that. Maybe go into an arts career. I'd like to be different. I think this is a sort of cycle that leads to a better life. It's necessary to pattern the rest of your life.'

Midge's picture was very delicate and colourful. It began on the left with little green shoots and tiny pink flowers just showing their head above the brown earth. Then suddenly, in the middle of the picture, a beautiful deep pink flower bursts forth. Then it begins to fade and shrivel as the bright yellow and blue sky turns dark while the green grass dwindles to a black dot.

Midge explained, 'I was thinking about time like a time line right through my life. And this part is like my earlier life which has had lots of colour and lots of happy times, but with things kind of bubbling which emerged finally when I was a young adult and when I met my husband. That's when I began to kind

of come to myself and struggle to find who I was as a person. I'm hoping that the rest of my life will be a continuation of that, but what I realize is that it will probably decline and end in that little black dot.'

Lou's picture was enormously vibrant. In the bottom right-hand corner there was a face looking in all directions. There's even an eye on the top of the head. From this head come red, blue and yellow lines and swirls, and to the left more blue and yellow lines and swirls.

Lou's picture of time was highly abstract. He said, 'My sense of time is my sense of history. I always feel that time is a maelstrom of dimensions or tunnels that each have a logic of their own, and we step in them and out of them like currents of a river. There are pictures of them that are incredibly subjective based on the current of work that you happen to be in when you're looking at something, something in the future or something in the past, something that's personal and something that's objective, cultural, larger, historical, and that it's filled with continuity, there are all these rhythms. It's only a unity as you try to conceive it to give it the name of time, otherwise it's just a series of discontinuities, it's a series of realities and contexts.

Somebody else might be somewhere else in this picture at this moment, they're over here some place, or over there some place and they're looking at the same periods but they see them completely differently. My family's history is off on axes that no one else would ever agree with me upon. Diana a couple of days ago asked me to tell her the story about why I entered a monastery. I've had at least three different currents of explanation in my life since then. What I will give her is the latest one. My latest vision of the sense of the time. I never think of these visions as being anything more than arbitrary and constructive and wonderful. I think this is what artists display all the time. They match up the discontinuities. That's what I like. I'm very much a spectator. I look at things in different directions. Much of my life is spent considering why the things that appear to me really aren't such at all.'

Ed, who was thirteen, explained his picture to us. He said, 'Basically, I see that time is flying. That's what I was thinking about when I drew that clock, and when I drew the egg timer that was losing all its stuff. The cuckoo clock that flew open and this thing that's going back and forth. All I can see is that time is just going crazy. If you really think about it, it doesn't

seem like it's that long, but if you think of the things that you've done, then it seems a lot longer than it might actually be. I drew a circle here because I thought a circle, not a circle but a continuous line that represented infinity. That's a pendulum clock that's gone crazy too. The pan is cooking time, frying time.'

'Why,' I asked, 'is it frying time?'

'That's the way it sort of seems that time goes. Time disappears. If you look at a clock and one second goes by, and you don't do anything but look at a clock in that second, if that makes sense.'

Ron's picture was full of colour and movement. He explained, 'My picture was macro and micro because again if I try to think of time as something, as if time is a thing, then that immediately equates with space, and I find myself in a vast space, and I'm just a dot in it, so there's the dot and there's the thing, and I've no idea whether time goes forward or backwards, whether it goes in a circle, but I don't stop thinking about it, it's just that the universe seems very, very, very big. If by time you meant the space of time of my life, or even of history, or this planet, or any event, that all seems very minuscule in terms

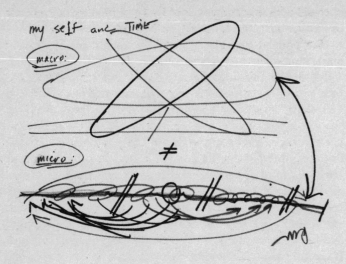

of what I've come to believe about what time is. But that belief doesn't have much shape. It just has vastness as a sort of quality. Whenever I've tried to read about or study or think about time the thing that stood out to me is that philosophically it is a massive thing to fool around with. The more you think about time the worse it becomes as a concept, and the most that happens is that you equate time with the universe, and the universe with vastness with your littleness and you're a very little being in that.'

Ron went on, 'That's fine, but that part of it doesn't equate with anything. So my macro is me. It seemed to me that my experience of life is that, my life and my time. It's not exactly going in a straight line. It's always going in looping time, and it keeps looping back over itself while moving forward at the same time. But there are disjunctions, and there are points at which there's a time where you sort of think forward, and then you spend a lot of the time, conscious time, thinking about time that passed, and then there are times when you think forward and you worry. Thinking forward is worry and thinking backward is guilt. There's a time where you realize you have to start repairing the things that didn't go right here, and you get obsessed with that and you spend a lot of time trying to repair or remake time, and it doesn't really work.'

Ron pointed to a place on the line caught in the looping line, 'Somewhere around here you realize this isn't working, and you start thinking at first, "How can I remake it?", and then you start getting worried because it's not just "How can I remake it?" but "What's going to happen?", because you realize at another point that you're not in control here' (he pointed to one part of the line caught in loops) 'and you thought you were in control here' (again he pointed to a part of the line), 'but actually you discovered here that you were more in control here than there, and you start worrying in general. Your worry from here to here is the worst worry. And then you pass into that space, and once you're in there these parts drop away like stages in a rocket, and you're just that little old thing hurtling forward. It has nothing to do with the clock. It has to do with layers. See the different colours here. There's a yellow, then orange and green and blue. There's always layers in any time.'

Diana's picture had a clock and an hourglass leaping out, high above a tiny house on the prairie – or at least that was my interpretation.

Diana said, 'What you asked me to do was what I was asked to do when I was a child in first grade when they would put on symphonic music like the Peer Gynt Suite and they'd say now draw what you feel about the Peer Gynt Suite. Which never made any sense to me. Given my druthers I'd rather write an essay than draw a picture. So I don't think I can draw a diagram where I can go to this point and this point. All I can do I can put down a form, so therefore I don't know how much I can explain. There's a house. I just sort of didn't try to make any construction. Anything I say now is true, but it wasn't necessarily true when I was drawing it. My explanation is an overlay on what I put down. My background as a painter is that I give it to you, and you tell me what you think of it because I did all this work and you have to do the rest of the work. So I don't really know. I picked nine o'clock because it's always almost nine o'clock in the past year when I have to get all my phone calls made.'

Ed said, 'I like what Salvador Dali did with the melting clock, with time sort of melting away.'

Diana said, 'I think my relationship to time has changed a lot in the past few months. I think I used to be much more hourly oriented during the day. Now I find that time just really flies. I can't keep track of time. It's always several hours later than I thought it would be, or that things take longer, or that I'm enjoying myself and I'm not as aware of time in a clockwise sense or in a linear sense. It seems to be about universal time, less bound in mechanical time.'

Diana had an eight-month-old baby daughter. There's nothing like having a baby to change your sense of time.

In an empty dining-room at the Groucho Club in London I talked to Michael Ignatieff about his image of time. Michael is a remarkable conversationalist. Most of us litter our speech with 'sort ofs' and 'don't knows' and stop and start sentences in the strangest places. Transcribing conversation for the printed page is usually a matter of translating and editing. But not when the speaker is Michael Ignatieff. He is not pedantic, nor does he think for an inordinately long time before producing a sentence, but his thoughts on a topic which he said he had not thought

about before came out in the clear sentences I have transcribed
here.

He said, 'I'm usually aware of time as stillness, standing beside
a lake, absolutely clear, unbroken skin of the water, absolute
complete silence, standing in a snowfield, very white horizon
and a pencil line between the sky and the ground. I'm listening
and hearing no sounds except the stillness of the air itself, or
looking out my window at the night through trees and just
stopping everything and just feeling my breathing, that beat of
the pulse, not so much my own mortality as is implicit in the
pulse, just time itself with a capital T brushing past my window.
That's when I feel closest to time. In fact, all the other sorts of
time, "It's time", "Have I got time?", "I've got to get home in
half an hour", the time discipline aspects of time seem to me
not part of that Time with a capital T at all. I think of Time as
an image of imperceptible movement within great stillness.
That's how I think about Time and always have. It's a very
beautiful experience, just being very still and feeling Time
moving. As you do if you're very still and you watch the sun's
shadow making the transit of a room, or you look through a
window a very, very long time at the sky and watch some diurnal
rhythm of the earth, very, very slow, that's when I feel I'm in
the presence of the big T, big Time. It's very beautiful. And
then, if you see yourself as part of that you feel reconciled to
quite a lot in your own passing along.'

I asked, 'Do you feel you're separate or part of that?'

'I think the nicest feeling is to feel part of that. To feel that
your pulse is connected to this rhythm of the rising of the sun
and the setting of the sun and the rising and setting of the
moon, to feel that you're not a special, detached, privileged
element of this at all, you're just another sort of grain of sand.
That I find a tremendously happy feeling. You feel joined to
something, but nothing spiritual, you're just literally, you could
be a rabbit or some marsupial in a tree with your eyes open and
just, you've got consciousness like them and no different. I don't
like the feeling of being outside and privileged and special. I
think it's an illusion. I often feel those feelings, I'm not saying
I don't feel them, but the greatest happiness is just being part

of this very, very slow rhythm that started long before you and will continue long after you, is without personality, is without direction, is without intention, means strictly nothing, but you see it because you feel that you're part of life and Time is that life. I've never talked about this before.'

He went on, 'I also feel that one is connected to the dead. I do believe my father and grandfather and grandmother are in the ground in a specific piece of earth, they're nowhere else, their bones are rotting away, but I feel very close to them, their memory and that there is that being in time, a human time and that's the most important dimension of time, that connection to the departed. I feel very close to all our family. I find some very obscure comfort in that, I don't know why, so I don't feel the losses are irreparable, as long as you remember. I think that's the most important reason to write. I'm not sure it's so very important to write. There are so many good lives that don't leave a single stick, a single trace behind them, other than the memory of being a good companion and a more or less decent person.'

This brought us to talk of time not as some abstract principle, or force, or path along which we travel, but time as the past, present and future.

EXPERIENCING THE PAST, THE PRESENT AND THE FUTURE

Michael said, 'I feel very close to my parents' generation in that I am the last generation who was marked by the war. Although I was self-evidently too young to experience the war, I felt by surrogate experience that it is part of my life somehow. One thing it left me with was the thought that my parents' lives were more real than my own. My mother had a very tragic and difficult war. They were both in London during the Blitz and interruptedly between 1938 and 1945, but I grew up with the stories of the war and always felt somehow that their emotions were more real than mine and their experiences were more real than mine; more authentic in some way.

'I don't feel that now, I feel that is part of the experience of growing older, that you grow out of that feeling of the inauthenticity, of the lightness and triviality of your own feelings. You learn to realize that they are your feelings, they are all you have got, you cannot wish you had other feelings than you had. I certainly was marked by a sense that real life began before I was born and that my life was a pale continuation. I am perhaps slightly unusual in that respect, I don't know. I think that may be quite a common experience that a child has. It is a kind of reality incarnated in parents' lives which your own life only slowly acquires. I think it was reinforced by the specific generational caesura of being the one after this great historical calamity. I feel that way because my parents talked about it, because they made it very real and I feel a great gratitude towards them for making it real as opposed to hidden or secret or unavowed.'

That part of the past which we feel is ours even though we were not alive to experience my friend Una Gault calls 'the historical cliff'. Over all the years I had known her (we met in 1948 when she was a psychology tutor at the University of Sydney and I was a terrified first-year undergraduate) she had often talked about this image, so for this book I resolved to ask her about it and to record her answer.

Una said, 'I have this distinct feeling that there's this historical cliff where things go back in your memory and in time that you know about, and then you come to a point where you drop over the cliff and beyond that is history. You might have read about it but it's far-off distant times, whereas everything else you can sort of integrate into yourself. I was born in 1925 and for me the historical cliff is just before 1914 somewhere. Perhaps earlier, about the time of Federation,[26] but before that it's all history. When I was at school I studied for Leaving Certificate on my own, private study. My headmaster had been a young soldier, and he introduced me to the war poets and the Georgians. For me modern poetry started with the Georgians and the war poets. I read a lot of war memoirs, works about being in the trenches and so on, all the people who wrote about that, and the First World War seemed very real to me. I was growing up among ex-service men, and although that was all before my time, it was part of my existence. Somewhere back there just before that the cliff starts, and Lloyd George and early Winston Churchill and all those things I learnt about, they were history.'

She went on, 'My father told me stories of when he was a young man and he was born in 1882, so in some ways the cliff sort of tapers off. You can talk about the Depression and I can say I remember the Depression. I can't remember the gay twenties because I was only a tiny little girl. That's a historical epoch I feel I was in then, and I feel I can look back on World War One because of these things I've absorbed. Before that I have to go to the history books, and I don't feel I have that sense of close familiarity and part of my being. My mother was born in 1896. She was a student teacher. She used to tell tales about that. That would have been the early part of the war. Then she came to the city and she used to talk about that, about her boyfriends going away to the war. I feel that's part of me. That's what I feel is the historical cliff.'

Michael and Una were talking about how the way they experienced the experience of other people became part of themselves and part of the story of their lives. Our memories contain much more than just what we have done. Our memories contain other people's stories.

We have two ways of remembering the past. We can, from the vantage point of the present, review the past like a mountaineer from the top of a mountain looking back across the valley and the plain. Or we can relinquish our hold on the present and go back into the past.

A very important person in my childhood was my mother's youngest sister. Her name was Doris, but my mother as a little girl could not pronounce 'Doris' and instead called her Doff, and all the family followed suit. After I was born Mother was not well and Auntie Doff looked after me. (That was the way the story was told in the family. Years later I worked out that Mother must have been depressed.)

Auntie Doff was always unfailingly loving and kind to me. When I was a child she often protected me from my mother's rages, but she was always loyal to her sister, and concerned about her welfare. If I was visiting her she would, for instance, make sure that I arrived back home at the time Mother expected me.

Now old and frail, Auntie Doff spends a good deal of time in a nursing-home where the staff are very kind but there is little going on to engage her interest. She knows that in the future lie increasing frailty and death, so she prefers to think about the past.

Whenever I am in Australia I visit her several times. On one occasion when I called to see Auntie Doff in the nursing home she was having difficulty in seeing clearly. Yet she recognized me and immediately greeted me warmly. We talked about what I was doing, and then we lapsed into silence. After a while she said in a tone I had heard many times before, 'What time's your mother expecting you home for tea?' I held her hand and said as gently as I could, 'You know Mum's not there any more.' Her face crumpled as she felt the loss of her sister and the shame of such a mistake, but then she recovered and we talked some more.

Suddenly the muscles around her eye went into spasm and she was in intense pain. I tried, ineffectually, to comfort her, and asked if her doctor had examined her eye. She said that he would come soon, and, after a pause, said, 'He's always good. He always asks after Mother and Dad. Perhaps he'll send Nurse Nelson to see me.'

Nurse Nelson had lived in the big house across the road from my grandparents' house. She was a respected woman, a bringer of comfort and security to the homes scattered through the bush. This time I didn't remind Auntie Doff that the people who were so real to her at that moment were long dead. When she asked me again what time my mother was expecting me for tea I assured her that I wouldn't be late.

After I left Auntie Doff I sat in my car and shivered and cried. She had spoken to me as she had spoken in the past, in my childhood. I could not have recalled that memory, but when I heard her say, 'What time's your mother expecting you for tea?' it was as if I was back in the past, a past which was now lost to me.

No wonder when people hear old people talking so they say

that they are 'wandering', 'mad', senile'. Such people prefer to categorize the old and distance themselves from them rather than experience these disturbing shifts of experienced time.

When I saw Auntie Doff next she was home for Christmas, surrounded by a talkative son, his three teenage children and a noisy dog. In her own home and with all this activity she was right there in the present. As she had always done, she gave me a cool drink, insisted I had a second slice of Christmas cake, and asked me about my travels.

At whatever age we are, whenever our situation in the present does not claim our attention we drift off into the past or the future. Fantasies about the future can be just as entrancing and demanding as memories, but they have a different quality. We know that our thoughts about the future, be they well worked out plans or the most grandiose of fantasies, are our constructions, the meanings we have created. However, we are often unaware that our memories are also constructions of meaning.

Our memory function is not like a filing cabinet into which we pop a memory like a sheet of paper to be retrieved when needed, and out it comes as it was the day we put it away. Remembering is always an act of reconstruction, and these reconstructions change over time.

Hearing Auntie Doff ask, 'What time's your mother expecting you home for tea?' filled me with sadness and longing. That certainly was not what I felt when I was a child and teenager and she asked me that question. What I felt then was impatience and irritation with these two old women (good heavens, they were in their forties!) who were always checking me, inhibiting me, criticizing me. Home to tea? I wanted to get away, to travel, to be free.

We look at some point in the future and believe we know what our life will be when we get there, but when we do get there everything is different, even the past. How foolish it is to dread turning thirty, forty, fifty, sixty, and so on. When you get there it won't be what you expect. So why ruin the present by imagining the horrors in the future?

There is always a surfeit of real difficulties in the present without needing to add imaginary ones. At whatever age we are, we live in the present, and visit the past and future only in our imaginations. We construct our past and our future.

We are what we remember. We are what we plan. We are our past, and our future, and, for every moment of our lives, we are our present.

CHAPTER 7

Time and timelessness

THIS IS the strangeness of our existence. We live in the memory of the past and the hope of our future, yet all we actually know is a string of present moments.

When we remember the past, it is in the present. When we hope for, or dread, or plan our future, it is in the present.

In present time we can pay attention to what is happening, or we can turn away from the present and lose ourselves in our constructions of the past or the future. To reside solely in any one of those times, past, present or future, is to court disaster. How much time we should spend in one of those special times, past, present or future, is one of those questions for which each of us has to find an answer.

It is not just that the universe is queerer than we think. Life is queerer than any universe we could ever know. Life requires us to live, as Sheldon Kopp said,

> *within the ambiguity of partial freedom, partial power, and partial knowledge.*
>
> *All important decisions must be made on the basis of insufficient data.*

Yet we are responsible for everything we do.[1]

We are totally responsible for ourselves. We can never be totally responsible for other people because we cannot be in control of everything which might affect them, and we can never control how other people interpret what happens to them. We cannot control most of what happens to us, but we do control how we interpret what happens to us. We can choose from a multitude of meanings. Thus we are totally responsible for how we interpret what happens to us, but, whatever interpretations we choose to make, certain consequences will follow.

Choose to fear time passing and growing old, and certain consequences will follow. You'll feel trapped and, one way or another, you will be unhappy.

Choose to see that the nature of life is change, and that to deny that everything changes and try to keep everything the same is to suffer, then other consequences follow. You will be free, and you will have a good chance of being happy.

'Suffering,' so the Buddhists tell us, 'is the attempt to make reality repeatable.'[2]

Perhaps there should be two words for suffering – the suffering others inflict on us, and the suffering we inflict on ourselves.

We cause ourselves to suffer when we fail to understand that the nature of life is change, and that the nature of human beings is to create and impose meaning on the everchanging interconnectedness of everything that exists.

We suffer when we fail to understand that time, like everything else we know, is a meaning which we have constructed.

However, everything that exists is not just a collection of our own individual meanings. There are real events (physical reality and other people's meanings) and our task should be to get as close as we can to understanding what reality is, even though we can never know it directly. If we do not constantly try to do this we become lost in our own idiosyncratic and increasingly unreal world.

To approximate reality we need to be able to compare our approximations of reality with those of other people. If we base our lives on the principle 'All the world's mad except me and thee, and even thee's a little mad' we cannot carry out the reality testing operations which enable us to make sound judgements about reality, and so respond to our perceptions of reality in ways which advance our interests. We need to develop an understanding of other people and of ourselves which allows us to be unafraid of being close to other people. If when young you hate the old, and when old you hate the young, you will go through life being unable to approximate reality to the degree you need to achieve in order to live safely, wisely and happily.

Our negative attitudes about time and age are just part of
the cruelty we inflict on one another. The suffering we inflict
on one another is immense. We should not turn away from it
and pretend it is not happening.

Nor should we, in acknowledging the existence of suffering,
sentimentalize the victims of cruelty, though many of us do,
especially when we have not been the victim but the observer.
Oh, the bravery of those who have gazed on other people's
suffering and allowed themselves to be upset! Oh, the nobility
of those who, having gazed, say to a large audience, 'This is
terrible. Something must be done'! Oh, the virtue of those who
claim to feel guilty for the suffering of those in distant lands!
Sentimentality is easier to generate than compassion. How
much easier it is to see the suffering of those people in far distant
lands than the suffering of those close to us.

There is no special virtue or significance in being the recipient
of cruelty. It does not in itself make anyone's life more significant. Why should it? The majority of human beings who have
existed suffered great cruelty. All that differs is the form. Some
suffered more than most, but only the individual can measure
the degree.

If suffering has a special significance, it is that it should cease,
that those ways of thinking and behaving, so ingrained in
human beings, should change. We should not spend more than
a minute saying and feeling, 'How poignant. How sad.' Instead,
we should ask ourselves, 'How can I change?' If we have the
talent to be sentimental, we have the talent to be cruel. If we
have the talent to dislike, hate, criticize and punish ourselves,
we have the talent to be cruel. Most of us have the talent to
intellectualize and justify our cruelty. How many parents and
teachers resort to, 'I'm only doing it for your own good,
darling'?

When we have looked at ourselves we can then ask, 'How
can I persuade others to consider these questions?'

I am not saying that you *must* go out and confront all the
purveyors of cruelty. There are so many, and you have your life
to live. If you feel you can't change the world (I don't, and I
feel nervous about those who think they might) let's just deal

with what comes our way. Just so long as we don't feel virtuous simply because we have witnessed someone else suffering, and, if we have suffered, feel that we must be recompensed.

It is sad that our increasing knowledge of the effects of the hole in the ozone layer, the population explosion, the destruction of the rainforests, pollution, and so on has not created in everybody an urge to put things right. Instead it seems to have created in many people a heightened selfishness with the attitude: 'I'll get as much as I can now, and the generations after me can fend for themselves.' This is another example of how parents, for their own benefit, sacrifice their children.

Some people would argue that human nature cannot be changed, for there is and always will be some force of evil in the world. I don't believe this, but I do believe that there are certain ways in which people behave greedily, selfishly, cruelly which can be grouped together under the word 'evil'. In my lifetime I have seen no diminution of evil behaviour. Hitler was defeated, but then came the cruelties of the Cold War. The power-hungry Chinese government was restricted if not defeated in Vietnam, but only at the cost of immense suffering which still continues. In the eighties Britain was supposed to have moved on to a more efficient business structure, but it was at the cost of suffering to the many with benefit to the few.

It would be easy to lose heart, but to lose heart would serve no purpose, other than to ruin our lives.

It is better to look after our own interests, but not in the silly, short-sighted way that ensures that vultures come home to roost. We need to look at our lives, not in the context of the short run – 'I want it now' – but in the context of 'What is best for me in the long run?' We should look at our lives, not in terms of a couple of years, or even a decade, but in terms of its full possible length. What will matter most in all that time and ultimately? We should look beyond our death. Do we want to vanish into the great unknown and leave not a ripple behind? Or will there be something achieved and friends to miss us? Only if we feel we are able to answer yes to the second question shall we be able to face our death with courage and acceptance.

Such a way of seeing our lives in time shows us how much

we need to care for one another. The better lives our fellows lead, the better lives we lead. To live in a well-educated society is a richer experience than living in a society where only an élite is educated. To live in a society where one class regards itself as better than its inferiors only serves to create false self-confidence and envy. To live in a society where everyone is healthy is better than living in a society where the sickness of others threatens the well.[3] To live in a society where everyone has an adequate income is better than living in a luxurious prison and in danger from the deprived who are inevitably angry and envious.[4] In all important aspects of living, by giving away we create our own superabundance.

When I was young I understood this only in so far as it applied to people generally. I didn't know how this understanding operated in my relations with individual people. I was frightened of other people, and I took everything a thousand per cent seriously. I remember when I was twenty-three and teaching with Nan in a secondary school where there was often cause for dismay. Something would be being discussed heatedly in the staff-room and Nan, to calm us down, would say, 'It'll all be the same in a hundred years.' I would be *furious*. The matter, whatever it was, was far too important to be dismissed in this way.

Now I find it extremely satisfying to have reached a point in my life where I can see in terms of a hundred years. Now I see things falling into place. Despite the horrors of what is happening in the world, I see – and many of my contemporaries see – that life and its issues are not as desperate as we thought they were when we were young. I want to pass this understanding on to those young people all of whom are struggling with issues which seem so real, so overwhelming, which I found so real, so overwhelming when I was there, but I find myself athwart two places at one time. I know, as much as anyone can know of another person, how those much younger than me feel, yet I cannot convey what I know to them. I want to say, 'Don't worry. Don't invest the issues in your life with such reality. It seems now that everything that presses on you is important. But it will pass. Everything passes. What is happening is serious but not critical – and certainly not eternal. Take life easily. Go, as the Taoists say, with the flow.'

Whenever I am talking to clinical psychology trainees and I say something like that they become furious with me. (My dad always said you only get back what you give away!) They want me to tell them the Secret which all qualified clinical psychologists are supposed to know, which is How to Make People Better. When I say, 'The Secret which all qualified clinical psychologists know is that there is no Secret' they want to lynch me. They are sure that there must be something more than the commonplace, uncertain wisdoms which have been around for ever.

Sometimes I feel like a ghost who witnesses all, but is unable to speak and be heard.

How much time do we need to discover not just that time passes but that it is good that time passes?

When I was a child I would come to my mother with a great idea and she'd say, 'We'll see.' That would infuriate me. Why didn't she say, 'Yes, we'll do it.' Laziness on her part sometimes, and sometimes a desire not to disappoint me – and an awareness of life's difficulties and unpredictabilities.

Now I have great ideas. 'I'll do a book on –' Or I think, 'I'll do such and such' – travel somewhere, interview someone, write to someone. And then I say to myself, 'We'll see.' It's a wise thing to say. I don't immediately spring into action, or feel frustrated because I can't. I know now that my brilliant ideas need time. Time withers some of them. Others grow and blossom. 'We'll see' means 'Don't commit yourself until this passing brilliant idea becomes grounded and real.' 'We'll see' means allowing for the world to show its many faces. 'We'll see' means conserving my energy for what matters. How comforting and reassuring it is that when I'm enthused with a brilliant idea I look in the mirror and my reflection says, 'We'll see.' We always do see, my reflection and me.

It is impossible to understand the wisdom and freedom of 'We'll see' when we believe that we live in a world of Absolute Truths and Absolute Realities.

Teaching children that they live in a world of Absolute Truths and an Absolute Reality has the consequence that, when, later in life, disaster strikes, when they feel that their life is unbearable, they are convinced that they are trapped for an eternity in their quagmire of pain. They are unable to comfort themselves and give themselves hope with the knowledge that everything passes. Nor can they lighten the darkness of their situation with the light rays of humour.

When we hold to absolutes nothing is funny. For instance, most of us like dressing-up. However, we need to remember that this is one way of presenting our fantasies, and aren't fantasies always verging on the ridiculous? How could anybody with a sense of the ridiculous dress like the Pope, or all those Church of England men in frocks? I shall say nothing of those Orthodox chaps in bulbous, glittering pots who are only marginally less ridiculous than the guys in smart suits persuading us to part with our money and prepare for being raptured into heaven.

Yet, if there is any aspect of our lives which fills us with joy, which draws us together in love and acceptance, which sets us above and apart from the misery and degradation we suffer, which reveals to us our potentially great intelligence and understanding, it is our capacity to look at what happens to us and see it in its ridiculous unimportance, and to laugh. Our laughter is the sublimest of our experiences. Life is tragic, and it is very funny. Adults damage and constrain children in many terrible ways. They starve and mutilate children, and that is probably the worst that a child can suffer, because if your body has been damaged it is hard to live properly. However, if you have survived physically, more or less, the next greatest damage you can suffer is to be taught that life is real and life is earnest, and that you must not laugh at your betters, no matter how ridiculous they may be. To be deprived of the right to laughter is the equivalent of depriving a diver of his oxygen supply. In the greatest and smallest of the tragedies which we can encounter, remedies are few, and survival depends on our capacity to laugh.

Teaching children that they live in a world of Absolute Truths prevents them from understanding that the reason the society we live in is so unjust is not because we are wicked and are being punished through the inevitable workings of a Just World design, but because we are lazy. We will not put our minds to solving the problem of how we, each an individual *and* a social animal, each a solitary structure of idiosyncratic meaning, can live together in groups. Such a solution could never be once and for all, but would have to be worked out time and time again.

However, such solutions would need to be based on the understanding that human beings – all human beings – are people, not objects. Children are people, and so are the old. Our capacity to be human is dependent on our capacity to see others as being human.

We need to understand that there may be no justice in this world but there are consequences, and if you make yourself less than human, if you see other human beings as no more than despicable objects which you can use, then, as night follows day, you will suffer. You will become a shrivelled skin of the human being you might have been. You will live and die alone. This is not a curse, or a working out of the Just World. It is a simple scientific fact. Human beings need food. Lacking food, they shrivel and die. Human beings need other human beings. Lacking other human beings, they shrivel and die. If you give up being close to other human beings, you might as well give up breathing.

So, even though there seems to be a great divide between the young and the old, we must try to build bridges.

Suppose, across the great divide between generations, someone did ask me, 'How can I face time passing and growing old?' what would I say?

Just the commonplace, uncertain wisdoms that have been around for ever.

Live as fully as you can. Don't, in old age, have to look back and regret the missed opportunities, the pusillanimous failure to do what you knew was important to you to do. Live in life. Life being what it is, you'll encounter disappointments, losses, failures, and the sheer unpredictability of life, but don't let any of these make you bitter because you foolishly expected to be rewarded for your goodness, or guilty and depressed because you, equally foolishly, believe that you deserve bad fortune. Remember that any contest with life that doesn't actually kill can make you stronger.

Don't burden yourself with stupid, wrong notions about age and time. Don't tell yourself you've got to have made it by the time you're thirty, or that you're finished at forty, or a fossil at fifty.

Be the age you are and make the most of it in the way you know is right for you. Don't feel that you have to prove anything about the age you're at. You don't have to prove that the thirties are successful, the forties are dynamic, the fifties are sexy, and the over-sixties are marathon runners. Be successful, dynamic, sexy and an Olympic champion if you want to, but don't feel that you have to so as to be accepted and allowed to exist. If you want a quiet life and to pass peacefully into gentle old age, do just that. And NEVER apologize for existing.

All you have to know is, 'I am here, I exist, and I belong.'

Growing old has some aspects which are very hard to bear. These are aspects which have no amelioration or recompense. But we are foolish in the extreme when we make these aspects, and every other aspect of growing old, even more difficult by our attitudes of denigration, rejection and contempt for the old. Throughout our lives we should remember that if we do not die young, we become old. Old age and death are inescapable. There are no exceptions.

Life is finite. We should make the most of it.

The finiteness of time gives everything an edge. There's nothing I like better than being with my friends Jill and Alan, Helen and Galen, Jo and Jeremy, Craig, Jacqui, Kevin and Hilary, Nan and John. They are the best conversationalists ever. Sometimes I think that Heaven would be an eternal summer day while we ate and drank, getting merry but not drunk, and talked about everything that had ever arrested our interest or taken our fancy.

But if that were the situation, if we knew that we could indulge ourselves there for ever and ever, the edge, the bite, the make-the-most-of-this, now-is-the-moment-to-make-this-point, the suddenness, the transitoriness, the once and onlyness would disappear. Instead of the brief sharpness of a tart vinaigrette we would be wallowing in jelly.

And even an eternity of bliss would not make life less strange. Life really is odd.

All that experience and then – boomph you've gone and it's all wasted. All that experience there's been – about how to survive in a cave in midwinter, or give birth in a medieval hut, or wheel and deal in the slums of London or Calcutta, or how to make scones that rise, or how to keep hens that lay, all that experience and knowledge that's stored in a skull, and boomph, it's gone. No point in saying you'll take it to heaven. What use will it be there? It's just part of that wonderful superabundance that comes and lives and vibrates – and disappears. There's no way of making it last for ever. Just appreciate it, live it while it's there.

Where we have to get to is the realization that other people and we are all that there is and that we need one another. Not in the way that extraverts need other people in order to feel that they exist. Not in the way that introverts need other people to tie them to external reality. We need other people – one another – because in recognizing, being with, being open to, loving, being close, is the best, the absolute and ultimate best of being alive. The best is not in singing hymns in heaven, or in being rich and famous. The best is in being with other people, feeling accepted, appreciated, and accepting and appreciating others. All else is dross, useless fantasies, lies and confusion. Loving, being close, we can die happy.

Do not sentimentalize what I say. To be close to others we have to drop all pretensions to sentimentality, the close companion of cruelty, its pretensions and lies. To be close to others we have to drop all pretence and be as we are, simply ourselves, neither good nor glorious, wicked nor special, abandoning delusions of God, heaven, wickedness, the devil and punishment. We are simply here, together, frail but loving, joyous, tremulous, simple, here-in-the-present-with-you pleasure and joy. We may not be here for long. In terms of time, our time is brief. But, as we reach out from our lonely, individual knowingness, if we abandon our isolating pride and the obedience-demanding admonitions of our society, we can reach other people, other selves like ourselves, and know that, while we have not lived long, we have lived.

When we live in such a present, time has no meaning.

OF COURSE there are people who understand what time is and don't need me to tell them. Poets know all about time. Seventeen-year-old Alysdair MacLean wrote this poem for his stepmother Jeannie on the occasion of her fortieth birthday.

Life is like your favourite hat
More threadbare as it ages,
More valuable for the years,
More comfortable, better known
But it doesn't get newer
Cleaner or fixed.
Life's a hat
Worn on the head
Lived by the head.
Old hat.

NOTES

1 THE FEARFUL PASSAGE OF TIME

1 Barry Norman on 'The Gloria Hunniford Show', BBC Radio 2, 16 March 1992.

2 Samuel Beckett, *Waiting for Godot*, Faber, London, 1965, p.49.

3 E. Slater and M. Roth, *Clinical Psychiatry*, Baillière, Tindall and Cassell, London, 1970, p.31.

4 Roger Penrose, *The Emperor's New Mind*, Vintage, London, 1989, p.291.

5 Ibid., p.386.

6 Stephen Hawking, *A Brief History of Time*, Bantam, London, 1989, p.133.

7 Paul Davies has popularized the strong anthropic principle in his book *The Mind of God* (Simon and Schuster, 1992). His article in the *Guardian* (15 March 1992) brought a response from Professor John Sparkes.

'Paul Davies wonders where physical laws "come from" and "why they have the form they do". He rejects the ancient idea that physical laws are "thoughts in the mind of God", but is unable to reject the idea that "the laws of nature are written in some secret code" which the physicists are trying to crack. He still believes that physical laws are somehow put there, though not by God. And he believes that the fundamental laws of nature can be "encapsulated in a succinct mathematical expression which you can wear on your T-shirt".

'There is no mystery about the origin of the laws of physics; they come from the physicists who created them and they have the form that they have because they provide the best basis so far devised for explaining and predicting the behaviour of that part of the universe which physicists study.

'But the domain of physics is really rather limited. All but confirmed, repeatable, human experiences, often obtained in a laboratory, are rejected by physics, which means that most human experiences – from personal relationships to

ESP – are excluded. Even some repeatable experiences, such as time going quickly when one is happy and slowly when one is bored, are rejected as evidence about time because they don't fit in with accepted theories.

'But the idea, implicit in the formula, of achieving a mathematical prediction based on physical laws of behaviour is in any case absurd: partly because the calculation would be far too lengthy even if the many billion causal equations could be set up and partly due to the effects of positive feedback. In systems where effects can affect the cause, causal explanations are inadequate – as weather forecasters know well, even when all the laws are understood.

'If Prof. Davies could believe that he and his colleagues were simply helping to devise principles and laws which work rather well in certain situations, he could jettison all the unnecessary mysticism that fills his article.' (*Guardian*, 24 March 1992)

8 Quoted by Peter Coveny and Roger Highfield, *The Arrow of Time*, Flamingo, London, 1991, p.250.

9 Henry Porter, *Observer*, 19 April 1992.

10 Hawking, op. cit, p.164.

11 Ibid, p.185.

12 John D. Barrow, *Theories of Everything*, Vintage, London, 1992, p.130.

13 Ibid, p.15.

14 Ibid, p.210.

15 Quoted by Coveny and Highfield, op. cit, p.281.

16 Penrose, op. cit, p.574.

17 Steve Longhorn, 'Volvo City', *The Cutting Edge*, Roy Acherman and Susanna White, Channel 4 Television, 4 November 1991.

2 FEARING TO GROW OLD

1 'Behind the concern with reform and "good practice" lurks the seemingly ineradicable old-fashioned misery of the aged in institutions, where apathy and depression are often taken for granted, and where the tendency, even when the staff are kindly and well intentioned, is too often still towards infantilising, patronising and depersonalising, "does he take sugar?" attitudes. But not all homes are even kindly and well intentioned – abuses abound, and trouble in homes for the aged which has long been commonplace in America is becoming commonplace here. The miseries of long-stay care are nowadays literally in our midst, for they are diffused in small units which, being so dispersed, easily become almost invisible, while being described as "in the community". There were not many virtues to the old institutions, though there were some, and at least in recent years they had become "visible" and open, and they

had rehabilitation departments and programmes (often slender) of stimulation. The pitfalls of long-stay care have not gone away, and will not go away, and it remains what long ago I called the Achilles' heel of the care of the aged.' Tom Arie, Professor of Health Care of the Elderly, Nottingham University, in the *British Journal of Psychiatry Review of Books*, January 1992, p.7.

2 Margaret Forster, *Have the Men Had Enough?*, Penguin, Harmondsworth, 1990, p.233.

3 'Britain has more over-65s than any other European Community country, a report out today shows. And people are living nearly thirty years longer than when Victoria was on the throne . . . The average life expectancy of a boy born at the turn of the century was 45.5 years and 49 for a girl. By the year 2000 men are expected to live to 74.5 while women can expect to reach almost 80.' *Guardian*, 26 October 1992.

4 Personal communication, 2 November 1992.

5 Ian McEwan, *The Child in Time*, Jonathan Cape, London, 1987, p.31.

6 Tony Parsons, 'First Person', *Guardian*, 28 May 1992.

7 John Milton, Sonnet VII, *The Poetical Works of Milton*, ed. Helen Darbishire, Oxford University Press, London, 1958, p.431.

8 Edward Pilkington, 'Enoch the Sceptic', *Guardian*, 12 June 1992.

9 John Williams, 'Soundtrack', BBC Radio 4, 10 March 1992.

10 Caroline Sarll, 'Rock of Ages', *Observer*, 23 February 1992.

11 John Lennon, in his song 'Beautiful Boy', 1979.

12 Colin Macilwain, *Observer*, 21 April 1991.

13 Otto Fenichel, *Psychoanalytic Theory of the Neuroses*, Routledge, London, 1963, p.575.

14 Rosalind Coward, *Our Treacherous Hearts*, Faber, London, 1992, p.161.

15 Anjelica Huston, *Chat*, 22 February 1992.

16 Emma Tennant, *Observer*, 23 February 1992.

17 Peter Coni, 'Soundbites', *Guardian*, 21 April 1992.

18 Tennant, loc. cit.

19 Melissa Benn, 'The Hite Report', *Guardian*, 3 April 1992.

20 Germaine Greer, *The Change*, Hamish Hamilton, London, 1992.

21 *Guardian*, 24 September 1992.

22 Greer, op. cit., p.337.

23 Emma Tennant, *Faustine*, Faber, London, 1992, p.139.

24 'Opinions', *Independent on Sunday*, 8 September 1991.

25 Marek Kohn, 'The perils in store for the late arrival', *Independent on Sunday*, 21 July 1991.

26 Phillida Salmon, *Living in Time*, Dent, London, 1985, p.40.

27 *Independent*, 3 June 1992.

28 'Pensioner power moves in on Euro parliament', *Guardian*, 3 March 1992.

29 *International Herald Tribune*, 4–5 January 1992.

30 Matthew Gwyther 'Britain bracing for the age bomb', *Independent on Sunday*, 29 March 1992.

31 Martin Walker, 'American Diary', *Guardian*, 9 September 1991.

32 Gwyther, loc. cit.

33 Ibid.

34 David Christie-Murray, *Observer*, 7 July 1991.

35 Nina Bawden, *Family Money*, Virago, London, 1992, p.52.

36 WE ARE NOT GERIATRICS!

Recently *Yours* reported that a distinguished professor had complained that there were two sorts of medical treatment, one for 'normal' people and one for elderly people. Enid and Frank Jordan found that their experience proved his point.

'My wife and I have noted the distinctive attitudes made between those under 65 years of age, and those over, in matters of health.

'We have both passed that milestone, but when recently my wife had to attend the local hospital to see a consultant, she was instructed to report to the geriatric unit, to which she took exception. She does not consider herself a geriatric. After some persuasion she did attend, but raised her objection with the specialist who was most sympathetic.

'We subsequently wrote to our Member of Parliament stating our objections, sending a copy to the hospital and our county councillor. From all quarters we received support. The Department is now called "Medicine for the Elderly", which is an improvement, but why, we ask, differentiate at all? We didn't change when we turned 65.

'We maintain that "geriatric" is a state of health, not an age criterion.

'Furthermore with consternation, that most elderly people of our acquaintance who have to go to hospital to stay seem to find themselves on a Geriatric Ward, often with patients suffering from senile dementia or the like. Although feeling extremely sorry for anyone who has this problem, by classing all over 65's as geriatric, and putting them all together, does have a very detrimental effect on those who are fortunate enough to be mentally alert.

'You attend hospital to be made better, not to be depressed and shown what could be your future.

'When will the authorities realize that at 65 you don't cease to be a valued member of society, and become a different person?

'Why, at that age, are you suddenly "geriatric"? We are not.' *Yours*, April 1992, p.28.

37 Richard Burton, *The Anatomy of Melancholy*, ed. T. C. Faulkner, N. K. Kiessling and R. L. Blair, Clarendon Press, Oxford, 1989, p.103.

38 Celia Hall reviewing
Understanding the Menopause by
Robert C. D. Wilson
(Consumers' Association and
Hodder and Stoughton,
London, 1992), *Independent*,
3 June 1992.

39 'The number of men
committing suicide is rising
dramatically, the Samaritans
said yesterday. The
organization was outlining
how it is trying to target its
counselling services on people
considered most at risk.
Vulnerable groups identified
by the Samaritans included the
young, the old, and ethnic and
rural communities. It is
estimated that four farmers a
week are taking their own
lives . . .

   'Suicide has always been
more common among men
than women . . . The age
group most at risk continues to
be the elderly, with a rate 50
per cent above the average of
the population as a whole
because of problems
associated with bereavement,
isolation, retirement and ill
health.' David Brindle,
Guardian, 16 May 1992.

40 Ruth Hughes, 'The one thing
they never tell you about
HRT', *Independent*, 8 June
1992.

41 Anne Karpf, 'The new face of
ageism', *Weekend Guardian*,
3–4 August 1992.

42 Jay Rayner, 'Daddy Cool',
Arena, Spring 1991.

43 *Guardian*, 24 October 1992.

44 *Independent*, 14 July 1991.

45 Chris Mihill, *Guardian*,
25 June 1992.

46 Greer, op. cit., pp.85, 285.

47 Ernst Cassirer, *The Philosophy of
Symbolic Forms*, Yale University
Press, New Haven, 1953.

48 The meanings we can give to
death, and the implications of
the meanings we choose, are
examined in my book *The
Courage to Live* (Fontana,
London, 1989).

49 Personal communication,
31 May 1992.

3 YOUTH AND AGE: A MUTUAL ANTIPATHY

1 Exodus 20:5, Deuteronomy
5:10.

2 Lloyd de Mause (ed.), *The
History of Childhood*, Bellew
Publishing, London, 1991,
p.1.

3 Julie Flint, *Observer*, 9 August
1992.

   'This is how a starving child
in Africa dies. It is not always
quietly, with round staring
passive eyes, like in the
television pictures. Nor can the
dictionary of suffering do it
accurate justice.

   'In the West, we have got
used to the pictures. The
suffering becomes almost
abstract. We have hijacked the
language of hunger, raided its
vocabulary, amortised its
meaning and robbed it of its
real impact.

   'Just miss one lunch and we
are "starving". We will
complain of "hunger pains" all
afternoon. By the evening we
will be utterly "famished". We

might even be "dying" for some food.

'The African children, too, are dying for some food. Or dying for the lack of it. From the moment they are deprived of food, their bodies begin to shut down, to economise, to cut out non-essentials. They become famished.

'Dr Andrew Prentice, of the Medical Research Council, says they are bodies "in recession". "They are in a defensive mode." Every expenditure of energy is subservient to the greater need to keep the brain going via the heart and liver.

'Metabolism is reduced, the body shuts down on unnecessary physical activity. This produces the familiar signs of lethargy. The heart slows down. Apathy is not a description, it is a recognized medical symptom of starvation.

'In Africa, the children have little reserves of body fat to start with, so the onset of protein loss is quite quick. Doctors estimate that a Western child would have to starve for three or four weeks before they would reach the physical condition in which an African child starts.

'Because of the protein loss, their guts atrophy, vital organs are reduced in size, vitamin deficiency increases, raising apathy. They lose any desire to move. Unable to produce glucose for the brain, the liver desperately produces an unsuitable chemical alternative. If anything, pain gets less as the brain, too, begins to economise, reducing its expenditure of energy on emotions and reactions. They are unnecessary.

'In this grimly efficient hierarchy of economy, the body now reduces further the amount it spends on defence, to protect its most vital functions. The skin stops repairing itself. The child acquires an immune deficiency syndrome.

'It then dies. It may not actually die of hunger but of some disease brought about by its inability to fight off the disease. Or it may die from actual hunger. It may die because, in the chilling words of Professor Alan Jackson of Southampton University, "the child no longer has the strength to breathe." Daily, more children are losing that strength.' Peter Hillmore, *Observer*, 23 December 1990.

4 de Mause, op. cit., p.27.
5 'Seven people accused of sacrificing a child, aged seven, in a satanic ritual to win political success in the forthcoming elections have been arrested by police in the southern state of Parana (in Brazil). They include the wife and daughter of the mayor of Guaratuba, a seaside resort 700 miles south of Rio de Janeiro, where the boy, Evandro Caetano, was kidnapped and killed in April . . .

'The mayor's name appeared in a notebook belonging to the leader of the group under arrest, Oswaldo Marceneiro, who is known in Guaratuba as a *pai de santo* or Afro-Brazilian spiritual leader. Instead of the usual animal sacrifices he confessed to using the seven-year-old as a human sacrifice. Police say that he has confessed to kidnapping another boy, Leandro Bossi, also aged seven, who disappeared in February in the same town . . .

'In a taped confession played to the press by the Parana police chief, the mayor's wife, Celina Abagge, said the boy was strangled and his throat was cut. His chest was then opened up with a saw and his heart was torn out and offered to the devil. His feet and hands were cut off.

'When the child's body was found in a wood the mayor's wife visited the child's parents to comfort them.' Jan Rocha, *Guardian*, 7 July 1992.

6 'It is a sweet and seemly thing to die for one's country.' Horace, *Odes*, III. ii.13.

7 'In the depths of the Thar Desert in north-western Rajasthan live the legendary Rajputs . . . This is a fiercely masculine culture, where *purdah* is enforced and all the women veiled. The birth of a boy is greeted with songs and celebrations; a girl, particularly among the Bhatti Rajputs, has a very different reception. For century after century,

newborn girls have been slaughtered, in what is perhaps the ultimate preemptive strike. The custom, which originated in the desire to prevent the family's honour from being tainted were the girl to be raped by invaders or make an unsuitable marriage, is now used to solve the problem of the dowry.

'"A piece of opium, some damp sand on the nose – it takes about 15 minutes, then she dies" . . .

'For the desert dwelling Rajputs, struggling to survive in an inhospitable environment, tradition-bound and isolated, the excuse of "backwardness" is made. When people are educated, I was told on innumerable occasions, they will no longer kill their female offspring. But throughout urban India, modern ultra-sound technology is adding a new twist to this penchant for slaughtering girls. My interpreter, a middle-class businessman, told me that when his wife was pregnant she wanted to have the foetal sex-determination test in Barmer, the nearest large town. Although the test can only be carried out at five or six months, if the foetus is a girl, it is invariably aborted. Across the country signs are springing up proclaiming, "Spend 600 rupees now, save 50,000 later" in a blatant exhortation to kill a baby to forestall a dowry payment. Out of 8,000 abortions carried out in one Bombay clinic following foetal sex determination, 7,999 were female . . .

'Most countries have more females than males, expressed as the number of females per thousand males. In India, the number of females dropped from 972 per 1,000 in 1900 to 935 in 1981, and the decline continues. In Rajasthan the figure is 811 females per 1,000 males. Overall, India has a deficit of 30 million females, equivalent to the entire UK female population.' Pamela Nowicka, 'India's Dowry of Death', *Observer* Colour Supplement, 2 August 1992.

8 John Boswell, *The Kindness of Strangers*, Penguin, Harmondsworth, 1988.

9 Ibid, p.3.

10 Ibid, p.428.

11 Ibid, p.430.

12 Ibid, p.429.

13 Barbara W. Tuchman, *A Distant Mirror. The Calamitous Fourteenth Century*, Knopf, New York, 1978, p.53.

14 de Mause, op. cit., p.16.

15 Alice Miller, *Thou Shalt Not Be Aware*, Virago, London, 1990.

16 Boswell, op. cit., p.430.

17 Ibid, pp.431, 433.

18 In London I am often accosted by children and adolescents asking for money. They are always sad, ill and embarrassed. However, they are part of a long tradition.

'In 1848 Lord Ashley (later, Lord Shaftesbury) compassed a figure of 30,000 *shelterless* street Arabs in London's population of 2.5 million . . . nearly thirty years later Dr Barnado could still estimate some 30,000 homeless youngsters in the capital. Child beggars in fact formed a high proportion of all beggars in the country. Just how eagle-eyed and rampant they were can be gauged from Charles Dickens's account in *The Uncommercial Traveller* (1865). Walking through the street, he once bumped into and knocked over a ragged little scrap. When he stopped to help him up and give him some money out of sympathy, fifty similar ragamuffins "were about me in a moment, begging, tumbling, fighting, clamouring, yelling, shivering in their nakedness and hunger. The piece of money I had put into the claw of the child I had overturned was clawed out of it, and was again clawed out of that wolflike grip, and out of that, and soon I had no notion in what part of the obscene scuffle in the mud of rags and legs and dirt, the money might be."' Lionel Rose, *The Erosion of Childhood: Child Oppression in Britain 1860–1918*, Routledge, London, 1991, p.80.

19 de Mause, op. cit., p.37.

20 Ibid, p.38.

21 D. E. Garland and G. L. K. , in *The International Standard Bible Encyclopedia*, 1988, Vol.4, 5, p.670.

22 Luke 2:7.

23 Garland and G. L. K. , loc. cit.

24 Ofra Ayalon, personal communication, 29 July 1992.

25 de Mause, op. cit., p.37.

26 Ibid.

27 Ibid, p.38, quoting William P. Dewees, *A Treaty on the Physical and Medical Treatment of Children*, Philadelphia, 1826, p.4, and Hester Chapone, *Chapone on the Improvement of the Mind*, Philadelphia, 1830, p.200.

28 Patricia Robertson, 'The Home as a Nest', in de Mause, op. cit., p.411.

29 de Mause, op. cit., p.37.

30 Ibid., pp.37–8, quoting Earle L. Lipton, Alfred Steinschneider and Julius B. Richmond, 'Swaddling, A Child Care Practice: Historical Cultural and Experimental Observations', *Pediatrics*, Supplement 35, part 2 (March 1965), pp.521–67, and Turner Wilcox, *Five Centuries of the American Costume*, New York, 1963, p.17.

31 Elizabeth Wirth Marvick, 'Nature Versus Nurture', in de Mause, op. cit., p.270.

32 Footbinding was not the only cruelty inflicted on girls. The Confucian scholar Chiang Yee visited China for the first time after forty-two years. He wrote:

'Another innovation struck me with particular force when I revisited China: I saw many men and women working together in the communes and factories. It showed me that the Chinese woman's position has been raised to equality with men. This is the greatest turnabout that has happened in China since the second century BC. Since the western Han period, when Confucianists became the administrators of the government, the difference between men and women had been highly stressed and, in fact, women were set apart on a lower level of society from men. The Confucianists had a saying that it is a virtue for women to be without intelligence. They stressed that a woman's life has three stages of obedience. At home she obeys her father's will; after marriage she obeys her husband's will; and, if her husband dies, she obeys her son's will. In other words, she has no will of her own and cannot live by herself for she has no knowledge of anything and would be unable to work. There had never been any jobs set aside for women to do except embroidering, housework, or serving as wet nurses. Throughout the whole history of China the very few women who were educated could almost be counted on the fingers . . .

I remember how in my young days many women I knew, among my relations, for instance, never had the chance or ability to get a job and they had to put up with whatever type of husband they happened to marry. Some men could be quite cruel or, being annoyed with the loss of a job or some other misfortune, could run into a temper and even beat their wives . . .

Apart from those women who were born into wealthy families, no woman enjoyed a proper life as a human being. If she was a second or third child in a poor household, she would not receive as much food as her brothers. If famine or drought occurred when she reached the age of ten or more, she would be the one to be sold to a rich family as a maidservant so that her parents could make use of the little payment to keep them alive for a time. The first day she entered the house to which she had been sold, years of misery began. It seldom happened that those who could afford to buy a maid would not try to get their money's worth; they would drive the tender-aged girl to work as hard as she could, though occasionally the girl might find a kind-hearted mistress. On top of all her troubles, the old master as well as the young master of the house would take advantage of her youthful face and innocent mind to seduce her. Should that happen and be found out by the mistress, the girl would be severely scolded or even half beaten to death. She could not run back to her parents or go to a nearby police station, for she would be sent back

immediately. Throughout the history of China, countless unhappy girls must have died by torture or for some misdeed for which they were not to blame. China in past centuries was always known to the west as being well ruled by great Confucianist scholars. And no Western students of Chinese philosophy would find these miseries for Chinese women in the Confucian classics. I am sure that Confucius did not mean that Chinese women should be treated in such a bad way. It was the later Han Confucianist scholars, who reinterpreted his words, who were to blame.' Chiang Yee, *China Revisited: After Forty-two Years*, Norton, New York, 1977, p.167.

(I find it surprising that Confucius did not know that when one group of people is defined as inferior, those people who regard themselves as superior feel that they have the right to be cruel.)

33 de Mause, op. cit., p.38.
34 See Andrew Scull, *Museums of Madness*, Penguin, Harmondsworth, 1972, and Elaine Showalter, *The Female Malady*, Virago, London, 1987.
35 de Mause, op. cit., pp.43, 45, 47.
36 Ibid, p.48.
37 Ibid, pp.40, 41.
38 For a longer discussion of this topic, see Dorothy Rowe, *Wanting Everything*, HarperCollins, London, 1991, pp.78–114.

39 de Mause, op. cit., p.41.

40 Rose, op. cit., pp.184, 181.

41 A. N. Wilson, *Evening Standard*, 25 September 1992.

42 *Guardian*, 4 August 1992.

43 Rose, op. cit., p.181.

44 But at least I was treated better than the first white children in Australia. In 1800 Governor King reported to the Duke of Portland, 'Soon after my arrival in this colony I had frequent opportunities of observing the numerous children of both sexes going about the streets in a most neglected manner. This observation was confirmed by the many distressing relations made to me of the early abuses the female part suffered, not only from the unprotected state they were in, but also from the abandoned examples of their parents, and those to whose care the orphans are committed.' Gwyn Dow and June Factor (eds.), *Australian Childhood*, McPhee Gribble, Ringwood, Victoria, 1991, p.7.

45 de Mause, op. cit., p.4, quoting from Charles Seltman, *Women in Antiquity*, London, 1956, p.72; Daniel R. Miller and Guy E. Swanson, *The Changing American Parent*, New York, 1958, p.10; Bayne-Powell, *The English Child in the Eighteenth Century*, London, 1939, p.6; Laslett, *The World We have Lost*, New York, 1965, p.12; Aries, *Centuries of Childhood*, pp.103, 105, Alan Valentine (ed.), *Fathers to Sons: Advice without Consent*, Norman, Oklahoma, p.xxx, Anna Robeson Burr, *The Autobiography: A Critical and Comparative Study*, Boston, 1909.

46 By 1897, 'Freud had altered the direction of his thinking. Earlier he had recognized the aggressive acts of parents against their children – for seduction is an act of violence. Now Freud had a new insight, that children had aggressive impulses against their parents; cf *Origins of Psychoanalysis*, p.207: "Hostile impulses against parents (a wish that they should die) are also an integral part of neuroses." Indeed, why should children not wish for vengeance for a crime committed against them? If the seductions had actually taken place, these "aggressive impulses" would have been a healthy sign of protest. But once Freud had decided that these seductions had never occurred, that the parents had not done anything to the child in reality, then these "aggressive impulses" replaced seduction in Freud's theories. An act was replaced by an impulse, a deed by a fantasy. This new reality became so important to Freud that the impulses of parents against their children were forgotten, never to surface again in his writings. It was not only the aggressive acts of a parent that were attributed to the fantasy life of a child; now aggressive impulses belonged

to the child, not the adult.'
Jeffrey Masson, *Freud: the
Assault on Truth*,
HarperCollins, London, 1992,
pp.112–14.

47 Sigmund Freud 'Infantile
    Mental Life: two lies told by
    children', *Collected Works*,
    trans. and ed. James Strachey,
    1950, quoted in *The Penguin
    Book of Lies*, Philip Kerr (ed.),
    Viking, London, 1990,
    p.290–3.

48 Ibid, pp.290–1.

49 Ibid, pp.292–3.

50 Rose, op. cit., pp.215, 216.

51 'The Children's Employment
    Commission of 1842–3
    exposed the horrors of child
    labour in the mines: children as
    young as 5 being sent below
    ground; multiple shifts
    creating spells of up to 36
    hours at a time underground;
    boys' and girls' cattle-like use
    as wagon-pullers in narrow
    shafts; beating and whippings
    by older workmen as regular
    and habitual; injuries from
    roof falls or wagons rolling
    over them; and industrial
    disease of the lungs and skin.
    Periodic mining disasters had
    claimed many tragically young
    lives among the victims. In
    1841 the 46 collieries
    shipping coal from the Tyne
    employed 7,261 adults and
    about 2,000 aged 13–18, and
    admitted only to employing
    nearly 1,500 children below
    13. Employers argued that the
    cheap and plentiful supply of
    child labour kept costs down
    and children were useful to

work the narrow seams. The
1842 Mines Act banned all
females and boys under 10
from underground work, but it
was widely evaded, and even
in 1860 boys of 6 were
working underground where
the seams were awkward or
thin.

'In the pottery trade
youngsters could work in
temperatures of 120–148°F.
They served as 'mould-
runners', carrying the article
fresh out of the mould to the
stove room, where the
atmosphere was charged with
particles of fine clay. This
contaminated and over-heated
atmosphere brought about
chest ailments, stunted growth
and premature death. In the
wall-paper staining trade
children worked from 6 a.m. to
9 or 10 p.m. and were in danger
from arsenic poisoning from
the green dyes used in colouring.'
Rose, op. cit., pp.11, 13.

52 Derek Brown, writing his
    Bombay Diary, reported, 'The
    kids who love the monsoon are
    those lucky enough to be able
    to play in it. There are others.
    This week the papers have
    reported municipal plans to
    mechanise the dreadful work
    of draining storm drains and
    sewers, now done manually.
    But, it is thought, the sub-
    contractors will resist the
    reform. Small boys and girls
    are so much more adept than
    machines are at crawling
    through the 18 inch drains.
    And, at less than 50p a day, so

much cheaper.' *Guardian*, 8 August 1992.

53 'From 1862 the Education Secretary Robert Lowe introduced more stringent criteria for subsidy as an economy measure to ensure "value for money". This was the Revised Code, known to the teachers as "Payment by Results", which was to bedevil the education system for the next thirty years. Individual school subsidies (upon which teachers' salary levels partly depended) were to be assessed for the year, upon the school inspectors' visits, according to pupils' performances in the three Rs alone; subjects like history and geography were left out of account and so suffered in the school timetable. Children were ranked in six 'Standards', according to age alone, from Standard 1 at age 7 to Standard 6 at age 12. Pupils had to satisfy the inspector of competence in the three Rs at the standard for their age, regardless (at least in the earlier codes) of their ability. Attendance levels were also taken into account in the grant assessment. Schools became high-pressure examination factories; all teaching was geared to the annual descent from Olympus by the awesome inspector.' Rose, op. cit., p.119.

54 'Teaching was inevitably authoritarian and the learning process regimented; it is significant that the earliest form of physical instruction was called "drill". Children were not only taught their place as children, but also taught their future proper place as adults. Elementary schoolchildren were intended to be operatives or clerks. This attitude was particularly strong in country schools, where the social hierarchy was strictly defined, and the local bigwigs on local councils and school committees. They wanted to turn out docile farm labourers and domestics respectful of their betters, not social aspirers. Flora Thompson recalled how in greeting their starchy schoolmarm each morning the boys pulled their forelock and the girls curtsied. When the rector had given them their Scripture lecture he delivered a lecture on morals and behaviour: "The children must not lie or steal or be discontented or envious. God had placed them just where they were in the social order and given them their own especial work to do; to envy others or to try and change their own lot in life was a sin of which he hoped they would never be guilty."' Ibid, p.134.

55 'The spaciousness of the upper-class villa permitted the relegation of children to the remote parts of the house, out of sight and sound; and the employment of staffs of servants to supervise them relieved parents of the need to

play a part in their early upbringing. Fathers were too grand and busy, and mothers too elegant and superior, to attend to the feeding and nurture of their numerous progeny. From the moment of birth a wet-nurse, or patent brands of baby food of dubious nutritious value, would be the instinctive and customary answer to the problems of feeding; mother's figure and time to socialize took overriding precedence. Many children, surrounded by nurses and nannies, were raised to feel that physical distance from the parent was right and proper. Gwen Raverat recalled; "I can never remember being bathed by my mother, or even having my hair brushed by her, and I should not have at all liked it if she had done anything of the kind. We did not feel it was her place to do such things." However, there were many children, too, who keenly felt their parents' remoteness and suffered mental dereliction from cold and perhaps uncaring fathers and social butterfly mothers. One psychological comfort was the sublimation of parents into idealized beings, idols to be worshipped from afar, who in children's fantasies would surely appear to rescue them from distress. The young Winston Churchill worshipped his socialite mother in this way: "She shone for me like the Evening Star. I loved her dearly – but at a distance."'
Rose, op. cit., p.222.

56 Ibid, p.227.
57 de Mause, op. cit., pp.11, 12.
58 Ibid, p.49.
59 Lucy Johnstone, 'Family management in "schizophrenia": its assumptions and contradictions', *Clinical Psychology Forum* 47, September 1992, p.3.
60 *Guardian*, 3 August 1992.
61 Amnesty International, *Report*, October/November 1989, p.12.
62 'Some African and Arab women are speaking out against the custom of female genital mutilation, but in the face of much opposition from "certain Muslim fundamentalists and some women who hold absolutely to the continuation of these customs in the name of ancestral values" . . .

'The types of mutilation used are

* **Circumcision** Cutting the hood of the clitoris, known in Muslim countries as Sunna (tradition). This, the mildest type of mutilation, affects only a small proportion of the millions of women concerned.

* **Excision** Cutting of the clitoris and all or part of the labia minora.

* **Infibulation** Cutting of the clitoris, labia minora and at least two-thirds of the labia majora. The two sides of the vulva are then pinned together with silk or catgut sutures, or thorns, leaving a very small

opening, preserved by the insertion of a reed or tiny piece of wood, for the passage of urine or blood. These operations are done with special knives (in Mali, a saw-toothed knife), razor blades, or pieces of glass. The girl's legs are then bound together from hip to ankle and she is kept immobile for up to 40 days to permit formation of scar tissue.

   * **Intermediate** Removal of the clitoris and all or part of the labia minora. Sometimes slices of the labia majora are removed and stitched, according to the demands of the girl's relatives.' Efua Dorkenoo and Scilla Elworthy, 'A cry in the dark', *Guardian*, 21 April 1992.

   'Iron deficiency, anaemia and chronic infections of the pelvis are the major causes of disability in women in poor countries. The latter is often caused by female circumcision – which affects at least 80 million young girls and women – and early pregnancy.' *New Internationalist*, July 1992.

63 'One in four children is living in poverty, according to official figures published yesterday which confirm that the gulf between rich and poor widened massively during the decade of Conservative government to 1989. They show that the poorest families suffered a 6 per cent cut in real income.' *Guardian*, 16 July 1992.

64 'The likeliest victims of a sudden unlawful death remain children under the age of one or people in the company of their family and friends.' *Guardian*, 4 August 1992.

65 *Daily Mail*, 4 August 1992.

66 John Illman, 'Suffer the child', *Guardian*, 5 June 1992.

67 Ian Katz, 'The despair of children who see no point in living', *Guardian*, 10 August 1992.

68 *Guardian*, 13 July 1992.

69 de Mause, op. cit., p.16.

70 Stephen Ramsey, who wrote and directed the television programme *The Baby Boomers' Picture Show* about the upbringing of the Baby Boomer generation in Australia, linked this kind of upbringing to 'our fondness for regimentation. As well as having fun in well drilled groups, Australians applied this love of routine to the sudden rush of post war children. Mothercraft nurses at baby health centres ordered our mothers to put aside only half an hour a day for mothering and to ignore our infants' cries to be fed. We had to wait four hours between feeds, and slept alone, often in distant bedrooms so our cries would not be heard.'

   Toilet training was strict. 'As we grew up regularity seemed like a way of life.'

   'Law and order was never questioned. We were always told that police helped old ladies across busy streets and protected our houses against robbers. They were always on the lookout when we got lost. They were models of morality for us to emulate.'

At school 'the emphasis was on obedience, God, country, flag, football, cleanliness, and school saving accounts.' A Co-Production of Film Australia and the Australian Broadcasting Corporation, 1990. Based on the book *Baby Boomers* by Helen Townsend, Simon & Schuster, Australia, 1988.

71 Candida Lacey, 6 August 1992.

72 Maggie O'Kane, 'Serb jihad in a Bosnian town', *Guardian*, 23 July 1992.

Marat Akchurin wrote, 'Frunze, the Kirghiz capital, which used to be shady and green, now looked like an active volcano at the moment of eruption. At the bus station where I came to find a seat for Tashkent, crowds of enraged Kirghiz youths were commandeering buses to go to Osh province and destroy Uzbeks. The general hysteria was inflamed by rumours that Kirghiz babies had been thrown on to bonfires by Uzbek crowds in Uzgen. It was clear that new and terrible violence had broken out in two city markets with casualties on both sides.' *Red Odyssey*, Secker and Warburg, London, 1992, quoted in *Guardian*, 6 August 1992.

73 Corinna Honan, *Daily Mail*, 4 August 1992.

74 I wrote to Claire to ask her whether she had been accurately quoted and whether she would allow me to use the interview. She wrote back:

'I've thought about it carefully, and the only comment I'm inclined to make is about the depression after childbirth. I honestly think, looking back, that my depression after each of those babies was almost entirely hormonal – or certainly 75% of it was! That there was some sort of psychological overlay, undoubtedly – but I'd be more inclined in this case to regard these depressions as very much chemical events rather than psychological ones. Certainly it was a tweaking of my hormone balance that got me out of it.

'Apart from that, your comments sound fair enough to me! And all the best with your new book.'

The question still has to be asked, Why is it that when we have a physical illness, some of us look after ourselves and let others look after us, while others of us turn against ourselves, won't look after ourselves, and feel guilty if other people look after us? The answer is not in our biology but in how we have learned to feel about ourselves.

75 Leonard Michaels, *I Would Have Saved Them If I Could*, New York, 1975, quoted in *Independent on Sunday*, 3 May 1992.

76 Roger McGough, *Defying Gravity*, Viking, London, 1992.

77 Sylvia Fraser, *My Father's House*, Virago, London, 1989.

78 Dorothy Rowe, *Living with the Bomb: Can We Live Without Enemies?*, Routledge, London, 1986.

79 R. I. Moore, Preface to E. Peters, *Torture*, Blackwell, New York, 1985. Quoted in Lindsey Williams, 'Torture and the Torturer', *The Psychologist*, July 1992.

80 'There are two common misconceptions about torture. The first is that the primary purpose is to inflict pain; the second is that the purpose of the pain is to elicit information. In reality, health care professionals have concluded that pain is used as a means to a different end, that end being the destruction of the individual as a person. Any information elicited is usually no more than a side benefit: often the victim has no information to give, or the information may be known to the authorities; and frequently talking is not rewarded by the cessation of the torture. The victim's powerlessness is demonstrated as the torturer continues regardless of what the victim says, regardless of what crimes he confesses or heresies he recants.' Williams, loc. cit.

81 Karl Maier, 'Free-market Africa's age of disrespect', *Independent on Sunday*, 12 July 1992.

82 Saeed Jaffrey, 'Who Cares', *East*, A Tartan Television Production for the BBC, 1992.

83 Forster, op. cit.

84 Charles Glass, *Independent Magazine*, 25 May 1991.

85 John Gittings, *Guardian*, 7 July 1992.

4 LAYING EGGS AND HATCHING VULTURES

1 David Richards, 'A life closed down too young?', *Guardian*, 18 July 1991.

2 Nick Thorpe, *Observer*, 4 April 1992.

3 See Dorothy Rowe, *Beyond Fear*, HarperCollins, London, 1987.

4 Louise Anike, 'Life Be in It . . . How?', in Louise Anike and Lynette Ariel, *Older Women, Ready or Not*, published by Anike and Ariel, PO Box 136, Bexley NSW 2207, Australia, 1987, p.19.

5 Judith Williamson, *Guardian*, 25 April 1991.

6 Derek Brown, *Guardian*, 24 July 1991.

7 Suzie Mackenzie, 'Answering a divine call', *Guardian*, 24 July 1991.

8 See Rowe, *Wanting Everything*, ch.7, 'Responsibility and Selfishness'.

9 Kate Kellaway, 'Dreaming on to paper', *Observer*, 23 August 1992.

10 Marjorie Hill, personal communication, 5 May 1992.

11 For a fuller account of this pattern, see Rowe, *Breaking the Bonds*.

12 From *The Real Thing*, Channel 4 Television, 23 August 1992.

13 For a fuller account, see Rowe, *Wanting Everything*, ch.2.

14 Tatyana Tolstaya, 'Tsar of all the answers', *Guardian*, 25 June 1992.

15 J. E. Lovelock, *Gaia*, Oxford University Press, Oxford, 1989.

16 The Twelve Steps of Alcoholics Anonymous are:

1 We admitted we were powerless over alcohol – that our lives had become unmanageable.

2 Came to believe that a Power greater than ourselves could restore us to sanity.

3 Made a decision to turn our will and our lives over to the care of God as we understood Him.

4 Made a searching and fearless moral inventory of ourselves.

5 Admitted to God, to ourselves, and to another human being the exact nature of our wrongs.

6 Were entirely ready to have God remove all these defects of character.

7 Humbly asked Him to remove our shortcomings.

8 Made a list of all persons we had harmed, and became willing to make amends to them all.

9 Made direct amends to such people wherever possible, except when to do so would injure them or others.

10 Continued to take personal inventory and when we were wrong promptly admitted it.

11 Sought through prayer and meditation to improve our conscious contact with God as we understood Him, praying only for knowledge of His will for us and the power to carry that out.

12 Having a spiritual awakening as the result of these steps, we tried to carry this message to alcoholics, and to practise these principles in all our affairs. (From Hugh Smith, *Depressed? Here Is a Way Out*, Fount, London, 1992, p.198.)

17 Zoë Heller, 'The Road to Recovery', *Independent on Sunday*, 14 June 1992.

18 Ibid.

19 HarperSanFrancisco, 1992. Anne Wilson Schaef dedicates this slim volume

'To all those persons who are suffering from this previously unnamed disease and who have not known that they have a disease that can be treated and from which they can recover.

'To those courageous enough to acknowledge having this disease and be willing to teach us about it.

'To those professionals who have stretched their conceptual boundaries to name and to treat this insidious and pervasive disease.

'To all of us who seek recovery and are joyfully recovering.'

Right from the beginning of the book she refers to co-dependency as a disease. I searched the book for some reference to or speculation about the biological basis of this disease, but I became only more confused. On page 4 she says, 'I have a disease process that I learned in society.' Do we learn to have a disease? Why did you learn to have measles? Why didn't you learn to have mumps instead?

We use the word disease in two different ways. 'Disease' can refer to a physical process caused by some biochemical changes in the body. Or 'disease' can be used metaphorically. Crime can be pictured as a disease in society. Is co-dependency a metaphorical disease? On page 10 Anne Wilson Schaef says, 'We are beginning to recognize that co-dependence is a disease in its own right. It fits the disease concept in that it has an *onset* (a point at which the person's life is not working, usually as a result of an addiction), a *definable course* (the person continues to deteriorate mentally, physically, psychologically, and spiritually), and, untreated, has a *predictable outcome* (death).' That sounds like 'disease' used as a metaphor, but on page 19 she rejects a co-dependency therapist who denies the disease concept of co-dependency and who defines a co-dependent person as 'human-relationship dependent and focuses her/his life around an addictive agent'.

I do hope you are not human-relationship dependent. Shall I tell you the other symptoms of this dread disease?

Dishonesty. Not Dealing with Feelings in a Healthy Way. Control. Confusion. Thinking Disorders. Perfectionism. External Referencing. Dependency Issues. Fear. Rigidity. Judgmentalism. Depression. Inferiority/Grandiosity. Self-Centredness. Loss of Personal Morality. Stasis. Negativism.

I think we all have this dread disease. We must repent and be saved.

20 Heller, loc. cit.
21 Lucy Johnstone, *The Uses and Abuses of Psychiatry*, Routledge, London, 1989, p.243.
22 Zoë Heller told of her meeting with Ethan who was in recovery in Prescott, Arizona.

'He was 43 years old – a handsome, slow-witted man with a sludgy southern accent and a puppyish manner. His route to recovery had been slightly bewildering, he told me. Six months previously his wife had left him – fed up, she said, with being married to a "spoiled baby" who refused to get a job. This had depressed him and for a few days he had drowned his sorrows in booze. When his elderly, protective mother saw what was happening, she feared he was having "a nervous breakdown" and offered to pay for him to go to Prescott. Before he knew it, he was in a clinic being diagnosed as an alcoholic and a "spending addict".

'He took this diagnosis seriously and applied himself enthusiastically to his programme. Working through his drink problem was not tough. He had, in fact, never been much of a drinker . . . The spending problem was much harder work, though. He had always been bad with money; a big part of his wife's complaint had concerned his extravagance with her earnings. But over the last six months, despite attending three 12 Step meetings a day, he had become more of a spendthrift than ever. Whenever he got bored, he said, he couldn't think of another way to entertain himself than to go and buy something.

'Ethan took me up to the house in the hills where he was staying, and showed me the garage, where he kept the collection of things he had been spending money on recently. It was junk: T-shirts with silly slogans, thrift-shop sweaters covered in stains and holes, cowboy chaps in case he ever decided to ride a horse. There were boxes and boxes of baseball caps, a CB radio that just needed tuning up. And a vast pile of shoes: bowling shoes, golf shoes, dress shoes, shoes to go fishing in, even "health" shoes shaped like cornish pasties. He stood in the middle of it all and smiled. "I've been kind of naughty, haven't I?" he said.

'It seemed to me that what Ethan needed was some self-discipline. But when I said so, he looked horrified. "God, no! They told me it's my desire to control my life that got me into this trouble in the first place." In accordance with the recovery dictum that self-control is a hubristic illusion, and that healing requires a surrender of self-will, Ethan had given up trying to stop spending and was waiting for the grace of his Higher Power. "It's Step 3," he said. "I've made a decision to turn my will and life over to the power of God."

'It didn't look as if identifying Ethan's lifelong profligacy as a disease had done him much good. But one thing was sure: the clinic he attended had made some money out of it. He might have been better served by a couple of weeks at boot camp, or by getting a job, but it was a lot more profitable to keep him in expensive sessions where he could release his repressed "rage" towards his mother.'

23 When I asked Alice Miller's publishers for permission to quote from two of her books, Helene Ritzerfeld of Suhrkamp Verlag, Frankfurt am Main, wrote to me to say, 'We have discussed your inquiry with our author. I am sorry to say, but Dr Miller does not want that parts or excerpts from her work are published in other

works. She feels that they
should not be taken out of her
own context' (1 November
1990).

24 Heller, loc. cit.

25 Richard Ehrlich, *Weekend
Guardian*, 7–8 March 1992.

26 Joanna Smith, *Guardian*,
27 August 1991.

27 I wrote this on the morning of
28 August 1992. That night,
when I was amending the
typescript of what I had
written, my sister Myra
phoned me from Australia to
say that Aunt Margaret had
died. I recalled that Aunt
Margaret had told me that she
wasn't sure if there was a
heaven but she hoped so
because then she would meet
her family again – her husband
Athol, her mother and father,
her sisters Anne, Elizabeth and
Adelaide (always called Annie,
Lizzie and Addie), and her
brothers, Joe and my father
Jack. I wondered if Mother
would join them in heaven. But
then Mother had told me she
didn't fancy heaven. 'All those
people!'

28 Lynne Barber, 'The Price of
Genius', *Independent on
Sunday*, 16 December 1990.

29 Maureen Sutton, *We Didn't
Know Aught*, Paul Watkins,
1992.

30 Suzanne Moore, 'Everything
you never wanted to know
about sex', *Guardian*,
3 September 1992.

31 Alick Rowe, *Friday on My
Mind*, Portman Television Ltd
and BBC TV, producer Philip

Hinchcliffe, May 1992.

32 *Guardian*, 19 May 1992.

33 For a full account of extraverts
and introverts, see Dorothy
Rowe, *The Successful Self*,
Fontana, London, 1989.

34 DONNA'S STORY
I'm a prostitute because I don't
know any other way of life. But
I hate it. I've done the rounds
– the saunas, the nightclubs,
the street. I have regular check-
ups and I always use a
condom. I'm as careful as
possible. I don't get in a car if
I sense danger. The blokes vary
– some are nice, some are
weirdos. I've had punters beat
me up. One took me to a lake
and I had to pretend to float
like I was dead. Twelve years
ago I was knifed in the stomach
in a man's car. His expression
changed from Mr Nice Guy to
Mr Psychopath. A taxi-driver
found me bleeding in the
gutter.

I suppose I look on men as
animals. I just turn off when I
have sex with them. Most want
oral or penetration – French
or sex. You get the odd one
who wants to do disgusting
things and I won't tolerate it.
I'll only do oral or straight or
hand. I'll whip them because I
can take my aggression out on
them, and there's more money
in S and M. It's £40 for straight
sex and French, £150 for S and
M, and £30–£40 for a hand
job. You can get it over and
done in a few minutes. If they
start taking their time, I say,
'Your time's up whether

you've come or not.' Some start telling you their problems and you say, 'Sorry, I'm not here for that.'

Men have got nasty with me six or seven times, but it's getting more frequent. The world is changing. It's because of the stigma against us because of drugs and Aids. The majority of men I see are happily married, but they don't want lovers because it means wining and dining them. It's cheaper to come to me, and they can go away with a clear conscience – they don't think of it as betraying their wives.

I refer to myself as a working girl, not a prostitute. I think I'm doing a public service and it's a tiring, dangerous job. The vice squad are supposed to protect us, but when I've gone to them as a rape victim they say, 'You're a prostitute.' But times are getting harder and there are more and more housewives out working to pay the mortgage. It's the recession. I meet them all the time.

I'm a normal person, I've got feelings. But I feel like an outcast, which is a terrible way to feel. I'd love to get out, but it's hard when you're used to the money. I'd love to pay tax. I think most of the other girls have stories something like mine.
Independent on Sunday, 13 September 1992.

35 *Guardian Weekend*, 12 September 1992.

36 Wendy Moore, writing about the Survivors Poetry group, four poets who have had spells in psychiatric hospitals, said,

'Although their poems often stem from this common experience, they find it almost impossible to produce good poetry while in the throes of a mental crisis, or taking heavy doses of drugs, or living in a psychiatric hospital. (Plath once said, "When you are insane you are busy being insane all the time . . . when I was crazy that was all I was.") "In hospital I get a lot of ideas," says Campbell, then laughs. "But I find it very difficult to write things because the atmosphere of living in an acute ward is so disruptive."

'The fourth survivor poet, Hilary Porter, wrote her first full length fiction, a play, while attending hospital daily after a breakdown. "But when it comes to writing about really painful things I can often only do that several years after. For me the process of writing clarifies the situation, which is often quite confused at the time. Once you clarify it for yourself the next stage is sharing it with others."

'Porter acknowledges that the creativity which fuels her poetry stems from the same place that produces the fears which lead to illness. But she adds: "I would not want to do without that side of my personality, particularly as it provides my poetry, even though it brings me pain sometimes.' *Guardian*, 5 June 1992.

37 John McVicar, *Weekend Guardian*, 11–12 January 1992.

38 Rupert Haselden, *Weekend Guardian*, 7–8 September 1991.

39 Nigella Lawson reviewed the so-called educational sex videos now available in newsagents and video shops. She wrote:

'In the bad old days, baffled boys and girls had to rummage through their parents' bookshelves to satisfy their sexual curiosity. They used to pore stealthily over tomes with titles such as *The Guide To Marital Happiness* . . . now they have freer recourse to W. H. Smith and the video stores.

'*The Lovers' Guide to Love*, *Making Love* and *Supervirility*: nearly every video guide to the delights of the bedroom – and beyond – may profess to be serious teachers of sex, but are they?

'This is the question raised by Detective Superintendent Michael Hames, head of Scotland Yard's Obscene Publications Squad, who this week attacked the censorship laws which allow pornographic videos to go on sale in the high street masquerading as sex education.

'Many such videos, he argued, would be illegal if they were not billed as educational.

'One thing is sure: never has the novitiate been able to receive so graphic a sex education. But having watched highlights from nine of these videos, it is impossible not to conclude that, just as much as Victorian pornography posed as items of anatomical interest or scientific research, these vehicles of supposed education are more likely to be viewed for their powers of titillation than education.

'Yet, ironically, they certainly do not promote promiscuity; the post AIDS virtues of commitment and fidelity are sung ad nauseam. And whereas the link between pornography and violent sex crimes seems apparent to most of us, even if still denied by many, the images these videos purvey are free from aggression, with their accompanying voice-overs insistently stressing the need for communication and understanding.

'In truth, the response of most viewers, I suspect, is more likely to be one of squirming embarrassment than pleasure. Sex is a private pastime, and to see it in this form is at best cringe-making.

'If parents are worried that their offspring are likely to be fired up for free love and go off on a rampage of pubescent sexual activity after watching one of these videos, they should rest assured that they are more likely to be put off it for life.

'A sudden shot of a woman

with magenta nail varnish pleasuring an orgasmically grimacing man is an aesthetically disturbing sight, as are the several hard porn channels' worth of pumping limbs and humping bodies . . .

'Dr Andrew Stanway, whose *Lovers' Guide* excited a spate of shocked disgust when it came out some months ago, has now brought out *The Lovers' Guide 2* to demonstrate, in his own words that "no one has to be a sexual bore." To that end, he and his performers show the varieties of sexual acts and techniques available.

'This may titillate, but the intention seems honourable. But though Dr Stanway may stress the need for commitment and care, many watching this may well discover that affection and sex are not the same thing . . .

'And Dr Stanway, for whom I have more sympathy than scorn even if he does look like a demented biology master, is rather hoist by his own petard when he instructs the viewer/voyeur "not to do anything ridiculous". That certainly rules out most sexual activity.

'And although these videos profess to promote sexual confidence, in many cases, I should think they would worry rather than reassure the viewer. *Supervirility* would hardly make those who may be self-conscious about their bodies feel any better about themselves as it earnestly intones about the importance of "looking good and smelling wonderful" and the necessity of "toning yourself up" to be good in bed.

'No, in themselves, I do not believe the tapes are dangerous in the sense that Scotland Yard's Michael Hames implies. What they are is sad. For the videos, sex is no longer seen as a private activity and an essential, intimate part of adult human life, but a leisure pursuit. Sex is a hobby much the same as DIY or stock-car racing.' *Daily Mail*, 2 September 1992.

40 *Guardian*, 4 September 1992.
41 Richard West, *Guardian*, 8 August 1992.
42 Nick Thorpe, *Observer*, 26 July 1992.
43 Alistair Mant, *The Leaders We Deserve*, Martin Robertson, Oxford, 1983.
44 Elena Barikhovskaya, 'Where the flag of racism flies free', *Guardian Europe*, 24 July 1992.
45 *Guardian*, 24 July 1992.
46 *Observer*, 26 July 1992.
47 *Weekend Guardian*, 14–15 March 1992; *A Soldier's Song*, Secker and Warburg, London, 1993.
48 Sheila Kitzinger, 'A child's view of a terrible war', *Independent on Sunday*, 30 August 1992.
49 *Guardian*, 23 January 1991.
50 Ryszard Kapuscinski, 'Canyons of the mind', from *Gazeta Wyborcza*, Poland, *Guardian*, 20 March 1992.
51 Sheldon Kopp, *What Took You*

So Long?, Science and Behavior Books, Palo Alto, California, 1979.

52 *Guardian*, 21 February 1992.

53 See Rowe, *Beyond Fear*.

5 FROM ABSOLUTE TRUTHS TO UNCERTAIN WISDOM

1 Sheldon Kopp, *No Hidden Meanings*, Science and Behavior Books, Palo Alto, California, 1975.

2 Ludovic Kennedy, 'The Book That Changed Me', *Independent on Sunday*, 20 January 1991.

3 Op. cit.

4 Sheldon Kopp, *What Took You So Long?*

5 Alan Brien, 'The Extended Father', in Sean French (ed.), *Fatherhood*, Virago, London, 1992, p. 21.

6 Mervyn Jones, 'Learning to Be a Father', ibid, p. 25–7.

7 *Guardian*, 24 June 1992.

8 *Motoring News*, 7 August 1991.

9 *Guardian*, 2 February 1991.

10 *Guardian*, 14 January 1991.

11 *Independent on Sunday*, 21 July 1991.

12 *Observer*, 25 August 1991.

13 Edward Pilkington, 'Why the dead don't like Tuesdays', *Guardian*, 5 September 1992.

14 Personal communication, 6 February 1991.

15 de Mause, op. cit., p.29, quoting C. H. Rolph, 'A Backward Glance at the Age of "Obscenity"', *Encounter* 32, 1969, p.23.

16 Personal communication, 5 July 1992.

17 *The Price of Everything*, Faber, London, 1994.

18 Routledge, London, 1986.

19 *Guardian*, 17 April 1992.

20 *Independent on Sunday*, 31 May 1992. This quotation was later amended by Daniel Massey, May 1993.

21 *Guardian*, 4 July 1992.

22 Personal communication, 15 July 1991.

23 Personal communication, 25 March 1992.

24 Personal communication, 11 June 1992.

25 Personal communication, 11 June 1992.

26 'Counselling' © Jean Medcalf, October 1990.

27 'Anger' © Jean Medcalf, March 1991.

28 Personal communication, 4 April 1991.

29 *The Dhammapada: The Sayings of the Buddha*, a new rendering by Thomas Byrom, Wildwood House, London, 1976.

30 Tuchman, op. cit., p.56.

31 *Guardian Weekend*, 17 October 1992.

32 *The World of Charles Addams*, Knopf, New York, 1991, introduction, p.ix.

33 Personal communication, November 1992.

34 *Independent*, 10 November 1992. The Cancer and Leukaemia in Childhood Trust is based at Clic House, 11–12 Fremantle Square, Bristol BS6 5TL.

35 *Independent*, 3 March 1992. Ian Waterman's full story is told in a book by his neurologist Dr Jonathan Cole, *Pride and a Daily Marathon*, Duckworth, London, 1992.

36 Piers Dudgeon, *Observer*, 17 November 1991.

6 FROM ABSOLUTE TIME TO CREATED TIME

1 Fintan O'Toole, 'Arts Diary', *Guardian*, 11 November 1991.

2 G. J. Whitrow, *The Natural Philosophy of Time*, Clarendon Press, Oxford, 1980, p.64.

'The idea of world-wide time was presupposed by Kant in his celebrated discussion of time in the formulation of the first of the four antimonies of pure reason. Indeed, Kant came to the central problem of his *Kritik der reinen Vernunft* by considering whether the universe could have had an origin in time or not. He believed that there were indisputable arguments for rejecting both alternatives, and he therefore concluded that our idea of time is inapplicable to the universe itself but is merely part of our mental apparatus for imagining or visualizing the world. It is essential to our experience of things in the world, but we get into trouble if we apply it to anything which transcends all possible experience, in particular the universe as a whole.' Ibid., p.27.

'The celebrated Austrian physicist and philosopher of science Ernst Mach (1865) maintained, in opposition to Kant, that time is not an *a priori* condition of mental functioning but is an *a posteriori* sensation. He believed that we have a specific sense of time and that the sense organ involved is the ear. He thought that our temporal awareness depends on the work, or effort, associated with the exercise of our powers of attention and the resulting fatigue of the organ concerned.' Ibid, p.60.

3 Ian Stewart, *Guardian*, 19 June 1992.

4 Les Murray, *The Independent Monthly*, December 1991, January 1992.

5 Susan Blackmore, Senior Lecturer in psychology at the University of the West of England has made a special study of the paranormal and out-of-body experiences. She wrote:

'Understanding out-of-body experiences means understanding our normal way of seeing the world. Normally we imagine that we are a self inside our heads looking out. In fact this is a mental construction. There is no little person in there. Rather our brains are constructing a model of the world from a viewpoint behind their eyes. The question then becomes: why should I suddenly seem to see the world from somewhere on the ceiling instead? The answer may be because I am dying and my brain can no longer construct a normal view of the world; because I am in terrible pain or am so relaxed that I feel I am floating. But why should even these experiences result in a bird's-eye view?

'The answer is that many memory models are in bird's-eye view anyway. For example, try to recall the last time you had to speak in public. Do you see the scene as though from where your eyes were? Or do you see yourself "down there"? Many people see themselves as though in bird's-eye view. It is my suggestion that this view is simpler for the brain to construct when under stress and so this bird's-eye view takes over and seems real. This fits with recent experiments showing that people who have out-of-body experiences have better spatial imagery skills, are better able to switch viewpoints in imagination and are more likely to see themselves in dreams.

'The tunnel too invites a normal explanation. In the brain's visual system there are far more nerve cells devoted to the centre of your visual field than to the degrees of what you can see. Imagine now that the brain is dying. The first cells to be affected are the inhibitory ones which damp down the activity of other cells, with the result that there is widespread random activity in the brain. In the visual areas this means lots of activity in the centre and less towards the edges. And what will this look like? Possibly a bright light in the centre which gets bigger and bigger as the activity increases, in other words a light at the end of a tunnel.

'If tunnels, out-of-body experiences and visions of various kinds can one day all be explained, doesn't that deny the very basis of spirituality? Certainly not. These experiences can have profound effects on people. Even if the light is a matter of brain activity, passing down that tunnel and feeling you have left your body can make you re-assess the meaning of your life and glimpse the very fragile nature of the constructed "self". All this, it seems to me, is the true basis of spiritual experience and should not be ignored.

'Hunting for the paranormal is not the way to understand the human mind: explaining our most puzzling experiences may be.' *New Internationalist*, November 1992.

6 G. J. Whitrow, *Time in History*, Oxford University Press, Oxford, 1988, p.4. Other books on our constructions of time down the ages are: Jeremy Rifkin, *Time Wars*, Henry Holt and Company, New York, 1987; Stephen Toulmin and June Goodfield, *The Discovery of Time*, Hutchinson, London, 1965; Donald J. Wilcox, *The Measure of Time Past*, University of Chicago Press, Chicago, 1987.

7 G. J. Whitrow, ibid, p.10.

8 Ibid., p.9.

9 Ibid., p.13.

10 George Steiner, *After Babel: Aspects of Language and*

Translation, Oxford University Press, Oxford, 1975, p.157, quoted in Whitrow, ibid, p.13.

11 Whitrow, ibid, p.65.

12 Tuchman, op. cit., p.55.

13 Whitrow, op. cit., p.139.

14 Ibid, p.139.

15 Daniel Boorstin, *The Americans: the Democratic Experience*, Vintage Books, New York, 1974, p.361.

16 Rifkin, op. cit., p.92.

17 Ibid, pp.91, 92.

18 Boorstin, op. cit., p.362.

19 Ibid, p.371.

20 Ecclesiastes 3:1.

21 Boorstin, op. cit., p.523.

22 G. Scott Budge and Ronald W. Janoff, 'Interpreting the discourses of family business', *Family Business Review*, Vol.IV no.4, winter 1991.

23 Jill Morrell, quoted in *Boston Times*, 10 August 1991.

24 U. A. Fanthorpe, 'Half-past two', *Neck-Verse*, Peterloo Poets, Cornwall, 1992.

25 Whitrow, op. cit., p.3.

26 The Federation of Australian States took place in 1900.

7 TIME AND TIMELESSNESS

1 Kopp, *No Hidden Meanings*, op. cit., pp.32, 33, 34.

2 Rowe, *The Courage to Live*, p.260.

3 Tuberculosis is now rife among the poor in the cities of the USA and is becoming prevalent in Britain among those who live below the poverty line. A strain of tubercular bacilli which is resistant to all antibiotics has developed. In Victorian England tuberculosis might have been the disease of the slums, but the rich died of it.

4 'As the globe teeters on the brink of catastrophe, anarchy and all kinds of beastliness, paranoid householders are wondering what more they can do to protect their little all from marauding hordes of criminals. On Merseyside "private police" patrol the streets, and communities from the Cotswolds to Cornwall are calling for similar experiments.

'The tendency is taken to extremes (as so many other tendencies are) in California, where they have resurrected the medieval idea of the walled town. Leisure World (population 21,000, average age 77) is surrounded by a breeze block and barbed wire barrier, with guards on every entrance. The residents pay £290 a month to cover their security services, a television station and buses. Elsewhere in California, residents (27,000) of Woodbridge Village must wear identity tags at all times, or they are banned from the town's amenities; houses can be painted in "approved" colours. Century Woods Estates, in west Los Angeles, is protected by 20ft high iron gates; any party attended by more than 15 people needs special permission.' *Observer*, 8 November 1992.

INDEX

Love Isn't Quite Enough

The Psychology of Male–Female Relationships

Maryon Tysoe

Finding out that love isn't quite enough is something most men and women do the hard way.

The traditional Western myth of romantic love has much to answer for. Both sexes can be devastated when they discover that, far from having the power of a psychological superglue, love is only one of many elements needed to sustain a relationship. Even those who are aware of – or reluctantly suspect – this are left floundering as to what other mysterious processes might be involved.

In *Love Isn't Quite Enough*, Dr Maryon Tysoe, widely admired social psychologist and journalist, has written an indispensable book for those seeking a better understanding of how relationships really work, why they fail and what we need to know to make them succeed. With characteristic wit and insight, she draws on a great deal of untapped psychological research to explore the route towards more realistic, and hence potentially more successful, relationships between the sexes.

'A wise, witty and highly readable book'　　　　Dr Anthony Clare

ISBN 0 00 637766 1

What Do Women Want?

Luise Eichenbaum and Susie Orbach

Many women today feel that they pour love, commitment and understanding into their relationships, but that it is not returned in kind. He seems secure and independent, she feels insecure and clingy.

The truth is that men and women are *both* dependent. But his needs are catered to so well – first by his mother, then by his girlfriend or wife – that he doesn't know he has them, while her needs – for closeness and tenderness – are constantly rebuffed as he retreats from intimacy.

Susie Orbach and Luise Eichenbaum set out to explore this crisis in the relationships of men and women. They explain how men have learned to 'manage' their dependency needs very differently from women, and *why* women feel dependent and hungry for love. Finally they show why dependency on both sides is the essential core of any successful relationship.

ISBN 0 00 638252 5

Sexing the Millennium

Linda Grant

'Linda Grant is on the side of women and sex, fearlessly making the case for passion . . . This is feminist writing at its imaginative best'
Joan Smith

Sex is under siege – sex is fighting back – sex has always been dangerous, to societies as well as individuals. It has always been the stuff around which utopias have been woven.

Charting the origins of sexual freedom in the anarcho-erotic sects of the English Civil War, through the hippie idealism of sixties counter-culture, to our present, postmodern bewilderment, *Sexing the Millennium* examines the intellectual, economic and technological movements that formed the sexual revolution, from the sixties to the present day.

In the age of AIDS, Madonna and Virtual Reality porn, the memory of the brief years when sex was free from the threats of both pregnancy and disease continues to shape our dreams. *Sexing the Millennium* affirms that the personal is still political. It calls for a new sexual revolution, which would at last liberate female desire from the thrall of male fantasy and allow women to pursue the passionate, erotic adventure of their own lives.

'Wise, witty – and wistful . . . I hope this warm book is as widely read and pondered as it deserves to be'
Angus Calder, *Scotland on Sunday*

Breaking the Bonds

Understanding Depression, Finding Freedom

Dorothy Rowe

'The light at the end of the tunnel'   Jill Tweedie

Depression: the imprisoning experience of isolation and fear which comes when we realize that there is a serious discrepancy between what we thought our life to be and what it actually is.

From birth onwards we create our own secure worlds of meaning. Challenged seriously enough, these worlds can crumble, leaving us despairing, frightened, isolated, helpless. But we are not helpless. We can resolve to save ourselves by embarking on a journey of understanding and self-acceptance, and finally and for ever break free of the bonds of depression.

Dorothy Rowe, the internationally renowned psychologist and expert on depression, brings together in this book what her twenty-five years of research have shown her about depression, and shows us how every one of us can take charge of our life and find the way to happiness, hope and freedom.

'Wise and witty, factual and poetic, and a luminous path to self-understanding for all of us'   Jill Tweedie

'Wisdom, says Rowe, is knowing your worst fear and why you have it. *Breaking the Bonds* takes us to it and, if we're smart, into the nirvana of beginning to know what we want . . . this is a smashing book'   *New Statesman*

'This splendid book is a vastly readable, greatly enjoyable lifeline. Use it if you're depressed, to help yourself. Read it if you're not, so that you can help others. Either way, *read* it'   Claire Rayner

ISBN 0 00 637565 0